WHEN THE WIND WAS A RIVER

Aleut Evacuation in World War II

WHEN THE WIND WAS A RIVER

Aleut Evacuation in World War II

DEAN KOHLHOFF

University of Washington Press   Seattle and London

in association with

Aleutian/Pribilof Islands Association   Anchorage

To the Aleut People

This book is published with the assistance of generous grants from
the ALEUTIAN/PRIBILOF ISLANDS ASSOCIATION,
the ALEUT CORPORATION,
the ST. GEORGE TANAQ CORPORATION,
the OUNALASHKA CORPORATION,
the ALEUTIAN & PRIBILOF ISLANDS RESTITUTION TRUST,
and the ETTINGER FOUNDATION.

Library of Congress Cataloging-in-Publication Data
Kohlhoff, Dean.
When the wind was a river : Aleut evacuation in World War II /
Dean Kohlhoff.
p. cm.
Includes bibliographical references and index.
ISBN 0–295–97403–6 (alk. paper)
1. Aleuts.   2. World War, 1939–1945—Alaska.   3. World War, 1939–
1945—Atrocities.   I. Title.
D810.A53K64   1995   95-17676
940.53'1503971—dc20   CIP

The paper used in this publication meets the minimum requirements of
American National Standard for Information Sciences—Permanence of Paper
for Printed Library Materials, ANSI Z39.48–1984. ∞

On behalf of the ALEUTIAN/PRIBILOF ISLANDS ASSOCIATION, the Board of Directors and staff continue to honor the Aleut people who were interned during World War II. We express our special thanks to Dr. Dean Kohlhoff, who chose to write the final chapter acknowledging the injustice endured by the interned Aleut people. We also recognize the University of Washington Press for publishing this book.

BORIS MERCULIEF, Board Chairman
DIMITRI PHILEMONOF, Executive Director

The ALEUT CORPORATION makes this contribution in memory of the Aleuts who perished in the evacuation camps in Southeast Alaska; those who did not survive to receive some remedy for personal damage and for harm to the Aleut culture and traditions; and all the Aleut people and to the future generations.

ALICE SNIGAROFF PETRIVELLI, President

ST. GEORGE TANAQ CORPORATION's contribution toward the publication of this story is dedicated to the memory of the sixteen people from St. George who died during internment and are buried in Funter Bay and Juneau, and to others who have since passed on. Memory Eternal!

ILIODOR PHILEMONOF, President

The OUNALASHKA CORPORATION is proud to participate in the publishing of *When the Wind Was a River*. Our donation is made on behalf of the World War II evacuees from the Island of Unalaska— the villages of Biorka, Kashega, Makushin, and Ounalaska. This publication will serve to document the tragedy, make people aware that it happened, and perhaps prevent its recurrence.

A. B. RANKIN, Chairman

Precious little has been written to document the suffering and inhumane treatment of the Aleut people during World War II. Finally comes a book, *When the Wind Was a River*, which tells this history. The Trustees of the ALEUTIAN & PRIBILOF ISLANDS RESTITUTION TRUST believe that by participating in the publication of this book, we will best be able to honor the people who died during the internment, and those who survived this tumultuous period. Now, the world will finally know of the injustices inflicted on a proud people during this sad chapter of our nation's history.

MIKE ZACHAROF, Chairman

Contents

Foreword

I was twelve years old in June of 1942 when Atka people were forced to leave their homeland and move to southeast Alaska. I was one of those people. Dean Kohlhoff asked me to write a foreword for his book *When the Wind Was a River: Aleut Evacuation in World War II*. At first I was resistant to the idea. But as I looked through the manuscript he sent to me, I warmed to the project. I found his book to be well documented; and I feel this book will open a few eyes.

Being an evacuee during World War II was a learning experience for me. When I say it was a learning experience, I mean that I learned the world could be very unkind to people just because they were not the same color as the majority. And I also learned if you really wanted to achieve your personal goals, an education was essential. An education opens doors that will enable you to fight for your rights and your goals.

It also taught me there are many different cultures in the world with which you have to learn to live; and one way isn't the only way to live. Therefore, you must adapt to be able to survive. Before the evacuation, I was surrounded by my family and community members. They were concerned about the well-being of all the villagers. When we were moved I found that not too many people were concerned with the well-being of the Aleuts. I feel they considered us to be a nuisance.

We were treated as second-class citizens. It was humiliating for independent Aleuts to be treated like children. The evacuation made Aleut people feel as though they had no rights whatsoever. Thank goodness we could take care of ourselves by working wherever and whenever we could. If we had waited for the government to take care of our medical, food, and housing needs, we would not have survived our three-year stay in these camps.

I cannot speak for the other camps, but at Killisnoo during the first year we were all busy working in the canneries and on fishing boats. We also baby-sat for cannery workers and gathered what little food we could in our new and unfamiliar surroundings. And we did not have time to be restless. Contrary to comments from the teachers at Killisnoo, Mr. and Mrs. Magee, that we were discontented and restless in the camp, I feel that was not true. We were busy working to make the houses livable, and working to earn money for food, fuel, and clothing. We were trying to survive the cold and the hunger that first summer and winter. The Magees were very lucky. They were living in a warm house and had plenty of food to eat. The comments made by the federal official and the teachers, who supposedly did an excellent job in caring for us and were also paid a bonus for their efforts, are insulting. This book is a revelation to me of how people reacted to our situation and what the people "in charge," whom we considered friends, really thought about the Aleut people.

Before the evacuation, I was very secure in my own little world and as far as I knew was content with my life. During and long after the evacuation, I was very insecure and very afraid of life. It was hard for me to understand the treatment I had received from people whom I did not even know. It was very puzzling.

One positive effect that the evacuation had on the Aleut people as a whole was exposure to the political process. This helped the Aleut people to become more self-determined about making decisions that affected their lives. It helped us achieve more independence from governmental agents who determined that we were incapable of planning our futures and carrying out our goals concerning the way we wanted to live our lives.

In spite of all that has happened to us we are still around, although gone are the secure Aleut lifestyles in which we were comfortable in our villages before World War II. I noticed that we were referred to as "these people" whenever there was a discussion about the evacuees. Well, "these people" are now in control of their own destinies, as much as any American citizen is, and will continue to do a good job preserving their culture and traditions.

Professor Kohlhoff has put together the missing pieces of the World War II evacuation puzzle with this manuscript. In the past, I've wondered about certain events that happened, and why they happened. Now, all the information concerning the Aleut evacuation is recorded for the public to read and to know what happened to us. The book tells the stories of the camps and the experiences of the Aleut people, who had previously felt too embarrassed to tell these things to their children. And if they did tell them, the children questioned the credibility of their stories. The children could not believe that the U.S. Government was capable of doing what they did at that time. In my own experience with my children, when I told my oldest daughter what happened to me and other Atkans during World War II, she did not believe me because it was not in the history books. Now, with the publication of *When the Wind Was a River,* the Aleut people will no longer have to explain why it was not in the U.S. history books.

Thank you, Professor Kohlhoff.

ALICE SNIGAROFF PETRIVELLI
President, the Aleut Corporation

Preface

In 1985, while undertaking a study of Native Americans, I attended a summer session at the University of Alaska Fairbanks. Greg Sawyer, an acquaintance and music teacher on Adak Island in the Aleutians, was the first person to mention the topic of Aleut evacuation to me. Then, in the course of the summer session, Professor Lydia Black lectured on it. I was drawn immediately to the subject. Upon looking into it, I learned that the story had not been written and that Aleuts wanted it told.

Because Alaska lies strategically close to Asia, it was eventually drawn into World War II. The Aleutian Islands region became the only American soil on which combat took place. The Aleut people on the islands were the area's most affected non-combatants when the war intruded into the North Pacific in the summer of 1942. After the Japanese bombed Dutch Harbor and invaded Kiska and Attu islands, the U.S. government evacuated 881 Aleuts from their homes to several locations in Alaska's Southeast. The Japanese removed 42 Attu Aleuts to Otaru city on Hokkaido Island.

It seemed to me that the evacuation story fit into phases reflected now in the organization of this book. Introductory chapters bring into focus Aleut people and government agencies affected by conditions in Alaska at the onset of the war. The heart of the book, however, is in the subsequent chapters on evacuation itself, life in the camps, and the process of return to Aleut island homes. The last chapter deals with Aleut efforts to win reparations.

My purpose throughout has been to fill a gap in our history by explaining as best I could why these events happened. But I also wanted to set out as much as possible the Aleut experience by incorporating Aleut voices into the text. This story has gone too long untold. I once thought that during the research I would interview camp survivors, but I changed my mind when I observed on videotape of earlier interviews the pain of recollection in their faces and heard it in their voices. I decided the record is clear without more personal testimony.

Although I am not an Aleut, I developed an increasing appreciation of them and of their tradition. Hence the dedication of this book. In one instance, though, I confess to an exercise of poetic license. The book's title is based on an ancient Aleut proverb, "A wind is not a river; sometime or other it will stop." I have modified the original "a wind is *not*" to "the wind *was* a river." Wind, often powerful and fierce in Aleut experience, is a metaphor for adversity applicable to evacuation. In the camps it seemed never-ending. Yet it did stop; and the story, true to the proverb, ended on a note of optimism.

While I still enjoy some proprietary claims to it, this book was truly a collaborative effort. First, my wife, Nancy, with swift, deft strokes and what seemed to me a magic touch, transcribed my drafts into the word processor. Next, by dint of editing, transposing, and clarifying, she created a more cogent manuscript. In the process this became her book, too, and I tender her the greatest thanks for her contribution.

Others helped immensely by lending support while suggesting improvements. My longtime friend and history colleague at Valparaiso University, Meredith W. Berg, read critically the first draft and was kind enough to give continued encouragement along with valuable direction on style and tone. Lydia T. Black of the University of Alaska Fairbanks delivered a "ruthlessly frank" (her phrase) appraisal. Her gimlet eye was indispensible in guiding me around numerous pitfalls. Alice Petrivelli, an Atka evacuee, provided important insights after reading an early draft. Not all the suggestions of the readers are incorporated into this final version, but they made it a better book and are herewith absolved of its remaining shortcomings.

I am also indebted to many who aided the research and now give them heartfelt thanks. The staff of Rasmuson Library at the University of Alaska Fairbanks provided wonderful service, especially Tom Couch, Ronald Inouye, Paul McCarthy, Marge Naylor, Ginger Polon, William Schneider, and Rose Sparanza. At the Aleutian/Pribilof Islands Association headquarters in Anchorage, the executive director Dimitri Philemonof graciously opened official files and contributed copies of needed materials. Virginia Newton and Lawrence Hibpshman of the Alaska State Archives and Phyllis DeMuth and Marilyn Kwock of the Alaska State Historical Library at Juneau helped retrieve materials. India Spartz was very helpful in locating photographs. Chris Campbell of the U.S. Forest Service in Ketchikan also provided a valuable file and photographs. Peggy Conversano of *Natural History* magazine kindly arranged for photos of sketches of Aleut faces. Michael Vigue at the Alaska Office Building worked diligently at uncovering mortality statistics. Joyce Justice, Susan Karren, and Janusz Wilczek of the National Archives—Pacific Northwest Region in Seattle worked tirelessly responding to my countless requests. Similarly, Don Jackanicz, Wilbert Mahoney, Mary Francis Morrow, Charles Roberts, Aloha South, and Richard Von Doernhoff of the National Archives in Washington, D.C., gave unstintingly to a sometimes dead-end search. Richard Boyland of the National Archives Modern Military Branch in Suitland, Maryland, literally led me down into the vast swamp of army and navy records there. David Bradley of the Foreign Claims Settlement Commission was particularly generous in tracing postwar claims records.

Woven into the text are numerous insights garnered from my Alaska teachers. They helped me understand the context. Lydia Black is a premier Aleut scholar, and I benefitted from her knowledge, sensitivity to Aleuts, and steady pressure to finish the project. Linda Ellanna, also at the University of Alaska Fairbanks, presented a clear anthropological picture of Alaska Natives. Both Mary Mangusso and Jonathan Nielson taught me Alaska history in correspondence courses. In a fruitful summer session Katherine McNamara introduced me to the importance of Native story telling and regard for homelands. I hope these teachers sense my debt to them in this recognition.

Material aid came my way, too, without which the book might never have been written. My brother Robert insisted on providing free of all sibling indebtedness a new—and our first—computer for word processing. BMW of Munich, Germany, produced but did not provide free a beautiful R80/7 motorcycle that carried me on research trips from Washington, D.C., to Alaska. Small but timely grants helped pay travel expenses. The Walter E. Bauer research fund of the History Department and a travel grant from the Committee on Creative Work and Research of Valparaiso University supported the venture, as did a semester sabbatical and a spring 1992 semester course reduction. Blessings often come in small portions, and I am thankful for them.

The maps were produced at the University of Waterloo, Ontario, Canada. Its Cartographic Centre is led by Gary Brannon, who was very cooperative and patient. The help of my colleague, Gottfried Krodel, was equally impressive. His specialty in Renaissance and Reformation history accompanies his editing skill and publication knowledge. The final manuscript copy came to life on his word processor and printer.

Naomi B. Pascal, editor-in-chief of the University of Washington Press, and Julidta C. Tarver, managing editor, eased the way and deserve thanks for their efforts. I thank Leslie Nelson Bond, my manuscript editor. Her sharp eye for detail and feeling for the language make her a model of excellence. Likewise, Pamela Canell Chaus lent her considerable aesthetic sense to the design. To them my gratitude for shaping what follows.

I would like to thank the following for grants that contributed to the production costs of this book: the Aleutian/Pribilof Islands Association, the Aleut Corporation, the St. George Tanaq Corporation, the Ounalashka Corporation, the Aleutian & Pribilof Islands Restitution Trust, and the Ettinger Foundation. I have assigned my royalties from this publication to the Aleut educational program of the Aleutian/Pribilof Islands Association.

WHEN THE WIND WAS A RIVER

Aleut Evacuation in World War II

In pre-Russian days our people, surrounded by many wonders of nature, worshiped, in their way, a deity who had the power to make mountains steam or erupt; the earth shake and sometimes crack; the wind blow so strong that a man could not stand up against it.

Aleut history is filled with tragic . . . disruptions beginning from the day the first Russian discoverer set foot on this land. . . .

Organized Aleut governments collapsed under the disruptions of World War II. In my own lifetime, I have seen the end of four villages.

In coming together we can remember and maintain the good things from our past and build and perpetuate a future that will not only sustain us economically but culturally as well. Then we will always be able to be proud that we are Aleuts.

What makes all those things meaningful to us of Aleut descent is the *remembering*.

—Lillie McGarvey, Aleut historian

Alaska Geographic 7, no. 3 (1980)

Of Aleuts and Alaska

> Mt. Cleveland breathed through a woman. That woman
> looked at Umnak from the top of Mt. Cleveland and
> saw Samalga Island appearing like floating kelp.
> In the evening she began to descend.
> —"The Chuginadak Woman"

Mount Cleveland in the form of the Chuginadak Island woman, an Aleut volcano guardian spirit, descended to find a mate. In her search, she traveled to important islands and into villages near familiar straits and bays. It was an intimate Aleutian landscape. Horsetail grass, murres, rosy finches, seals, and whales—members of a great family of life—lived there or nearby. Her adventures coupled the supernatural with this natural world and ended when she married the son of the chief of Akutan village. The marriage united in kinship a powerful volcano and the Aleut people of two island communities.[1]

Telling and remembering such stories reinforced Aleut attachment to their homes, villages, and islands. This oral tradition accentuated love of particular places. Father Ivan Veniaminov, the first ethnographer to record their stories and study their language, was impressed by the extensive Aleut nomenclature featuring the palpable environment. Their vocabulary, he noted, was "so very rich in place names . . . for every little cape or small point of land, inlet, recess, deep water area, brooklet, rill and rock." Individuals "were generally named for birds, fish and the like" found in the varied local assemblage of living things. They adopted names of animals, birds, or a "feature of the terrain" for a "link with the Creator." The largest group of Aleut primary names described landscape. They tied together place and home. Adak Island, for example, was thought to be "the great father," the family head named after its highest point, Mount Moffett. The land form where it stood, Cape Adagdak, was a "dear father," and a nearby hill was identified as his would-be wife.[2]

"The people," their collective name expressed in three dialects (*Unangan, Angagin,* or *Angaginas*), could be taken to mean the people related to these very islands. So strong were the ties between Aleuts and their homes that some of them "obstinately declined" invitations to a "better life" elsewhere. When a group of them were temporarily moved in 1874, "they became homesick immediately."[3]

Ancestors of these Aleuts, some believe, had lived in the Aleutians reaching back 9,000 years or more, "a longer continuous existence as an identifiable people in one place than any other people in the world."[4] There they had achieved a long record of adaptation. Kayaks, marine vessels of ingenious construction, were maneuvered with extraordinarily skill for transportation and harvest from the sea. Aleuts had for ages used successful hunting, fishing, and gathering techniques on land and in the intertidal zones. Their knowledge of human anatomy, medicine, and mortuary science; their complex spirituality, expressed in story, song, and ceremony; and an elaborate practical and aesthetic artistic tradition were marks of creativity. Rather than merely surviving, Aleuts enjoyed long and meaningful lives.[5]

These strides were made in a region not given to easy living. Their treeless islands were mountainous outcroppings of a chain of volcanoes that had deposited layers of ash, now overlaid by soggy tundra. Steep gorges indented the interior. Coastal cliffs plunged sharply into the sea. There was little flat land and few good harbors. The surrounding sea often became wild with turbulence. Capricious currents and riptides abounded near shore. This arc of islands was a cyclonic frontier dividing a cold Bering Sea and a warmer Pacific Ocean. The resulting clash caused frequent fogs, rain, and overcast. Winds—the Aleutian williwaws—used the islands for playgrounds, blowing snow and rain horizontally with gale force. Veniaminov remembered not one day of complete calm and called the region "the empire of the winds." There was no cornucopia in the Aleutians. Scarcity of food often threatened the Aleuts with starvation. Etched into the Aleut language itself was a grim reminder of this reality associated with the month of March: its Aleut name, *Qisagunax*, meant "when they gnaw straps" or "month of hunger, gnawing thongs," followed by April, "the near hunger month."[6] Natural catastrophes—earthquakes, seismic sea waves, and volcanic eruptions—struck with destructive force. Violence, moreover, took a toll when Aleuts engaged in combat against non-Aleut neighbors or in internecine warfare. Yet at the time of Russian encroachment in the 1740s, Aleut population according to some estimates totaled from around twelve to sixteen thousand. They flourished in what many would regard as a most inhospitable environment.[7]

Aleut people were confronted over time by many external challenges that tested this resiliency. Challenges came both in the Russian period from 1741 to 1867 and in the succeeding United States administration of the region. Aleuts suffered in these interventions what other

Native Americans and indigenous people around the globe experienced in "contact": disease, population decline, loss of tradition, uprooting, and foreign rule. By the early 1800s, Aleut population had shrunk by as much as 80 to 90 percent. In the face of such loss, however, Aleuts were tenacious. Like other people—particularly European immigrants to the New World whose communities also changed immensely—Aleuts adjusted to change just as they were changed in the process. William L. Laughlin, a scholar acquainted with Aleuts, described their modern adversities as a "chamber of horrors." He surmised, however, that they were nevertheless likely to survive for at least another nine thousand years.[8]

Their religion was a significant expression of Aleut adaptability that linked past to present. Although Russians introduced Aleuts to Christianity, what emerged was a Russian Orthodoxy with characteristics distinctly Aleut. It was the core of their identity as Aleut people.[9] Their church was the institution they treasured most. Worship services included lay readers, choirs, and a liturgy using the Aleut language. Church sanctuaries and religious icons reflected a spiritual world transcending the mundane.[10] Emblematically, their churches were, and still are, the most prominent village structures and provided the central focus of community life.

This Aleut community life was disrupted when war came suddenly to the North Pacific in the summer of 1942. Its impact was felt by Aleut people who lived in ten villages on eight scattered islands, remote from the major population centers of Alaska. Before the war, life there had been rather stable, although several communities had lost population between 1920 and 1939, reflecting the process of community breakup that had begun with Russian-Aleut contact. Census figures, however, showed an increase in total Aleut population during this period of nearly two hundred people.[11] Traditional attachment to their island homes remained intact and brought, in the eyes of one observer, "security, comfort, and peace."[12]

Attu village on Attu Island, the most distant tip of the Aleutian archipelago, was typical of these communities. Forty-four Aleuts lived there, separated from the Alaska mainland by two thousand miles. Attu Island lay only 650 miles northeast of Japan's Kurile Islands. The Japanese had conducted scientific investigations in the area, some of which were documented by signatures of Japanese ship captains in the Attu church registry. American biological surveys were led into the area in 1936 and 1937 by Olaus Murie, who was aided by the "friendly cooperation" of Mike Hodikoff, the Attu leader. A village school building was constructed in 1932, but until late in 1940 no governmental education program was provided for its fifteen school-age children except for an occasional summer visit by a teacher. The community's largely self-sufficient economy was based on fishing, trapping, and a relatively lucrative fox farming operation. Following a nineteenth-century practice, United States Coast Guard vessels supplied medical aid and communication, usually reaching Attu between April and October each year.[13]

Nearest Attu, the village of Atka lay six hundred miles to the east on the shore of Nazan Bay on Atka Island. In 1940, eighty-nine Aleuts lived there in sixteen houses near a picturesque church. Although there was occasional bickering, life in Atka was harmonious. The village was incorporated in 1938 and governed itself through a council and an elected leader, William Dirks, Sr. Atka Aleuts had a cooperative store where supplies were purchased with profits from trapping of blue foxes on Atka, Amlia, and other neighboring islands. During the summer, some Atkans hired themselves out for sealing operations on the Pribilof Islands. Although hunting, fishing and trapping were carried out using privately owned dories, outboard-motor boats, nets, guns, and gear, the whole community shared the proceeds. By 1941, Atka villagers had accumulated nearly $24,000 of credit in an account administered by the Alaska Indian Service, a government agency that also employed two resident Caucasian teachers. As was the case with Attu, doctors on Coast Guard cutters provided medical services on summer visits.[14]

Nikolski, a village of ninety-seven Aleuts on the western tip of Umnak Island, stood east of Atka about two hundred miles. It was only about 150 miles from the hub of Aleutian activity, Dutch Harbor on nearby Unalaska Island. Nikolski's twenty Aleut houses were clustered around a church and cemetery, a schoolhouse, a recreation hall, and a cooperative store. Like Atka, Nikolski was incorporated and self-governing. The livelihood of its people derived from seasonal work supplemented by subsistence hunting and fishing. Some earned money by fox trapping. Several men were employed full-time, others part-time, at the Aleutian Livestock Company's sheep ranch less than a mile from the village. Others worked each summer in sealing operations on the Pribilof Islands and in various jobs on Unalaska Island. Because of poor fur harvests in 1939 and 1940, Nikolski Aleuts experienced hard times, but except for several widows whose husbands died in accidental drownings and left behind dependent children, the village was a self-supporting community.[15]

The village of Kashega on the northern shores of Unalaska Island was about eighty miles to the east of Nikolski. Twenty-six people lived at Kashega in eight houses, with a church and an empty school building and teacher quarters, abandoned sometime around 1936 by the Alaska Indian Service for lack of enrollment. A sheep ranch run by the Aleutian Livestock Company provided some employment for Kashega's Aleuts, and like Nikolski's Aleuts, they also relied on work elsewhere, fox trapping, and subsistence harvesting of fish and game. Because they did not have a cooperative store, they were dependent on supplies from the town of Unalaska, also the closest source of medical help. In 1942, the Aleut leader in Kashega was George Borenin.[16]

Makushin village, to the northeast of Kashega approximately thirty miles, was located on Makushin Bay, Unalaska Island, forty-five nautical miles from the town of Unalaska and fifteen by air. Only eight Aleuts lived there; six were members of the Eli Borenin family. John P. Olsen, the Caucasian owner of a sheep ranch, store, and other buildings in the village, was married to an Aleut woman. Not all of the seven Aleut houses were used, but the church and a small electrical generating plant were. The Borenins apparently supported themselves by working on the sheep ranch and by hunting, fishing, and trapping.[17]

The city of Unalaska on the eastern end of the island of Unalaska was the Aleutian chain's largest community, diverse and almost cosmopolitan, very much unlike Makushin. Not as remote as the other island communities, Unalaska was nevertheless separated from the territorial capital, Juneau, by over 1,100 nautical miles, from Anchorage by 740, and from Seattle by 1,700. Its 289 people were split almost in half ethnically, 151 of them being Caucasian. The 138 Aleuts occupied thirty-eight houses, some interspersed among Caucasian-owned dwellings and business establishments. In 1941, soldiers from nearby Fort Mears and navy personnel from Dutch Harbor, the naval base across Iliuliuk Bay, frequented the town, as did civilian employees engaged in the area's military construction projects. Unalaska was provided a school, a hospital, a post office, and a commissioner and deputy marshal. Aleuts of the town lived on wages earned as longshoremen, commercial fishermen, and construction workers, and by hunting and fishing as most Aleuts did elsewhere in the Aleutians. The town included restaurants, taverns, a movie theater, and a large general store. Unalaska's Aleuts were especially proud of their beautiful Church of the Holy Ascension of Christ. Their leader was William Zaharoff.[18]

Biorka village on Sedanka Island, twenty-five miles to the southeast of Unalaska Island, stood in stark contrast to the town of Unalaska. Eighteen Aleuts lived there in four family houses and worshiped in the Aleut church. The leader of this tiny community, second smallest after Makushin, was Alex Ermeloff, head of a family of five. His and the other families were sustained by trapping, subsistence harvesting, and employment at Unalaska. No school or store existed there; medical help had to be obtained at or from Unalaska.[19]

The village of Akutan on Akutan Island was situated fifty miles to the northwest of Unalaska and was in some of its characteristics similar to it. Just over one-half of its eighty residents were Aleuts, forty-one of them living in fifteen houses. The village contained a church, Indian Service school building and living quarters, store, post office, recreation hall, and hydroelectric plant. One of its industries, a small fish saltery, was owned by Hugh McGlashen, an Aleut who also ran the store and post office, although regular mail runs were eliminated in 1940. McGlashen's role in the community was important, but Mark Pettikoff was the Aleut leader. A major part of Akutan's wage economy was based on its two boat repair shops and a whale processing plant one mile from the village. Some of the village Aleuts joined in summer sealing on the Pribilof Islands, and many supplied their tables by fishing and hunting. Akutan had no medical services except those available on Coast Guard cutters or at Unalaska's hospital.[20]

The Pribilof Islands, northwest of Unalaska and Akutan about 250 miles into the Bering Sea, were home to over one-half of the Aleuts most affected by World War II. The village of St. George on St. George Island, the smaller of the two inhabited islands, was occupied by 183 Aleuts. In St. Paul village on St. Paul Island, forty-five miles north, lived 294 Aleuts who, like those on St. George, were essential employees of the United States government's enterprise in the harvesting of fur seals and fox. Both communities had Aleut churches, relatively modern houses, schools, community halls, cooperative stores, and movie theaters, and both were dotted by numerous buildings for the processing of thousands of pelts and seal by-products. The operation, a government monopoly in partnership with the Fouke Fur Company of St. Louis, Missouri, was supervised by agents of the Department of the Interior's Fish and Wildlife Service. St. George and St. Paul Aleuts were dependent on wages earned for the skins they helped take and process. Unlike other Aleuts, Pribilovians were provided houses by the government and certain food staples, but these had to be supplemented by seal meat harvested by the community. Repairs, furnishings, and fuel for these government houses, and clothing and personal belongings were not provided. There was a resident physician and four teachers. St. Paul, the most accessible island, had a rudimentary airplane runway, but access to the island was usually by ship. The Fish and Wildlife Service ship the *Penguin* made regular runs for supplies. Pribilovian Aleuts were valuable assets to this government operation, using considerable skill in handing the fur seal herd and curing pelts.[21]

Aleuts of the Aleutian and Pribilof islands obviously were not all alike. The war that encroached on them in June 1942 struck also in a variety of ways, affecting individuals and their villages differently. But what it meant to all was a painful change in the quality of their lives as described by an observer before the war: "People of the islands were not desolate and lonely. In their souls was a deep contentment that comes only to those who live close to the things they love."[22]

For many non-Aleuts, this area had long been shrouded in obscurity. In the annals of exploration, the Aleutian and Pribilof islands were part of the "Northern Mystery," a territory of conjecture and fanciful cartography. When the region belatedly began to emerge in the European consciousness, the images conveyed were as foggy as the climate itself. Even after considerable Russian exploration, ignorance persisted as "European scholars continued to publish erroneous books and maps about the lands of the North Pacific."[23] United States coastal and geodetic studies starting at Unimak Pass on the chain's eastern end and moving slowly westward were initiated as late as 1934. By 1940, only about 30 percent of this hydrographic work had been completed.[24]

Other officials of American government also moved slowly in these waters, and rather infrequently. Descriptions of Alaska's governance indicated dual control—federal and Territorial—but Aleuts and other Alaska Natives were barely touched by Territorial government, seldom if ever receiving its protection or support.[25] Furthermore, although over six hundred Aleut citizens were of voting age, they were not provided precinct voting facilities except at Unalaska, effectively disenfranchising all but a few.[26] Classified as "wards," they were the responsibility of federal agencies in Washington, D.C. The agency most active in their lives was the Department of the Interior, but its relationship to Alaska's Natives, unlike to American Natives elsewhere, was not defined by treaties. The New Deal's Indian Reorganization Act of 1934, the Wheeler-Howard bill, which sought to revitalize Native Americans, was not extended to Alaska until 1936.

Working under Secretary of the Interior Harold L. Ickes, the Commissioner of Indian Affairs, John C. Collier, superintended Aleutian Aleuts, while the Director of the Fish and Wildlife Service, Ira N. Gabrielson, oversaw the Pribilovians. The demands of their offices—administrative and political—were concentrated in the nation's capital, far from Alaska.

For the sake of efficiency and better service, the Bureau of Fisheries and the Bureau of Biological Survey were combined to form the new Fish and Wildlife Service in 1940 under the President's Reorganization Act.[27] In spite of the reformist nature of this move, it had little effect on

Pribilovian Aleuts. It kept intact several old divisions and brought no change between Aleut employees and their supervisors in fur seal conservation and hide production. This operation under the Fish and Wildlife Service was controlled by its Division of Alaska Fisheries with headquarters in Washington, D.C. The division's chief, Ward T. Bower, reported directly to Gabrielson.

In this government chain, the organization directly responsible for Pribilovian Aleuts was one of Bower's divisions, the Seal Division, whose superintendent, Edward C. Johnston, administered the Alaska sealing business from Seattle. On the islands, Johnston's most powerful representatives occupied the managerial positions of resident agent and caretaker: Daniel C. R. Benson on St. George and Lee C. McMillin on St. Paul. Although the organizational chart might seem cluttered, Fish and Wildlife Service lines of command were clear: Director Gabrielson to Chief Bower to Superintendent Johnston to agent and caretaker—Washington, D.C., to Seattle to the Pribilofs.[28] This rather simple administrative structure had worked for many decades, but its effectiveness would be tested severely in the wartime 1940s.

Non-Pribilovian Aleuts were under the jurisdiction of John Collier's Office of Indian Affairs, sometimes called the Bureau of Indian Affairs. The bureaucratic line followed from Collier through Assistant Commissioner of Indian Affairs William Zimmerman, Jr., in Washington, to a subdivision, the Alaska Indian Service. Its general superintendent was Claude M. Hirst, whose office was in Juneau. The Alaska Indian Service's mission was to provide education, health care, monetary assistance, and reindeer management for Alaska's Natives, who in 1939 numbered 32,458 people.[29] Activities of the Indian Service, established in 1884 as part of the U.S. Office of Education, had evolved over the years into more areas than education. In response to these additional roles, the Alaska Indian Service had been transferred in 1931 to the Office of Indian Affairs, and its Seattle office was moved to Juneau. Reform of the agency began in 1934, when six district educational superintendent offices were consolidated into two. The bureau was finally unified under one person in 1939 when Hirst was appointed its first general superintendent.[30]

Although this agency's responsibilities for the care of Aleuts were similar to those of the Fish and Wildlife Service Sealing Division, there were important differences. The Alaska Indian Service was a not-for-profit agency having no employer relationship with Aleuts. Its staff was much larger, served more people over more territory, and faced greater diversity and complexity.

At the Juneau office in 1941, Hirst supervised forty-six administrators and staff, including his administrative assistant, Fred R. Geeslin, Medical Director Dr. Langdon R. White, Director of Education Virgil R. Farrell, Acting Supervisor of Social Welfare Dr. Evelyn Butler Dale, and Senior Organization Field Agent Donald W. Hagerty. Its smallest divisional force in the field, the Reindeer Service, was composed of ten employees with headquarters in Nome and six stations starting in the north at Barrow and spreading along the Bering Sea coast to Bethel on the Kuskokwim River. Next largest, the Medical Department employed forty-nine field nurses, seventeen part-time dentists, and four full-time and five part-time physicians. Difficulties in health care delivery were apparent from the number of vacancies: twenty-two nurses and five physicians.[31]

The largest share of the Service's effort was spent on education of Natives. For educational tasks, Hirst had in the field nearly 270 personnel—teachers (about three dozen vacancies), their spouses, principals, housekeepers, mechanics, and miscellaneous assistants. These employees were assigned to 123 teaching stations in all sorts of communities listed alphabetically from Afognak to Yakutat, scattered geographically from the Arctic Ocean to Metlakatla on Annette Island in the temperate Southeast. Indian Service teachers exercised governmental and social influence because they were often the only officials and Caucasians living in these Alaska villages.[32]

Of the Alaska Indian Service's approximately four hundred employees, more than 10 percent were administrative personnel residing in Juneau. In spite of its size, the Service's presence in the Aleutian Islands was minuscule. Just over four hundred of the area's Aleuts in 1941 were served by three nurses in a twelve-bed hospital at Unalaska; the hospital's physician post remained unfilled. Teachers on the chain were extremely scarce: one each at Akutan, Atka, Attu, and Nikolski, all with male spouses as "special assistants"; a male principal, his wife, and another woman as teachers at Unalaska. Such austerity was related to budget cuts initiated in 1938.[33] Care of Aleuts cost the Alaska Indian Service relatively little before the war.

While few village conditions had been improved by the government before World War II, there was one notable exception. A report by the Bureau of Fisheries, "The Fur Seals and Other Life of the Pribilof Islands, Alaska, in 1914," revealed that Pribilovian houses were ramshackle and overcrowded. Better dwellings were consequently provided.[34] Other moves held potential for improvement. A series of conferences in 1937 at Washington, D.C., determined that Alaska Indian Service teachers were to be agents of reform.[35] An agreement clarifying responsibilities in cases of mixed marriage, desertion, incarceration, and divorce was worked out between the Alaska Indian Service and the Territorial Department of Public Welfare. Its intent was to assist needy Aleuts. One of its key provisions was that the Office of Indian Affairs would "be responsible for the care of any person one-quarter native or more and his or her dependents."[36] This one-quarter blood quantum test modified a long-standing one-eighth blood quantum standard.

But significant improvement in the Aleutians was difficult because old problems persisted. Scholars investigating the system argued in 1935 that Juneau was too isolated to serve as headquarters for the best interests of Natives. Aleutian airplane travel was extremely difficult because of inclement weather. Mail-boat service was infrequent. Unalaska, they determined, should be the Aleut service center of the federal government, not Juneau. An Aleutian base would help, among other things, in the dispatch of government boats to service remote Aleut villages. These observers also noted "inequalities and discriminations against natives" in the government's allotment of fox hunting privileges in the Aleutians.[37]

Other problems existed within the Alaska Indian Service organization. Its officials held distinctly negative attitudes toward the Aleutians and Aleuts. Jay Ellis Ransom, a young teacher slated for service at Nikolski on Umnak Island, was told by Superintendent Hirst in 1936, "It is impossible for me to convey adequately to you all the troubles and problems which will confront you." Conditions there, he warned, would be "anything but savory." Another employee described Umnak as "a terrible place . . . no white people . . . no electricity . . . the last teacher had trouble with the natives . . . the weather is awful." Hirst admitted that some problems there were caused by teachers. However, Ransom himself claimed that the Alaska Indian Service was weakened not only by educators but by "politicians," and "too many inefficient and irresponsible men" who "bungled" and "mismanaged" and "do not care about natives." Aleuts, he noticed, were proud of their heritage, resented "white oppression," were disrespectful of American government, and regarded themselves as "exploited people."[38] As a consequence, many of them, like those at Akutan, resisted efforts to participate in an adult education program. "We have carried on considerable agitation for such classes," a field worker reported, "but so far we have had no response."[39]

Other accounts of Aleuts were decidedly deprecatory. Typical was a Roman Catholic priest's judgment in 1935 that "old Aleuts were a blood thirsty lot" who "did not get very far in the cultural arts," were "probably Asiatic degenerates," and had "hardly advanced beyond" the

"Stone Age." Modern "pure-blooded Aleuts," he thought, "are either dying out or else have become so mixed with alien blood as to hide their racial characteristics completely."[40] Similar sentiment was expressed by a storekeeper's wife, a school teacher from New Mexico, who wrote about her experiences in Atka between 1935 and 1936. She never really liked Aleuts, was condescending, and contrasted them with "civilized" people. She regretted they did not possess a competitive, capitalistic instinct. Her husband, however, predicted she would "get used to them soon enough" because "they're really just like kids." In his estimation, they were "lazy" and "irresponsible."[41]

Some observers were simultaneously admiring and suspicious of Aleuts. The popular New Deal writers' project guide to Alaska, for example, declared that "Aleuts . . . look more like Russian mujiks than the remnants of a great Eskimauan people. Like the Czar's peasants, they have a stoic capacity for suffering in silence; like the peasants, they are subject to terrible swift rages."[42] One newspaperman in 1942 saw it differently. He asserted that "Aleuts might be described as sawed-off Indians with slant eyes. They have an admixture of Oriental blood, which may be an additional reason why they hate the Japs."[43]

Pribilovians were viewed the same way as their Aleutian relatives, although they generally were regarded as more privileged. Catherine Benson, wife of the St. George agent and caretaker, claimed that "you have to do everything for them, even think for them." After twenty years of service at this post, she and her husband had come to view the Pribilof Aleuts not only as "adopted children" but as "extravagant" and wasteful beneficiaries of governmental largess.[44]

A like-minded opinion from outside the Sealing Division appeared in a widely circulated monthly journal, *Alaska Sportsman,* commonly referred to as "Alaska's Magazine." An article in 1941 by Ralph A. Ferrandini, entitled "They Sing, Dance and Play," described these islanders' blissful lives as a gift of a generous government. Besides singing, dancing, and playing, they "work . . . a little . . . throughout their simple lives" and are superstitious, pampered, ignorant, sexually immoral, "actually . . . unmoral," and primitive. Ferrandini charged, moreover, that Pribilovians were by birth locked into inferiority. Nothing that "well-meaning doctors or school teachers" tried in "social reforms and moral education" materially helped matters. All "such attempts ultimately" were doomed to "failure," causing the Aleuts to "become suspicious and resentful. They lose their respect for their white overseers," he wrote, and become "sullen and rebellious."[45]

Because fur seals leave the Pribilof Islands every autumn and do not return until spring, some people, according to Ferrandini, proposed that Pribilovians be removed in the winter to lessen the burden of governmental costs. Ambivalently, he opposed this suggestion, wondering, "Where could the natives be sent? They know nothing of outside conditions . . . have no other occupation, . . . will always be wards of the Government," and will always "have to be taken care of by some Government Agency." Despite these concerns, Ferrandini felt that the Pribilof situation was a proud "example" of what could be accomplished by "generous, just management and understanding cooperation." He ended on an apprehensive note: "The haunting shadow of insecurity . . . banished from these fog-bound little islands, should never again be allowed to return. . . . Let us hope that . . . no destructive outside factors will steal in to trouble the hearts of these simple people, happy in their unique occupation of herding seals through the misty dawns across the rocky slopes of the Pribilofs."[46]

2

Rumors of War

Some day they [will] come to Attu. . . . They [will]
come here; you see. They [will] take Attu some day.
—Michael Hodikoff, Attu Aleut Prisoner of War
in Corey Ford, *Short Cut to Tokyo*

Hodikoff predicted an ominous Japanese invasion. But Aleuts seemed
so secure on their island homes that hardly anyone anticipated what
would happen to them if war came. This changed little even as talk of
war's likelihood increased. The emerging Pacific powers, the United
States and Japan, gave the Aleutians scarcely any military attention until
the early 1940s; then they moved into the area rather precipitantly. On
close analysis, a clash in the Aleutians appeared natural given the expansion of both countries in a span of several decades. United States annexa-
tion of the Hawaiian Islands, cession of the Philippines as a result of the
Spanish-American War, and Japan's victory in the Russo-Japanese War
and subsequent Asian conquests were omens of impending conflict.

Until actual fighting made speculation irrelevant, several positions
emerged concerning the military value of the Aleutian and Pribilof
islands. One held that the islands were not very important because the
area was a virtual cul-de-sac that was so remote it was strategically
worthless. Furthermore, it needed little or no defense because rugged
terrain and adverse weather were deterrents to military action. Armies
would find there a special kind of hell.[1] But another position disre-
garded such factors and stressed Aleutian military importance. William
"Billy" Mitchell of the Army Air Force was a chief supporter. An advocate of the airplane, Mitchell, armed with a world globe and Mercator
projection map, advanced to Major Henry "Happy" Arnold the argument that we "could swoop down on Japan, following the long finger
of the Aleutians." Conversely, the Japanese could beat us to this route
"first by dominating the sky and creeping up the Aleutians."[2]

Actually both theories contained valid points—one about Aleutian
isolation, difficult terrain, and weather; the other about the potential of
airplanes to conquer the area's vast distances. But the one tended to
exaggerate the improbability of war there, while the other failed to

realize that, although on maps the islands look like convenient stepping stones, in reality they were more like roadblocks.

Our military planners considered these arguments but were slow to develop strategy for the Aleutians even when driven in the 1930s by prospects of war. Army strategists in 1935, according to one version of "Plan Orange," our contingency response to war, drew the nation's defense line from Alaska south to Hawaii and thence southeast to the Panama Canal. Navy planners countered with a more offensive strategy emphasizing naval engagements west of Hawaii in the central Pacific.[3] These issues remained in limbo and the Aleutians were left an undeveloped military area.

The Japanese military, on the other hand, speculated that the United States might use the Aleutians for invasion or air raids on military bases at Paramishiro in the northern Kurile Islands. A Japanese occupation in the North Pacific would prevent this and anchor a protective arc stretching from Kiska Island to New Guinea. Apprehension over American intentions deepened in the 1930s as Japanese citizens were subjected to increased anti-American propaganda and scare rumors of supposed new American military bases in the Aleutians. The Japanese army and the press, in years before the war began, "used America as the hypothetical enemy in order to whip up a war psychosis."[4]

Similarly, Alaskans were stirred in the 1930s by anti-Japanese rhetoric and provocative scenes of imminent war. Anthony J. Dimond, Alaska's elected delegate to Congress with voice but no vote, repeatedly predicted direful consequences for the undefended Territory should Japan or the Soviet Union attack. Such disaster-filled warnings were aimed at promoting military expenditures and building Alaska's underdeveloped infrastructure. Alaska's legislature had little tax revenue for this. Washington, D.C., with the larger purse, was therefore solicited to fund Alaska's internal improvements.[5] These requests were based on the assumption that preparation for war fit hand-in-glove with progress for Alaskans.

Actual battles in the North Pacific, referred to throughout the war as "the Aleutian campaign," began with the Japanese bombing of Dutch Harbor on June 3 and 4, 1942. The Japanese occupation of Kiska and Attu followed several days later. Preliminary to that, starting in 1941, unprecedented numbers of wartime personnel had arrived with material for construction projects. This phase of military buildup ushered in a new chapter in Aleut history that would last well beyond World War II. From an Aleut perspective, the story of the war in Alaska started when fortification brought outside influences to their islands and effected substantial changes in their way of life.

The buildup began with a program of fortifying Alaska strongholds near or on the mainland: the army's at Fort Richardson outside Anchorage and the navy's on Kodiak Island and at Sitka. Fairbanks, deep in the interior, was also slated for considerable military expansion. The initial directors of this military enterprise occupied stateside headquarters: Vice-Admiral Charles S. Freeman in Seattle, Commandant of the Thirteenth Naval District, and Lieutenant General John L. DeWitt in San Francisco, Commander of the Western Defense Command. Under them in Alaska stood Navy Captain Ralph C. Parker, Commander of the Alaska Sector, and Army Colonel Simon B. Buckner, Jr., Commander of the Alaska Defense Force. By the end of the war, these officers and their successors—the military establishment—had superintended the expenditure of $1.25 billion for the building of a new "Fortress Alaska."[6]

This sudden infusion of personnel and money reversed a decline of the armed forces in the Territory since the turn of the century and revitalized an old tradition—the military as a shaping force in Alaska history. It meant military activities in defending, garrisoning, policing, and building.[7] Many Alaskans felt the effects of these functions. Military command directives were governmental in nature and involved travel restrictions, communication censorship, and civilian evacuation. The rationale for these measures was based on safety and effective pursuit of the war to its victorious end. Military officers were often ill at ease when exercising civil administrative power, however, for they felt insufficiently trained for it and regarded such tasks as diversionary.[8] Moreover, the military preferred to prepare for war without civilians getting in the way. But there was no such luxury in Alaska. By dint of ample supplies, monetary resources, and power over civilians, the military became the lords of Alaska, a status reluctantly held but made necessary by the circumstances of war.

At first, relations between military and civilian officials were complementary, both being interested in the defense program. Alaska's newly appointed governor, Ernest Gruening, joined Delegate Anthony Dimond as an avid supporter of military construction. They enthusiastically endorsed efforts of Colonel Buckner at Anchorage, the majordomo of this military buildup.[9] His arrival in July 1940 and subsequent promotion to Major General signaled the increasing importance of the Territory. The new general became Alaska's "Mr. Defense" and also its "General Offense," arguing that the Aleutians should be used as an avenue to Tokyo. In their first meeting, Gruening, who was commissioned to organize Alaska's National Guard, was impressed by Buckner. But this attitude changed. Eventually, Gruening complained about censorship, unnecessary travel restrictions, and Buckner's restrictive policies vis-à-vis Alaska's Natives.[10]

Buckner nevertheless jumped into his asssignment with characteristic gusto. By October 1940, a personally conducted reconnaissance for airfield sites introduced him to the Aleutians. His first goal was to develop air protection for the area's military linchpin at Dutch Harbor. Recognizing the chain's drawbacks for military action and not wanting to incite the Japanese, Buckner recommended no defensive projects beyond Umnak Island, close to Dutch Harbor.[11] This meant that the majority of Aleuts—those at Attu, Atka, Kashega, Makushin, Biorka, Akutan, St. George, and St. Paul—would not see any prewar military buildup.

The fledgling defense program was also affected by monetary constraints. It was not until 1942 that a U.S. Navy aerological unit was established on Kiska Island two hundred miles east of Attu because weather data and surveillance reports were becoming more significant with the possibility of war.[12] But Attu Island is our closest territory to Japan. It is the westernmost and easternmost piece of U.S. territory, lying at 173 degrees east longitude, as far east as New Zealand. Attu harbored no weather-reporting facility until civilian agencies placed one there in 1940. The Washington, D.C., office of the U.S. Weather Bureau urged the sending of a teacher and radio operator but offered to fund only part of the expense. Responding patriotically, Superintendent Claude Hirst recommended that, in spite of more serious need elsewhere, the positions be filled and then fully funded in the Alaska Indian Service budget of 1941 for "national defense needs."[13] In this roundabout way, the Aleut schoolchildren of Attu also benefited.

Military activity in the early 1940s was concentrated on the other end of the chain from Attu. Troops numbering three thousand were dispatched there, and defense construction increased.[14] Only two Aleut communities, however, would be affected directly by these military developments: Nikolski and Unalaska. Of the two, Nikolski's involvement was the smaller and the impact on it considerably less, partly because its location was not as strategically important as Unalaska's.

The problem facing General Buckner was how to defend military installations at Dutch Harbor on Unalaska Island, for the surrounding mountains made airfield construction impractical. He chose a site at Otter Point on nearby Umnak Island, twelve miles across Umnak Pass from Chernofski Harbor, to serve as a staging area. Then began the secret construction of Fort Glenn, sixty-five miles from Dutch Harbor. Its "occupation by U.S. Army troops" in January 1942 was ordered by General DeWitt, who "prohibited the inclusion of Orientals in the movements."[15] By the end of May, the post housed "173 officers, one warrant officer, and 4,450 enlisted men."[16]

Never before had Umnak Island contained so many people. Its oldest inhabited community, Nikolski, located sixty-miles from Otter Point, was near one of the most ancient of known occupied sites in Alaska. Now it was to be occupied by a regiment of the Army Engineering Corps. On March 25, 1942, the United States Army transport ship the *Delarof* delivered five officers and 141 enlisted men to Nikolski, making it a "subpost of Fort Glenn," increasing its military importance, and introducing Nikolski Aleuts to the military.[17]

But Aleuts in the town of Unalaska on neighboring Unalaska Island received the brunt of this kind of military development. Even before great numbers of military personnel arrived, construction workers had inundated the area to build the army's Fort Mears and the navy's Dutch Harbor facilities. These were located on Amaknak Island, a stone's throw across Iliuliuk Bay from the town.[18] Starting in September 1940, workers arrived to transform Dutch Harbor into an Aleutian defense center. The Siems-Drake-Puget Sound construction consortium under a $44 million contract—$20.5 million for the army and $23.5 million for the navy—was designated the general contractor. By June 1941 both facilities were operational, and a year later wrap-up duties were assigned to navy construction battalions.[19] Inevitably, these civilian workers and military personnel crossed over Iliuliuk Bay and encountered Aleuts settled at Unalaska.

Strains on the community surfaced soon after this and grew in magnitude until Unalaska's Aleuts were evacuated in July 1942. Problems they had not experienced before were thrust upon Unalaska residents. The massive military project brought labor disputes and tensions. A lockout of union carpenters by management produced idle laborers walking Unalaska's streets; some filled empty time in saloons. Many workers became disgruntled over high costs of living, foul weather, dangerous working conditions and lack of medical facilities. They remembered promises of overtime pay and recreation offered by company recruiters in Seattle.[20] Their mood was surly, an attitude most Alaskan workers did not hold because they were familiar with Aleutian conditions.

Governor Gruening and the Territory's secretary, Edward L. "Bob" Bartlett (acting governor in Gruening's absence), were interested in seeing Alaskans placed in construction jobs. Both were frustrated, however, because contractors often preferred "outside" labor. Although some Alaska Natives, including nineteen Aleuts, were employed as civilians on Dutch Harbor military projects, Gruening and Bartlett complained in March 1941 when eight Aleuts from Umnak Island who were regarded as good workmen were denied employment. Discrimination by employees of Siems-Drake-Puget Sound surfaced as labor-management problems. A report on working conditions by two laborers told of a supervisor who, noticing a Native riding in the front seat of a company truck, threatened, "Get out of there, you black son of a bitch, before I pull you out. I'll teach you to respect your superiors." The supervisor then took the vacated seat.[21]

Other problems developed at Unalaska. By the spring of 1941, no agency had been designated to coordinate federal government bureaus responsible for health, education, and welfare of military dependents soon to be arriving in ever-increasing numbers.[22] Anticipating this influx, Unalaska's U.S. commissioner, Jack Martin, and the deputy U.S. marshal, L. Verne Robinson, both of whom exercised legal and quasi-governmental powers, became alarmed over lack of federal aid for schools, recreational facilities, electrical generating capacity, sewage and garbage disposal plants, and fire and police protection. They were joined by the commanding officer of Fort Mears, Brigadier General Edgar B. Colladay, who informed General Buckner that the influx of military families would create a school problem and "sanitary menace." Unalaska, he reminded his superior, "is not incorporated," and "consists of a collection . . . of dilapidated buildings occupied by people of a nationality other than white." It seemed to him hardly a place fit for military families.[23]

Nevertheless, Buckner confirmed the "permanency of the garrison" and ordered installation of additional army housing and two grade schools for an increase of 500 students. He suggested that Governor Gruening consider improved housing, power, water, and sewage facilities for the civilian residents of Unalaska and "also for the common good of the Army, the Navy and the Coast Guard garrisons." But funding from the federal or territorial legislatures for the material improvement of the remote town was not forthcoming. Buckner nevertheless promised the governor his cooperation "toward making this one of our many ideal spots in Alaska."[24]

In response to military pressures and the absence of federal and Territorial aid, Unalaskan citizens themselves adapted strategies for community improvement. By the fall of 1941, the population had grown to over four hundred, nearly doubling since 1940. Feeling that something had to be done, Commissioner Jack Martin informed Delegate Anthony

Dimond of "a growing under-current of rumor" that Unalaska might be placed in a "naval reserve" by executive order and that "martial law" could be established, curtailing individual freedoms. These fears led to a petition and vote to incorporate Unalaska as a first-class city.[25] The measure carried, and in December 1941 Unalaska became a city with a seven-member council and an acting mayor. In April 1942, John W. Fletcher, a Caucasian, was elected as Unalaska's first chief executive.[26]

Yet in the political maneuverings of these years, U.S. Commissioner Jack Martin, not John Fletcher, played the major role touching Aleut lives. More than anybody outside the military, he focused attention on Unalaska and attracted the scrutiny of officials in the Department of the Interior. He projected an image of Unalaska as a problem area. Martin thus unwittingly spotlighted Aleuts as a troubled people. Like many pioneers who came to Alaska for its riches, Martin was a shrewd operative, government official, politician, businessman, associate of Unalaska's white establishment, friend of Aleuts, and worker for the good of the community. He was thoroughly at home there. Controversy surrounded him because he seemed to mix public good with private gain. This rankled some but impressed others. Some admired Martin as an Alaska variant of a Yankee entrepreneur.

Because of the flurry of military buildup, Unalaska was ripe for bonanza profits in real estate and the liquor business. Many citizens saw property values move skyward and welcomed the growth as enthusiastically as the businessmen who luxuriated over profits in selling liquor and supplies, providing housing, and entertaining the new arrivals. Monies gained could be used for community improvement. The challenge, however, was to keep the new opportunities from degenerating into a frenzy of exploitation.

All segments of Unalaska society—the most diverse of Aleut communities—were interested in the escalation of property values. Many of the town's approximately forty property-owning Aleuts and a like number of its non-Natives stood to reap a windfall.[27] Ownership of land, which theretofore had been claimed by aboriginal and occupancy rights, could be deeded to Aleuts beginning in 1941 under supervision of the Interior Department. Title to approximately one-third of Unalaska's undeveloped and residential town sites was held by Aleuts, and the rest lay in the hands of the Methodist Church, which once ran an orphanage and school there, the Russian Orthodox Church, the Northern Commercial Company, and Caucasians with houses and business establishments.[28] In this situation, Jack Martin saw an opportunity; and like Tammany Hall's finest, he took it.

Catering to heavy demand for housing and business lots, Martin and his associate, L. Verne Robinson, leased property from Aleuts. They then subleased it for increased rates to business interests—all quite legal, it seemed at first. Suspicion over Martin's activities led Unalaska's Indian Service schoolteacher and principal, J. C. Wingfield, to a closer investigation. He claimed that Aleuts were being bilked because they signed leases for a pittance and for too many years, not accounting for appreciation of property values. Alarmed by this, Wingfield appealed to the Alaska Indian Service's legal counsel, G. W. Folta, for an opinion early in April 1941. Shortly thereafter, Folta informed Wingfield that Aleut deeds to property were restricted by a provision that they "could not be alienated or encumbered without the approval of the Secretary of the Interior." Because no one in the Department of the Interior had knowledge of these goings-on, such leases held by Martin and others "were void." Folta directed that Martin be so informed and that Alaska Indian Service officials take his place as intermediaries in future transactions.[29]

The fat was now in the fire, and the resulting imbroglio made Unalaska a hot spot in more than military building. Government officials interested in Aleuts were drawn there as never before. In Juneau, reactions of Alaska Indian Service officials to the Martin leases exposé were decisive. Superintendent Claude Hirst assigned Wingfield to be the agent in subsequent lease negotiations. After Wingfield resigned in June 1941, the town's physician, Dr. W. E. Corthell, replaced him as watchdog of Aleut interests. By late July, when matters seemed under control, Fred R. Geeslin, Hirst's assistant, visited to survey the situation. Unalaska's problems had seldom attracted as much attention, nor had they been addressed with such dispatch. Investigators agreed later that the crisis required a bigger Indian Service staff for Unalaska.[30]

Besides Martin, John A. Yatchmeneff was a catalyst in drawing government attention to Unalaska. He was "Secretary of the Unalaska and Aleutian Islands Native Community," an organization that existed in name only. Nevertheless, Yatchmeneff was the only elected Aleut city council member. He became the key figure in highlighting Aleut concerns before the war. His credentials were based on an old tradition of Aleut self-expression and leadership, exemplified by his father, Alexei Meronovich Yatchmeneff. The elder Yatchmeneff had been fluent in Aleut, Russian, and English, and before his death in 1937, had established a reputation as the most famous Aleut leader of the twentieth century, "Chief of all the Chiefs from Kodiak to Attu."[31] John Yatchmeneff did not inherit his father's mantle, but he took unto himself the role of Aleut spokesman in a long letter of May 16, 1941, addressed to President Franklin D. Roosevelt and delegate Anthony Dimond. He also sent this letter a few days later to Eleanor Roosevelt.[32]

The background to the letter was the Alaska Indian Service's nullifica-tion of the Martin leases, which Yatchmeneff viewed as meddling into Aleut affairs, despite the beneficial intent. Martin and Yatchmeneff had connections going back many years. Yatchmeneff's father had honored Martin in 1934 by presenting him with a gavel for conducting his court.[33] Now Yatchmeneff the son served as a court interpreter, one of Martin's employees. When Aleuts were evacuated from Unalaska in 1942, Yatchmeneff was allowed to stay, not because his court position was vital to national defense, but because of Martin's clout. Although motives for his writing to the President were mixed, a government investigator acknowledged that Yatchmeneff's beliefs were sincere and that he was articulate enough to be the letter's author.[34]

Although some felt that Yachmeneff did not speak for all Aleuts, his letter was a catalog of long-standing grievances against government discrimination. Officials of the Alaska Indian Service and the Fish and Wildlife Service were major culprits. In Yatchmeneff's eyes, federal bureaucrats treated Aleuts as inferior, second-class citizens. Officials persisted in calling them "Indians," when in fact they were *Aleuts,* an important distinction. Their ethnic identity was threatened in 1940 when Unalaska's school was transferred to federal hands, the Territorial government having refused to fund Native education. A promise was made then that the Aleut community would be provided two high school grade levels. But Yatchmeneff pointed out that this arrangement was soon abandoned when the government installed a program of Indian-like crafts not pertinent to Aleut students.

Other government action reduced Aleuts to "dependency and help-lessness." In contrast, Yatchmeneff praised Jack Martin for obtaining trapping rights for them on Carlisle Island and supporting their trans-portation and stocking of blue foxes there. This venture, which pro-duced six thousand dollars for the community in 1940, was terminated in the fall of 1941 by the Department of the Interior. Aleuts saw this as unwarranted encroachment and resented the order that they remove all their equipment from Carlisle Island to preserve bird life. To govern-ment officials, apparently, birds were more valuable than Aleut well-being. Yatchmeneff also complained that Atka's people were forced to give up trapping on Amchitka Island, ostensibly in an effort to save birds.

These allegations of infringement of rights, unkept promises, decep-tion, and lack of concern were old charges against Interior Department officials. But Yatchmeneff's request of the President for help was un-precedented. Behind it was the feeling that Caucasians were afforded constitutional guarantees while Aleuts were not; Aleuts were held in lower status because they were born Aleuts. Using imagery from Lincoln's "house divided" speech, Yatchmeneff pleaded that Aleuts "cannot be half wards and half free men," only serving "the purposes of the Indian Office." To counter notions of ethnic inferiority, he claimed that since Russian days, whites and Aleuts had "become so inbred" that except for Attuans, "none of our people are full blood Aleuts. Most of our people have more than half white blood in their veins."[35] If this were true—and it likely was—the blood quantum test defining Aleut-government relationships would apply to very few Aleuts.

But Yatchmeneff's letter to the President caused only slight concern among Indian Affairs personnel in Washington, D.C. Assistant Commissioner William Zimmerman, Jr., who handled Alaska problems for Commissioner John Collier, did not send a copy of Yatchmeneff's letter to Hirst until early September. By then, Zimmerman had learned that Dr. John P. Harrington of the Smithsonian Institution planned to be in Unalaska in the fall with a young anthropologist-linguist, Joseph J. White, Jr. Zimmerman employed these two as undercover investigators of the Martin affair and the Yatchmeneff letter, hoping these outsiders would not be "embarrassing either to Dr. Corthell or any other Indian Service people" at Unalaska. Their investigation into the episode concluded with a final report issued November 25, 1941.[36]

Harrington and White found in Unalaska a spoiled opportunity for Aleut betterment. The guilty parties were Jack Martin and associates, Yatchmeneff being their dupe. Although the two anthropologists recognized Yatchmeneff as a "gifted person" whose grievances were sincerely held, they felt his views were not shared by other Natives even though they attended a meeting he called and joined a committee to promote Aleut causes. It was Martin's ploy, fomented for "private purposes," that represented a "very extensive abuse of office" and was examined by the Federal Bureau of Investigation. Martin was not formally charged, but his activities had caused "Native factionalism."

The report by Harrington and White praised Indian Service activities and the hard work of Wingfield and Corthell. Martin was an easy target. The hostility of John Yatchmeneff was not, but the two failed to probe into it. They regarded complaints about Carlisle and Amchitka islands to be beyond their scope because trapping came under the Fish and Wildlife Service, and they had been hired by the Bureau of Indian Affairs. They accused Aleuts, including Yatchmeneff and Aleut leader William Zaharoff, of chronic "heavy drinking." Uncontrolled liquor consumption and subsistence hunting and fishing took Aleuts away from the town, making Indian Service work among them extremely difficult. One of the report's conclusions was that "natives were unable to protect their interests."[37]

More and more this assessment of Unalaska's problems was forwarded to Washington, D.C. Defense projects were making Unalaska infamous for its unhealthy society. Secretary of the Interior Harold L. Ickes was so worried about the effect on Alaska of the building boom that he sent a personal field representative, Dr. Ruth Gruber, to investigate conditions at Kodiak and Dutch Harbor. Her written report left a poignant impression of Unalaska in 1941. She contrasted its beautiful physical surroundings with an ugly social scene that would make a gold mining camp seem tame by comparison. It was a "Defense Town" in "upheaval" and had psychologically "gone berserk" when "money flowed and liquor overflowed." Young women there, she asserted, were "prostituted at 12 and 15" years of age; "the Russian priest and Methodist missionary" were engaged in "manipulating land," while drunken workers stumbled on its streets.[38]

Furthermore, Unalaska's deteriorating condition was likely to worsen because more than eight thousand military personnel were slated to arrive beginning in 1942. The Division of Territories and Island Possessions in the Interior Department was made aware of this crisis in civilian governance. Its director, Benjamin W. Thoron, who reported to Secretary Ickes, was assisted by Alaska's Territorial governor, Ernest Gruening, and in Washington, D.C., by Supervisor of Alaska Affairs Paul W. Gordon. The Division was briefed about the Unalaska situation by a representative of the War Department who met in November 1941 with Gordon and a member of the Division's Solicitor's Office. The "overshadowing defense development," they agreed, had led to "problems of law and order" that Secretary Ickes would have to address.[39]

Unalaska's problems, as they saw them, could not be solved by relying on federal or Territorial government. First, Deputy U.S. Marshal Robinson and U.S. Commissioner Martin as "enforcing officers" posed a "considerable question" about being "equal to their task." Martin was known as a minion of liquor interests and was guilty of "operating a disorderly house." Military police, who could be very effective, had no jurisdiction over the civilian population. Furthermore, Unalaska's need for schools, sewage facilities, water, and electricity could not be met by tax levies because the largest taxable base, the Northern Commercial Company, generated inadequate tax revenue. Finally, to incorporate the community for municipal government would not bring necessary protection for Aleuts since the new regime "would undoubtedly be controlled by other than natives." The conferees concluded "that the future of Unalaska cannot be separated from that of the Naval reserve." They noted that serious consideration had been given "to the possibility of extending the Naval reserve to include the site occupied by the town of Unalaska."[40]

These Department of Interior discussions soon bore fruit in a decision about Unalaska. On December 2, 1941, Secretary Ickes endorsed a policy written by his staff. The impetus for the policy, however, had been supplied by the War Department. Government and military officials agreed that Unalaska could not avoid being crushed by an impending large influx of people. This "interchange of activities will present serious problems of civil administration." The solution was "to leave these civil problems in Unalaska for the military authorities to solve."[41]

Government officials felt that they could not themselves solve Unalaska's problems. Incorporation of the town would be inadequate. They did not pursue legislation for strengthening Department of the Interior powers in civil administration, for which there was precedent. They did not seek presidential approval for Lanham Act funding to build defense-related housing and public works projects. Overwhelmed by Unalaska's situation, the policy-makers recognized "some danger in approving the extension of the military reservation, and thereby permitting the military authorities to have a hand in civil functions." But this danger was overshadowed "by the risks which inevitably would accompany the Department's assumption of responsibility for the administration of local affairs in the area."[42]

Aleut relations had been frustrating for the government. Interior Department officials had "difficult problems of adjustment and regulation in supervising the affairs of the Aleuts and in regulating the fisheries," officials stated. Pessimism ruled: "The community lacks essential resources, both material and human. In most part, the residents are Aleuts and the few white people living there are considered not to be sufficiently dependable to be entrusted with the delicate and difficult problems of civil administration that undoubtedly will confront the community."[43] By turning to the military, Interior Department officials unloaded their Unalaska responsibilities. This abandonment reflected traditional Aleut–government alienation and would be repeated in the evacuation of Unalaska city some months ahead.

3

Responses to War

> After the military had established themselves on Unalaska Island,
> they did erect a barbed wire fence that separated us from what
> they called the reservation. We were subject and had to
> conform to military curfew and blackouts,
> had to carry unwieldy gas masks. . . .
> —Philemon Tutiakoff, Unalaska Aleut Evacuee
> Commission on Wartime Relocation Hearings

Of Alaskans made vulnerable by the start of war in early December 1941, Aleuts occupied the most precarious positions based on proximity to Japan. This proximity already had brought Aleuts and Japanese together in less-than-amicable contacts. No strangers to the Aleutian and Pribilof islands, Japanese fisherman were not welcomed there by Aleuts. A bloody tradition was begun in 1906, when St. Paul Island Aleut sharpshooters killed two Japanese seal poachers and organized a guard force that later shot three other poachers to death. In a subsequent "battle fought between the Japanese invaders and the natives" who policed the seal herd, eleven Japanese lost their lives. In the Aleutians, intruders faired somewhat better, but there, too, "the Aleuts regarded the Japanese with extreme distrust even before the war."[1] Suspicion stemmed from "evidence of Japanese landings on uninhabited islands," and what were seen as frequent snooping visits of a Japanese fisheries training ship, the *Hakuyo Maru*, and a scouting companion, the *Hakuho Maru*, that were spotted sometimes in the waters of Attu, Atka, St. Paul, and St. George. After the Japanese attack on Pearl Harbor, hatred for the enemy was dramatized in the Aleut "Masked Dance" ceremony, in which, symbolically, Germans and Italians were merely shot, but "Japanese were shot, hung, and then cut to pieces."[2]

Aleut ritualism aside, many Alaskans feared a Japanese invasion and predicted it would be successful. Alaska was virtually undefended, an appealing lure to the enemy. Even before Pearl Harbor, Alaskan military and civilian morale was decidedly low and the mood pessimistic. At the army's Alaska Defense Command headquarters in Anchorage, reporter William Gillman noticed that "officers had a disciplined form of jitters." The Japanese could "cut the sea lifeline with submarines, leaving Alaska a frozen, withered plum to drop into [the enemy's] lap." Army officers "had to take orders from a designated Admiral . . . giving the Navy primary control in the Aleutian theater." This led to "sometimes laughable, sometimes tragic muddling." To Gillman, the system "reflected Washington's unhealthy attitude toward Alaska."[3]

Similar dismal news from Alaska was sent by Secretary of the Interior Harold Ickes's informant, Ruth Gruber, who saw newcomers there struggle against debilitating boredom. Their "evenings hang heavy," she commented, as "new saloons open almost over night; the red light districts spread and flourish while men and women search desperately for time-killers." In the military, she reported, "there have been a distressing number of suicides and insanities."[4]

Alaska's climate—its powerful winds and lack of winter daylight— was blamed for many aberrations. One of the military's key officers, Major General Charles H. Corlett, observed: "All of us have our dampers down. We are all depressed."[5] An avid Alaska booster, General Simon B. Buckner, Jr., also seemed deflated by Alaska's considerable problems. The most serious was "the difficulty of transportation and supply." Also, General Buckner felt Alaska's air power was shamefully inadequate. Noticeably disturbed on the day after Pearl Harbor, he wrote: "At dawn this morning I watched our entire Alaska Air Force take to the air so as not to be caught on the field." This weak little squadron was composed of only eighteen "obsolete" aircraft.[6]

Nobody ventured to point out where in this God-forsaken place the worst conditions prevailed. But had a poll been taken, the Aleutian Islands undoubtedly would have won. Except for Aleuts, very few appreciated the Aleutians or the North Pacific. The military knew little about the area, and what was known indicated that nobody in his right mind would chose it as a battlefield. It had never been completely charted and remained a foreboding land in the military mind. Soldiers stationed there found it a remote haven for malaise, foul weather, and social problems. Many sent there were "from Southern States like Alabama, Florida and Texas, and were spending their first winter in tents."[7]

When the war started, however, Alaskans buckled down to the task of winning it. Their leader was Governor Ernest Gruening. Although he believed that "Alaska was woefully unprepared" and would be Japan's next conquest, he was determined to fight. The four National Guard companies Gruening had helped to organize became part of the army's 297th Infantry. He then organized a Territorial Guard in early 1942 for protecting strategic sites. Based on military contacts, Gruening concluded that "many of the army officers stationed in Alaska had a depreciatory attitude toward . . . Indians, Eskimos and Aleuts." During the war, he launched a crusade to abolish civilian and military race discrimination. The military, he felt, failed to recognize valuable contributions of Natives serving in the armed forces. He complained that Buckner embraced "the color prejudice of the deep South and held it strongly," influencing Alaskan military policy detrimental to nonwhite Americans.[8]

Gruening was, nevertheless, Buckner's civilian counterpart in the defense of Alaska, and was confronted by many serious problems. The shocking news of Pearl Harbor caught the governor in Juneau ready to leave for Washington, D.C. Postponing his trip, Gruening set in motion security measures to protect an Alaska he felt was in jeopardy. Federal buildings were to be blacked out and Alaska Native Service teachers were instructed "to be on alert for enemy planes and notify headquarters" if any were sighted. Superintendent of the Alaska Indian Service Claude Hirst and the governor concluded that mainland Native villages were relatively secure. Maritime areas, however, needed more attention. Consequently, an important liaison was established with Admiral Charles S. Freeman in Seattle when Gruening requested navy escorts for civilian ships crossing the Gulf of Alaska.[9]

In this new role, Gruening refused to be a mere lobbyist or bystander. He could have chosen to be passive based on a narrow interpretation of the governor's powers. Instead, he was every Alaskan's advocate, concerned about all segments of society. He acted for them with considerable resolve and attempted to bolster morale. Only to his superior in Washington, D.C., Secretary Ickes, did he confess to pessimism about Alaska. He doubted that the United States had any plan at all to defend it. What little defense Alaska enjoyed was rendered ineffective by ill-conceived sites chosen for the three naval bases at Sitka, Kodiak, and Dutch Harbor. The Japanese would take the Territory, he predicted, in an offensive thrust sure to come in the spring of 1942.[10]

Governor Gruening also sensed a threat to Alaskans from within. War conditions might lead to U.S. military encroachment into civilian affairs. He felt in December 1941 that martial law would be imposed, with loss of personal freedoms. This would reduce the office of governor to an empty shell devoid of problem-solving power. The military would fill the vacuum. Gruening's dilemma became apparent when General Buckner requested that the governor order all saloons and liquor stores to close at midnight for civilian and military well-being. Gruening admitted to the under secretary of the Interior Department that he had no authority to act on this "reasonable request," but at the same time did not want "the military to assume this power." The solution was to strengthen the role of the governor. Besides liquor control,

Gruening argued that he needed authority to shape civilian health policy concerning water pollution, garbage disposal, and regulation of prostitution.[11]

Yet Gruening was wary about advocating this policy. There were considerable risks in suggesting that the governor assume more power. He feared that in sharpening the issue it would become obvious that the military must in fact exercise a more active role in civilian life. In addition, a move by Gruening might cause civilian outrage over a perceived power-grab by a governor who was regarded by many Alaskans as a pawn of Washington, D.C., bureaucrats. Governors had often been perceived as inimical to the Territory's best interests. These risks notwithstanding, Gruening suggested a direct solution. He wanted to take the initiative, to "get a psychological jump" on the War Department and avoid being presented with "a fait accompli."[12]

Gruening suggested the Departments of War and Interior agree on a plan for coordination of the military and Alaska government. He proposed that the "prestige" of the governor's office be "enhanced as a civilian instrument of the Federal power for the conduct of the war by tying it closely with the military." This would enable the governor "to keep the civilian branch of the government flexible and capable of meeting military demands"; it would also allow presidential and congressional veto over the governor's actions and avoid the appearance that Gruening exercised "tyrannical powers, or that there is no court of appeal." Also, the governor's expanded powers would be "contingent upon the request of the commanding military or naval officer," to meet "purely military requirements," while retaining "civilian control over civilian activities." It would keep "channels of appeal and contact with the Governor" open, thereby preventing "abuses of executive authority."[13]

In the end, Gruening's plan was not adopted, nor was Alaska placed under martial law. Nevertheless, he feared an overweening military and was sensitive about his powerlessness and Alaska's lack of direction. In January 1942 his friend, delegate Anthony Dimond, asked Secretary of War Henry L. Stimson and Secretary of the Navy Frank Knox to assign Gruening military aides. Dimond argued that Juneau, where the governor resided and conducted legislative affairs, was too isolated from army headquarters in Anchorage. Military aides would tie the two more closely together. He reminded Stimson and Knox that the governor of Hawaii had been granted a similar arrangement. Yet this request was denied.[14]

In spite of this, Washington, D.C., became increasingly concerned about Alaska wartime administration. A policy was eventually adopted to remedy lack of coordination. It was developed by the Executive

Branch and signed on June 11, 1942, by President Roosevelt as Executive Order 9181, "Administration of the Federal Government Services in Alaska." This order reflected Gruening's concerns but not his solution. Its source was the National Resource Planning Board, whose Alaska counselor, James C. Rettie, expressed "grave concern" over the Territory's "administrative paralysis and lack of clearly defined responsibility." The Japanese would soon attack Alaska, he predicted, and "we shall be worse than fools if we do not anticipate it. . . . The record of inaction, delays, inter-agency squabbles and bickering and lack of proper liaison with the armed forces will be terribly ugly." This was a crisis, and "utmost speed and resolution" were needed to coordinate military and civilian administration. A policy, Rettie contended, should be adopted "*before* and not *after* the bombs begin to fall." In response to this emergency, the Bureau of the Budget developed the order, and by May 25, 1942, it had been approved by the Secretary of War.[15]

Executive Order 9181 was intended to promote the safety of civilians, improve governmental administration, and coordinate civil and military agencies. To accomplish this, it created the Alaska War Council, composed of the three Alaska commissioners, one appointee each of the Federal Security Administration and Federal Works Administration, one designee of the U.S. attorney general, and one resident of Alaska elected by the War Council. Its chairman ex officio was Governor Gruening. Meetings were to be semimonthly, at the call of the chairman or elected vice-chairman or at the request of the military. The council's major goal was "to maintain close liaison with the military authorities." Military concerns were primary: "For the duration of the war the conduct of Federal civil activities shall be brought into closest possible conformity with military requirements." The council could recommend policy to the military; the governor as chairman reported directly to the president; and the Secretaries of War and Navy designated two military liaison officers to attend its meetings.[16]

This arrangement made the military the tail that wagged the Alaskan malamute. A military commander could flick off as fleas War Council recommendations. There was no martial law in Alaska because none was needed: the military did in fact rule. It could justify this power as an instrument for winning the war, improving morale, or establishing justice in the Great Land. Late in 1941, a feisty General Buckner took on the Alaska Game Commission in court to press for his and the military's rights to harvest big game. Yet he denied wanting "the burdens of the civil government" for fear that "it would involve him in endless local disputes" and might "bring on a feud with the Secretary of the Interior," a prospect he did not relish.[17]

Such hesitancy seemed uncharacteristic of Alaska's leading general, whose power was apparent. In Gruening's case, however, power to effect policy was questionable. The Alaska War Council's attempt at effective civilian governance, laudatory as it was, failed. There was little support for it. A navy officer in May 1942 judged that "the majority of civilians in Alaska would prefer to see the government vested in a military governor for the duration of the war."[18] Efforts by Gruening were valiant attempts to forestall such military governance. But with a war going on, there was already a de facto "military governor" of Alaska, making the official appointment of one superfluous. The governor's exclusion from this system meant that Alaskans were affected all the more by military policy without recourse to civilian intervention.

Admittedly, having to protect citizens in wartime put the military in an unenviable position. War tensions increased as Alaska's strategic importance escalated after Pearl Harbor. First, Buckner's Anchorage-based Alaska Defense Command was placed under General DeWitt's Western Defense Command headquartered in San Francisco. Alaska was declared "a theatre of operations." Then on December 15, 1941, DeWitt declared Alaska "a combat zone." In March 1942, Secretary of War Henry Stimson extended to Alaska his own authority under Executive Order 9066. He authorized Buckner to designate "prohibited and restricted" military areas, from which civilians could be removed or excluded. The order's purported intent was to minimize espionage and sabotage.[19] Although "military necessity" was not mentioned, this phrase was used to justify actions taken by military commanders under Executive Order 9066.

Armed with this newly acquired authority, Buckner moved rapidly against supposed threats to Alaska security. Between April 7 and June 30, 1942, he issued four "Public Proclamations" based on Executive Order 9066. In the first, removal of Japanese, German, and Italian aliens plus Japanese American citizens was ordered. In all, 230 Alaskan Japanese, over one-half of whom were U.S. citizens, were sent to stateside internment camps. Next, he empowered military commanders to exclude from their areas any "undesirable person" who might "imperil or impede military defense of other military operations." Following that, a system was established to register and issue "certificates of identification" for "citizens and subjects of foreign countries at war." Finally, Buckner restricted civilian travel and transportation to, from, and within Alaska. These measures were judged by Buckner to be necessary wartime precautions. Although Aleuts were not removed from the Aleutian and Pribilof islands under Executive Order 9066, they could have been had the military chosen to invoke it.[20]

Another response to war came in the removal of women and children dependents of armed services personnel and base construction workers. It was the easiest kind of evacuation, requiring only transportation and a minimum of planning. Most of these dependents had stateside relatives and homes. This simplified the procedure and made it unnecessary to provide care after they were removed from Alaska. The challenge was to anticipate the need for such a move and to complete it before hostilities or enemy invasion.

The navy took the early lead in developing removal plans for these dependents, and for some workers and some permanent Alaska residents. At the beginning of August 1941, well before Pearl Harbor, Captain Ralph C. Parker, commander of the navy's Alaska Sector, wrote to Governor Gruening expressing concern about "possible enemy raids on the Bering Sea Coast and the Aleutian Chain." He was worried about "curtailment of crucial supplies and medical care from outside." These circumstances, Parker thought, "might dictate the evacuation of the white inhabitants" of these areas, "wholly or in part." Preparation was necessary. "Tentative plans" should be made which would "avoid having to seek information hurriedly after the emergency." Parker asked Gruening to provide an estimate of "the numbers and locations of . . . white inhabitants" in the event that "special arrangements for their supply, protection or evacuation become necessary." This information, he suggested, could be "compiled and maintained by some Federal or Territorial office in Juneau" rather than by the army or navy. "Copies of it, however, should be sent to Admiral Freeman and General Buckner" and would "in no way commit the Federal or Territorial government to a definite policy of supply, protection, or evacuation." Parker added that "data on natives (round numbers only) would also be desirable."[21]

Captain Parker's inquiry came almost two months before Secretary of the Navy Frank Knox ordered all navy district commandants to plan for evacuation of navy dependents from outlying bases. These plans were to provide for "limiting the amount of household goods" taken by evacuees "in case shipping space is limited." Provision would be made for storage of personal possessions "at Government expense" until transportation was available. The commandants were directed to comment on "the effect of a failure to evacuate dependents" if there were military engagements. Food, supplies, health, morale, defense, and civil rights would have to be considered.[22]

This planning resulted in the flawless departure from Alaska of hundreds of military dependents shortly after Pearl Harbor. "As fast as ships could handle them," according to an observer, "women and children were being removed"; 250 from Dutch Harbor, including "forty-five babies." Of 700 people evacuated from Kodiak, 150 were children. In such a massive movement, of course, some inconvenience could not be avoided. Families at Dutch Harbor, for example, were first dispatched into "dugouts to await removal by convoy." Between there and Seattle, a storm pressed an army officer into washing "diapers when mothers became seasick." Excluding Aleuts, all women were removed from Unalaska except for one hospital patient. "Even the prostitutes left," allowing "the Navy to take over the brothel for storage space." Evacuation from Unalaska was mandatory for all "non-resident" women. But only those for whom the military felt directly responsible were subsidized. Removal to safety would "mean fewer mouths to feed" and would improve military morale because "in a raid," General Buckner reasoned, "I want the men to think of their posts, not their families."[23]

Although this removal worked smoothly, government officials did not consider applying it to other citizens until the spring of 1942. The Japanese raid on Pearl Harbor generated a flood of telegrams from civil defense directors to Governor Gruening asking for the government's evacuation plans. "Civilians," one of them claimed, "are Territorial obligations. Please advise full particulars." Gruening was empty-handed and, moreover, persistently declined to work out any evacuation plan. His policy was actually to have no policy at all and to defer instead to military judgment. "No plans for evacuation now," he wired back. Any "decision would be made by Army and you would be notified." The acting governor, Secretary Bob Bartlett, was in full accord. "We have no declaration of policy," no plans, he insisted. The army and navy would be in charge of any removal. They have "full control."[24]

Gruening and Bartlett refused to develop plans because they opposed civilian evacuation. They feared if women were removed, morale problems would result. Male defense workers might cast aside Alaskan jobs to follow their women. Furthermore, a mandatory civilian evacuation would "break down the economy of Alaska." Responding to this possibility, Gruening broached the topic with Secretary Ickes and asked him to ponder it. He cited a "fabulous labor turnover" endangering Alaska defenses. Instead of shipping people out, "there is an urgent need for additional people in Alaska to carry on many services helpful to the defense of the Territory." Captain Parker's concerns for civilian safety were unrealistic, Gruening felt, because the navy's Alaska bases were located on "offshore islands" and navy officials consequently "had relatively little, if any, experience with conditions" in the rest of Alaska.[25]

While their basic resistance to evacuation was motivated by economics, Gruening and Bartlett were also concerned about the military's role in setting policy. Evacuation would restrict Alaskan freedom of choice. The governor's office battled the military in January 1942, for instance, in a controversy involving John W. Fletcher, an Unalaska businessman, soon to become its first elected mayor. His wife, visiting in Seattle, was refused permission by military authorities to rejoin him at Unalaska. Concerning this, Admiral Freeman indicated that General Colladay, commanding officer at nearby Fort Mears, wanted all women, children, and construction employees removed from areas close to military installations. Furthermore, Colladay "requested all public domain around Unalaska be transferred to military reservation." Like other Unalaska citizens, Mrs. Fletcher would be in the way of military operations near her home.[26]

Taking up the gauntlet for Fletcher, Gruening criticized this restriction as "unwarranted and inadvisable." Every Alaska citizen, he claimed, "should be allowed freedom of movement even if they expose themselves to possible danger." The Governor lectured several military authorities: "the responsibility" for citizen decisions which might in wartime circumstances bring them harm, "is their own, not yours or mine." When the navy resisted this logic and appealed to Washington, D.C., Gruening enlisted Delegate Dimond and the Department of the Interior in what turned out to be a victory. Both General DeWitt and Admiral Freeman bent reluctantly, admitting that neither military organization had "any legal authority to prevent Mrs. Fletcher" from going home. They "strongly" urged, however, that she not go. In the decisive telegram message about this, Freeman bluntly stated: "I consider presence of women and children in Unalaska handicaps my ability to sustain and protect that area."[27]

Dramatic flap that this was, by pushing it the governor inflated its importance. In reality, it was an insignificant episode involving one person and no precedent. However, evacuation—determining if, when, and how it should occur—involved substantive questions. During a long stint as acting governor early in 1942, Bartlett opened a discussion of evacuation with military authorities. He asked a Coast Guard officer about military plans and was referred to Admiral Freeman, the navy's most interested party. The admiral sent Bartlett a copy of Captain Parker's August 1941 letter calling for information from Gruening about removal of "white inhabitants." The governor's office had responded with an incomplete list. Freeman asked Bartlett to comply with the initial request. Bartlett did so by recruiting George Sundborg of the Alaska regional office of the National Resources Planning Board to complete what Bartlett depicted as an "evacuation study which the Navy Department desires."[28]

It was one thing to cooperate with the navy, yet another to engage Juneau officials in working out civilian evacuation plans. Both Bartlett and Gruening tried steadfastly to avoid accepting that responsibility. They were torn between a need to respond to the Japanese threat and worries about the Alaska economy. They faced damaging risks if they failed to act at all. Evacuation, they believed, should be a military or federal government decision and obligation. Although removal of civilians would restrict individual freedom and be a distinct drag on Alaska's economy, they felt the choice was not a Territorial matter. But by the middle of March 1942, Washington, D.C., indicated that things were not quite that simple. In effect the subject was tossed into the Territory's lap.

News reached Acting Governor Bartlett that the Federal Security Administration had designated the Federal Social Security Board as the agency for "voluntary evacuation of individuals and families" from Alaska. The Territory's Social Security director, Hugh J. Wade, would have at his disposal twenty thousand dollars from the U.S. Treasury for evacuation and would be aided by the Territorial Department of Public Welfare. Funds could be used for transportation, "meeting boats, interviewing evacuees and providing temporary care," including "emergency medical care where necessary." It seemed too good to be true, generated and funded by the federal government. Skeptically, Bartlett wired Gruening in the nation's capital: "Message not sufficiently comprehensive to determine if this is start of general plan evacuation civilians or if it merely means shifting population from certain areas on voluntary basis." Gruening responded emphatically: "No general plan of civilian evacuation. Shifting is made on voluntary basis. Believed it should be discouraged. We need all the population possible in Alaska."[29]

In spite of Gruening's stance, planning for evacuation had begun. Preliminary discussion of civilian safety had concerned Caucasians, not Natives. Yet there was increasing likelihood of enemy attack along the Bering Sea coast and in the Aleutian and Pribilof islands area. Eskimos and Aleuts far outnumbered other civilians in this region. Their safety called for special attention. They were most vulnerable to suffering in the event of enemy attack.

In retrospect, Alaska held up well under great strain in the early months of war. But chaos and disaster frequently seemed imminent. Because the United States won the Aleutian campaign and the Territory survived, it is tempting to minimize Alaska's problems. In fact, they were legion and prevented many citizens and most units of government from engaging in "business as usual" in what were seen as threatening, unprecedented circumstances.

After the war began, Unalaska's school principal, Homer I. Stockdale, not knowing how to proceed, wired Superintendent Hirst for directions. What was to be done in this emergency about the school program and its teachers and equipment? Juneau headquarters ordered him to continue according to routine and to cooperate fully with military and civilian authorities. A day later, Stockdale informed Hirst that the school was closed because the building was to be used as a medical unit. Consequently, Indian Service headquarters at Juneau directed that school property be inventoried and stored unless it were needed by the military. Teachers were to remain at Unalaska to assist the war effort and Natives.[30]

Likewise, on the Pribilof Islands, Fish and Wildlife Service managers faced stiff wartime challenges when navy transportation was diverted elsewhere. According to Secretary Ickes in a letter to Secretary of the Navy Frank Knox, the Fish and Wildlife Service wanted protection for their supply vessel and navy security for Pribilovian people, fur seals, and blue fox, an "extensive investment" that produced millions of dollars for the U.S. Treasury. In addition, Ickes asked for continuation of navy transportation that shipped coal, materials, food, personnel, pelts, meal, and oil by-products.[31]

In conferences with Admiral Freeman concerning these needs, Sealing Division Superintendent Edward Johnston learned that the navy would not, indeed could not, be generous in its protection. No navy escort would be provided the *Penguin,* the Pribilof supply ship, but it would "probably be armed" and carry "a crew of five Navy men." The Pribilof Islands, due to "the absence of harbors and harbor defenses," would receive "no additional protection." However, "in case of attack, all assistance possible" would be "given by planes and ships," Freeman promised. Also, "all skins and supplies of value to the enemy" would have "to be destroyed." The admiral granted one request: the navy would provide a supply ship, but he demanded that it leave in early July, not August.[32]

In all of this, some of Admiral Freeman's problems, too, became apparent. His few ships could not possibly cover Alaska's vast waters. When the navy needed civilian ships in December 1941 to evacuate military dependents from Dutch Harbor, it commandeered the *Penguin* and incurred a $1,530 charge, the amount needed to pay for alternate transportation arranged by the Fish and Wildlife Service. Freeman resisted payment because he knew of no navy appropriation covering the cost and was not convinced the navy was obligated. Similarly, he was rankled at the Siems-Drake-Puget Sound Company when they refused to pay for evacuating employees, thereby passing the bill to Freeman. Admitting that the company "was not consulted" before these evacuations, Freeman nevertheless justified his move on "the exigencies of war and the imminence of attack." These conditions, he argued, "neither required nor permitted time-consuming bickering as to how and when the evacuees should be removed."[33]

The army, as well, found unusual challenges in wartime Alaska, not the least of which was to establish a smooth-working relationship with the navy. General Buckner appreciated the cooperation of Captain Parker but complained that the navy's shortage of personnel deprived him of a liaison officer and a representative for his Fort Richardson "joint information center." Buckner and Parker were advocates of Alaska's offensive importance and prepared a plan touting it. Theirs was a friendly, working partnership.[34]

In the Aleutians, General Buckner's goal preliminary to an offensive campaign was to protect the westernmost military centers, Fort Mears and Dutch Harbor, on Amaknak Island close offshore of Unalaska city. Building Fort Glenn on nearby Umnak Island under the cloak of secrecy was a masterful stroke in this strategy. This project was Buckner's claim to fame in the Alaskan theatre. But delays in shipping of construction materials for Fort Glenn and stormy weather in Umnak Pass plagued its progress. Adjusting to Aleutian realities, Buckner adopted scaled-down goals. "We should give up any idea of developing elaborate posts," he concluded, "and should limit construction to bare field necessities," reducing "the amount of freight . . . to an absolute minimum." Buckner thought there was a useful example in his father's experience. Before the Civil War, the elder Buckner had commanded an army company "among the Indians on the northwest plains" and used "sod huts, roofed with wagon covers," making "his men very comfortable." His son, the general, thought this idea could be "carried out in the Aleutians, using a few timbers and tarpaper as roofing material." Buckner observed that "since the Aleuts and Eskimos use similar structures, it should be well adapted to conditions in the Aleutians."[35]

The military housing problem was solved when barracks, cabanas, Pacific huts, and Quonset huts were installed. More important was the defense of these positions; and this weighed heavily on the mind of the commanding general of Fort Mears, Edgar B. Colladay. He announced to Buckner in May 1942 the undertaking of a general study of the area, a view of "the big picture," with defense of the entire Unalaska Bay area in focus. The Fort Mears garrison was bursting at its seams already and might receive three additional battalions. To make matters worse, there were plans "for increased Navy activity on Amaknak Island, without any consideration whatsoever of Army installations." His solution was to "leave Amaknak Island . . . in the hands of the Navy," except for some gunnery installations, and move army defenses "to the outlying shores."[36]

Other weighty matters faced Buckner, and he wrote frankly to General DeWitt about them. Frequent mistakes weakened the supply system; airplanes arrived late; mechanical problems and poor pilot skills abounded. Yet Buckner remained determined to overcome these difficulties. Unlike many military personnel from the South, this Kentucky general liked Alaska, appropriated it as his own, and planned after the war to fish and hunt in his newly adopted territory. His response to the war was resolute and pragmatic. But his problems were soon to take on new dimensions.

4

War on the Aleuts

> We were having church services in the little Russian church
> in Attu on Sunday morning, June 7, 1942, when boats entered
> the harbor. When the gunboats got closer to the village we saw
> that they were Japs. They started machine-gun fire on the village.
> Some of our boys ran for their rifles to fight the Japs but Mike Hodikoff,
> our chief said, "Do not shoot, maybe the Americans can save us yet."
> —Alex Prossoff, Attu Aleut Prisoner of War
> in Ethel Oliver, *Journal of an Aleutian Year*

In early June 1942, nineteen Japanese fighter pilots in one attack and thirty-two in a second strafed and bombed Dutch Harbor on Unalaska Island. Soon afterward, a Japanese Navy force landed on Kiska Island and overpowered its only inhabitants, ten United States Navy aerological personnel. The next day twelve hundred Japanese soldiers advanced on Attu Island, captured its people, and took over the village. These attacks abruptly shattered Aleutian isolation. Occupants of these two small islands became the first prisoners of war in Alaska, and the event marked 1942 as a year of conquest. It brought dramatic change to Aleut people. Up to then they had been relatively untouched by world affairs; now their homes lay in the path of hostile forces in a world war.

The attack on Dutch Harbor was connected to the Midway Island operation. Two Japanese aircraft carriers, two heavy cruisers, and three destroyers were sent north to "strike Dutch Harbor a paralyzing blow." The Japanese hoped this would divert U.S. Navy forces, confuse the military, and throw off our timing at Midway. The ploy failed because we had intercepted the plan and refused the bait. Kiska and Attu occupation was part of a larger strategy to prevent bombing attacks on Japan and strain American war efforts.[1]

This new phase of the Aleutian campaign brought the area its first large-scale violence in over 150 years. Stakes for both sides were high. Yet some assert that the outcome was insignificant. One judgment is that "operations in the North Pacific were not only of little importance in themselves, they had little influence on events elsewhere." The theatre's naval historian, Admiral Samuel Eliot Morison, agreed. "Both sides," he concluded, "would have done well to have left the Aleutians to the Aleuts."[2]

But the balance sheet of this conflict is difficult to reconcile and is open to debate. Both sides were mired down and could have used these forces to better advantage in the central Pacific. The United States committed more men and material, but the Japanese suffered more casualties. Not calculated in these assessments, however, are Aleut losses. A purely military analysis tends to make the Aleutian campaign trivial. In reality the campaign was a significant anvil's edge shaping Aleuts, Japanese and American soldiers, and civilians. Their lives were deeply affected by it.

Before the Japanese invasion, Attu Island was a pleasant Aleut haven. A visitor in 1937 recalled the generous hospitality afforded her party by Mike Hodikoff, the Attuan leader, and fellow Aleuts on "the shores of their little Eden." Coast Guard officers who knew the area claimed that Attu's people "are by far the happiest and best of all the natives, because they live in such a remote situation and bad influences don't come so easily their way. They . . . don't want to be brought into closer touch with the world. They are always the most friendly and helpful . . . lending a hand if required."[3]

Their teacher, Etta Jones, felt that Attu's Aleuts had created an impressive community. "They are progressive, intelligent, clean and friendly. . . . There are no indigents. . . . The houses are models for construction, neatness, and furnishings," she reported to Indian Service Superintendent Claude Hirst. "Their nine houses . . . are beautifully painted, inside and out. . . . The yards are neat . . . and the American flag flies from the village flagpole. . . . They have a beautiful church," she wrote, and "they are a proud people, who dislike and distrust the Japs. They accused them of stealing their foxes, and even of killing some of their trappers years ago. But for three years they haven't seen a Jap or a Japanese boat."[4]

That was the calm that preceded a storm. When Mike Lokanin returned to Attu in February 1942 from trapping on Agattu Island, he noticed changes in his village. Tension had replaced tranquility. Talk of war and rumors of invasion were common. Blackouts had become standard procedure. Attu's men were being drilled "as a little military force" by Charles Jones, the teacher's husband and Attu's aerological reporter and radio operator. Lokanin felt the war would never touch Attu because its smallness would fail to attract the enemy. Nevertheless, he and others packed their belongings in April for evacuation by the U.S. Navy. Storms prevented a landing and the evacuation was canceled. Another ship arrived at the village in May, the navy's seaplane tender USS *Casco* (AVD 12). The ship, however, was not assigned to evacuate Attu but to deliver supplies and ten navy weathermen to Kiska. Before departing, it took Mike Hodikoff and Alfred Prokopioff on a reconnaissance of shoreline landing spots for naval intelligence. Then in late May, a U.S. Navy submarine surfaced off the village coast and invited the men of Attu aboard. Its officers asked whether Japanese had been sighted in the vicinity and reminded Attuans that Dutch Harbor should be notified immediately if the enemy approached.[5]

In June, after the bombing of Dutch Harbor, Lokanin changed his mind about Attu's prospects of escape. His optimism changed to ominous premonitions. The day before the invasion, he was struck by Attu's quiet beauty. Green plants adorned its mountains and fragrances from spring flowers wafted toward the village. He noticed that "mountains on each side of Attu looked clearer than . . . even before with little fog strips around their bases." Strings of smoke rose from village dwellings, and the smell of salmon cooking was heavy in the air. He enjoyed the birds: "the seagulls and sea parrots flying and little birds waving beside the old ravens flying over the village and crawing. . . . I can hear chipee birds still chiping and seagull cloks," he remembered.[6] He savored his beloved Attu.

When Lokanin sat down for supper that night, his infant daughter, Titiana, was sleeping nearby, and his wife, Parascovia, remarked that "things look very quiet . . . today." But "one thing was in my mind steady," Lokanin recalled. The "Japanese will be here tomorrow." Parascovia replied, "I hope not, they might kill everyone."[7]

Japanese troops stormed Attu early the next morning, June 7, 1942. They fired into Lokanin's house, riddling the stove, doors, and windows. They looted his storage trunks and stole his valuables. Other Aleuts suffered similar treatment from these "young kids," whom Innokenty Golodoff called "pretty bad." Annie Hodikoff, age twenty-four, was shot in the leg. Etta and Charles Jones were disarmed and incarcerated, and Charles Jones died. Some Japanese and Aleuts believed that he committed suicide by slitting his wrists rather than submit to captivity. But Lokanin, who was ordered to bury Jones next to the church without a coffin, was convinced that he had been deliberately killed by his captors. Later examination of his remains revealed that Jones in fact had been shot in the head. Some of the Japanese soldiers accidentally killed their own men.[8]

After Japanese military officers appeared, the shooting stopped. Aleuts were ordered into the schoolhouse, where they were held without food or water until that night. One of them remembered the children crying while adults were indoctrinated about Japanese rule. The next day the commander, Colonel Yamazaki, arrived. He made the village off-limits to soldiers and returned stolen food to the Aleuts. They were placed under house arrest, guarded constantly, and allowed outside only occasionally for fresh air and fishing. Aleuts relied on their own supplies, not having "to give the Japs any food." Relieved, Innokenty Golodoff added, "They didn't bother our women."[9] Given Japanese atrocities elsewhere, the Attuans were fortunate.

Although many of them were good marksmen, Attuans "put up no resistance for it was hardly possible," remembered John Golodoff, then age fifteen. "We were surrounded and they were firing their guns very rapidly." Afterward, some Aleuts considered armed resistance. Youngsters wanted "to fight the Japs" and assembled guns and bullets in secret. Lokanin and his friend Fred Hodikoff, however, feared that Japanese ships might be "laying outside the bay," ready to discharge more troops should trouble start. "Then one of the old men came and talked to us and told us not to fight." The Aleuts were outnumbered. He concluded the only recourse they had was to "think of our God."[10]

Although open resistance was ruled out, some Attuans responded to captivity with clandestine activities during the three months of occupation. They mocked the Japanese flag, "the Rising Sun," referring to it as "the Japanese meatball." Lokanin and Alex Prossoff said it looked like a "target" under which the Japanese took identification photographs of the Aleuts. It was the only authorized flag, and Aleut fishing boats were required to carry "the meatball." But one Aleut stole and hid the American flag for safe-keeping. Aleuts called it "our flag" and resented that it had been taken down. Alex Prossoff gave misdirected advice which made him a type of saboteur. He told the Japanese to store their goods at a certain place on the beach and then waited for a storm he knew would wipe out the cache. It did. The Japanese threatened him with death should he deceive them again. Undaunted, Prossoff hid church funds and concealed them throughout his prisoner of war years.[11]

The Japanese considered these newly acquired Aleutian Islands to be permanent additions to Greater Japan. Their maps included them in the Empire. Ancient Aleut names were changed. Attu became Atsuta Island, a reference to the Japanese Atsuta religious shrine at Nagoya, where the Japanese celebrated June fests. (Nagoya had been bombed by American "Doolittle" raiders on April 18, 1942.) Kiska was designated Narukami Island, a derivation of *Narukamizumei* or Thunder Month, the name for the month of June. On this island various locales that had gone nameless under American ownership were assigned simple place names attached to inlets, ponds, and bays. Some of them evoked the familiar: Big Inlet, Bright Pond, Sweet Potato, Girlfriend, and Sweetheart bays. Also, the Japanese built "six Shinto shrines" on Kiska. In contrast to military construction, however, these were done with an artistic flair.[12] Thus, the western Aleutians were touched by another of the world's major religious traditions, following original Aleut spirituality and transplanted Russian Orthodox Christianity.

Of all Aleuts, the Attuans suffered most in the war. Three months after the Japanese invaded, the Attuans were taken as captives to Japan. They were never to return to their island home. No one in the United States learned of their fate until the war ended. For wartime security, the Japanese military would not tell of this "lonesomest spot this side of hell," as Attu was called in a popular book on Alaska at the time. It was as if Aleuts in this "no-man's-land" had fallen off the face of the earth. When Assistant Secretary of War John McCloy told Interior Secretary Harold Ickes about the Japanese attack on Alaska, Ickes wrote in his diary, "Word came down yesterday that a landing had been made on two of the furthermost and utterly useless islands."[13]

To the east of enemy-occupied Attu, the Aleuts and two Alaska Indian Service employees of Atka village on Atka Island waited to be evacuated. They had expected the removal as early as March 1942. Now with the Japanese close by, their rescue seemed imminent. It appeared that Atka's people might not be drawn into the war. There was no United States military base there to attract attention, no airplane landing field or naval facilities, no garrison, no arsenal or artillery implacements. Japanese military planners had not included it in a list of "important areas in the Aleutian Archipelago." Pinpointed instead were Dutch Harbor, Adak, Kiska, and Attu, "desolate" places about which "available data on the military topography were inadequate and out of date."[14]

But Atka's geographical position did draw it into the war, and its Aleuts were the first to be evacuated. The Japanese occupation of Attu, some 600 miles to the west, did not affect Atka; but occupation of Kiska, 360 miles away, did. Possessing a sheltered harbor, Atka was the midway point between the Japanese garrison on Kiska and U.S. military forces at Dutch Harbor. After learning of Kiska's invasion, the navy decided to use Atka's Nazan Bay for landing seaplanes. There they could be secured to buoys, refueled, rearmed, and repaired by seaplane tender crews. The tenders also provided food and rest for exhausted pilots. After dispensing all fuel and ammunition, the tenders returned to Dutch Harbor, 350 miles away, for replenishing. Atka became a strategic part of this loop in Aleutian maneuvers.

Early U.S. offensive strikes at Kiska were delivered not by army B-17 bombers from Umnak Island's Fort Glenn, but by navy PBY patrol planes stationed at Dutch Harbor. These PBYs could be refueled easily in Nazan Bay. They were organized as Patrol Wing Four, armed with one bomb on each wing. To support these missions, Task Force 8.1 was formed on June 9, 1942, as an air search group of four seaplane tenders to scout the Atka vicinity and serve the pilots of Patrol Wing Four. The U.S. military action aimed at Japanese-occupied Kiska beginning on June 10 brought to Atka two navy vessels, the destroyer class USS *Gillis* (AVD 12) and USS *Hulbert* (AVD 6). Their crews helped tend twenty-four seaplanes moored in Nazan Bay. In addition to these personnel, Patrol Wing Four itself consisted of sixty-eight officers and over 170 men.[15]

Atka's eighty-three Aleuts had never seen such numbers of arms and personnel or the kind of military action the Kiska offensive brought to the island. They had seen airplanes before—calling them "ducks"—but never so many birds as these and never so fierce. On June 11, Admiral Chester Nimitz, commander-in-chief of the Pacific fleet, ordered "maximum effort to bomb the Japanese out of Kiska." Patrol Wing Four "was directed to attack the enemy in Kiska continuously with bombs and torpedoes." This assault "was kept up day and night until *Gillis* had issued all her supply of bombs and every pumpable gallon of aviation gasoline. She was then relieved by *Hulbert*." These raids, called by one Aleutian campaign historian the "Kiska Blitz," also engaged Atka's Aleuts, their teacher, Ruby Magee, and her husband, Charles, the radio operator. They fed and housed some of the navy crews. School pencils were donated to stuff bullet holes in the pontoons of riddled seaplanes damaged by heavy anti-aircraft fire over Kiska. Numerous planes languished in the bay. Three were damaged beyond repair. Two were sent to the bottom, and one was beached and torched to prevent use by the enemy. One Patrol Wing Four crew member was killed and two were wounded.[16]

Although this offensive lasted only forty-eight hours, it foreboded ill for Atka's Aleuts. Most expected the entrenched Japanese garrison on Kiska to retaliate. A day after beginning the blitz, navy PBY crews stopped at Kanaga Island, about 120 miles west of Atka. They evacuated a navy aerological group and then "destroyed everything there which could be of any possible use or assistance to the enemy." Pilots reported "an increasing concentration of Jap vessels and shore activity at Kiska." Admiral Nimitz and Rear Admiral Robert A. Theobald of Task Force Eight, the navy's special force for defense of Alaska, believed that remnants of Japan's Combined Fleet defeated at the Battle of Midway were "now active in the North Pacific." As a consequence, "maximum submarine activity in the western Aleutians" was ordered.[17] Enemy attack on Atka seemed imminent.

As a precaution, the navy ordered Aleuts to leave Atka village, making it off-limits. They were sent to campsites and joined others already there for summer fishing. This movement out of Atka village preceded the eventual evacuation of Atka Island. Vasha Nevsoroff, who was fourteen years old, remembered leaving with her father for a camp and then departing to another one about two miles away for better protection. Aleut tents at the camps were ordered by the navy to be camouflaged. It seemed as if Japanese fighters would soon raid Atka.

On June 12, Alice and Vera Snigaroff, plus the Dirks and Galley children in camp, heard an airplane approaching. Their custom was to run up a nearby hill to wave at American aircraft engaged in the Kiska Blitz. This one, however, was Japanese. The children scampered down and hid as instructed. At that time Cedar Snigaroff and his son, Poda, spotted the Japanese scout. They were on the way from camp into the village in a motor-driven dory for supplies and personal belongings. Navy personnel met them on the beach—guns and bayonets drawn— and ordered them to hide because other enemy aircraft might be coming from inland on bombing runs. The scare passed and the Aleuts were given gasoline, flour, and sugar by the navy, but were kept from entering their homes for personal belongings. William Dirks and Cedar Snigaroff, however, picked up some clothing when sailors relaxed their watch. People were not safe in or out of Atka village.[18]

With the enemy occupying Attu and Kiska, and Atka verged on siege, what would follow? Were any of the other Aleutian Islands safe? The U.S. military had foreknowledge of the Japanese gambit at Dutch Harbor but knew nothing of their overall Aleutian strategy. It might be purely defensive; but nobody could be certain what their intentions were, or when or where their next move would be. Many felt they would move eastward along the island chain toward the Alaska mainland.

Before the war, U.S. military leaders had steadfastly avoided extending U.S. posture westward past Unalaska and Umnak islands. If war was to be there, the Japanese would have to bring it. The United States did not lure them into the confounding Aleutian fogs. To the contrary, as late as March 1942 General George C. Marshall, chief of staff, opposed construction of airfields in the Aleutians because this would bring "more of menace than of advantage." His policy for Alaska was "strategic defense." Both he and Admiral Ernest J. King, chief of naval operations, favored efforts "against the enemy in the Solomon Islands." The

attack on Dutch Harbor and occupation of Attu and Kiska changed
U.S. planning: we resolved to retake Attu and Kiska, built new naval
facilities in the Aleutians, and sent troop detachments to the chain's
isolated islands. Closer to the Alaska mainland there appeared little
threat of Japanese aggression. In the middle of June 1942, Admiral
Theobald wrote to Admiral Nimitz, "It is hard to envisage a serious
campaign by the Japanese in the Aleutian area from Umnak . . . to the
eastward." Such attack would bring "too heavy a strain on amphibious
forces of Japan and supply vessels."[19]

Still, there was an underlying uncertainty about the Aleutians. Japan
had used surprise before. The possibility of sneak attack raised the level
of apprehension. The islands most secure seemed to be the Pribilofs.
Unlike the Aleuts of Attu and Atka, the nearly five hundred residents of
St. George and St. Paul islands were far removed from Japanese forces.
They were located about six hundred miles northeast of the Japanese
entrenched at Kiska and could be given protection by U.S. bases on
Umnak and Unalaska islands some two hundred miles to the south. The
United States had no military presence in the Pribilofs. The value of
these islands in war was questionable. On a map it appeared they were
approaches guarding Unalaska Island to the south, Bristol Bay and
Nunivak Island to the northwest. They also seemed to be stepping
stones to the northern islands of St. Matthew and St. Lawrence, point-
ing toward the Bering Strait and Nome, one of the transfer hubs for
lend-lease planes flown to Siberia. But in reality, they were practically
useless for military purposes because they lacked good harbors. Their
open anchorages were made hazardous by heavy waves and riptides,
and their shorelines were steep and dangerous. Japanese familiar with
the area knew this but exaggerated the area's inclement weather as they
did also in the western Aleutians.[20] Pribilof topography, moreover, did
not lend itself easily to air base construction. There were no docks along
the rugged coasts.

The United States Navy, nevertheless, was convinced of the Pribilofs'
strategic importance and worried about a Japanese takeover. Anticipating such a move, Admiral Freeman at the end of May asked the Fish and
Wildlife Service to use "scorched-earth" actions on both St. George and
St. Paul islands should the Japanese invade. "All supplies of value to the
enemy, including seal skins," were to be "destroyed." Of all Aleut communities, St. George and St. Paul contained the most government property. They had the only facilities for producing seal industry profits for
the U.S. Treasury. Because destruction of Pribilof properties would
mean extraordinary losses, Seal Division Superintendent Edward C.
Johnston had to clear this policy with Washington, D.C. After extensive

discussion, Director Ira N. Gabrielson ordered that "destroying supplies or other property . . . must be in conformance with the instructions and wishes of Naval authorities." Seal oil, fuel, the by-products plant, "and some of the electrical, mechanical, refrigeration, and transportation facilities" were to be destroyed "if such action appeared necessary to competent Navy personnel." Only foodstuffs, coal, and medical supplies should be exempt from destruction. They would be hidden in "caches for emergency use." Fish and Wildlife Service people would have to exercise their own judgment on the scene "in the best interests of the Government."[21]

Such talk naturally heightened tension in the two Pribilovian villages. To reduce nervousness at St. Paul, wartime policy was adopted by a village committee composed of Aleut leaders and Carl M. Hoverson, the Service storekeeper-in-charge. They met on June 4, 1942, to "talk about war matters and many rumors which have caused some unnecessary uneasiness." They posted on the workshop door measures aimed at "more safety and peace of mind for the community's Aleuts." In this posted notice, the most dangerous contingencies were capitalized: "WHEN AIRPLANES ARE SEEN COMING" and "IF ENEMY BOATS COME." The suggestions were scary.[22]

Because it was difficult to determine friend from foe, at the sight of any airplane, St. Paul Aleuts were to seek the safety of buildings and avoid standing by windows that might shatter, spewing "broken glass or flying fragments." Outside, "you may be shot down with machine gun bullets," St. Paul's people were warned. "It is best to wear clothes which are not too bright colored" and to "lie down flat on the ground, in a ditch, behind a rock, under a truck or tractor" for protection. If the enemy appeared by boat, Aleuts with firearms were directed not to commence firing or to "take matters into their own hands." Those "who are in charge" would decide on action and give others "advice and instructions." Aleuts would "be told when and where" to begin fighting.[23]

Life in the entire St. Paul community was affected. A 9:00 P.M. curfew was imposed: Blackouts were enforced. Movies and dances were banned. Children were to stay close to home. An all-night watch-force was organized to make the community feel safer. Certain members of this watch, "for instance, Iliodor Kozloff," were put "in charge of a row of houses each." Fire extinguishers were prepared. "An air raid shelter" was "being constructed for the hospital staff and the patients." It was suggested that others should dig shelters for themselves and their families and use driftwood and sandbags for cover. Aleuts were reminded to "keep a cool head." The village committee reassured the community: "We have your welfare at heart."[24]

But it was difficult for Pribilovian Aleuts to remain calm after they learned of the Dutch Harbor attack. Some thought they had detected Japanese war planes in the early summer flying over St. Paul. Some like Sergie Shaishnikoff wondered whether they "were going to be shot or bombed." After Dutch Harbor, "the fear set in." Would the people be evacuated? When Shaishnikoff was told that "only the white people would be taken off the island"—possibly a plan discussed by Fish and Wildlife Service personnel—he passed the disheartening news to his wife. "She cried." Shaishnikoff then lodged a complaint about this policy with Lee C. McMillin, St. Paul's agent and caretaker. St. George resident Flore Lekanof believed that, regardless of the tension, Aleuts would never be removed from the island.[25]

Aleuts on Unalaska and the surrounding islands should have been extremely uneasy. However, outside Dutch Harbor, life went its routine way with only minor adjustments. In nearby Akutan village on Akutan Island, Aleuts "weren't worried about Japs," George McGlashen remembered, because five navy airplanes in the harbor there seemed protection enough. The men were sufficiently occupied with work at the Akutan whaling station and were not bothered by military activities at the United States Navy station or the fueling station used by Russian ships plying the Bering Sea on lend-lease duty. These facilities were not connected to the village by a road.[26]

Near Nikolski village on Umnak Island, a small army garrison had been deployed for protecting the U.S. airfield at Fort Glenn. Servicemen policed the village to enforce a blackout and entered Aleut homes when violations occurred. The military required underground shelters to be built and conducted regular air raid emergency drills.

The morning of the Dutch Harbor raid was etched into the mind of Leonty Savoroff, a Nikolski Aleut. His two-year-old daughter died that morning just as he heard airplanes to the north. Shortly thereafter, "the Army came in the village and shot their rifles three times as a warning and alert that Dutch Harbor had been bombed." Four United States fighters flew over the village to "engage the Japs."[27] It was June 3, 1942. War had come to the eastern Aleutians.

It was no surprise that Dutch Harbor received the blow. The U.S. knew that military facilities there would attract Japanese fire. Only the area's chief force—"Admiral Weather," in the form of fog and clouds—prevented greater damage in the two-day attack. Although there were no Aleut casualties, the Alaska Indian Service hospital in Unalaska city, across the bay from Dutch Harbor, was destroyed. That made health care more difficult.

The Aleuts of Unalaska had been exposed the longest to U.S. military presence. In spite of their being farther away from the Japanese than Aleuts in the western Aleutians, Unalaskans faced the greatest risk of attack. But they were the most prepared and protected. Their city status helped because it carried political weight. United States Commissioner Jack Martin, for example, wrote to the governor's office in May 1942 complaining about "a distressing lack of any fire-fighting equipment, fire hose and gas masks" for civil defense in the city. He asked for funding, and it was arranged.[28]

After the Dutch Harbor attack, an Unalaska Defense Council was formed, but no Aleut served as a member. Alert drills were conducted. Taverns and liquor stores closed. "Hospitalization of military personnel in case they need to be evacuated from the military hospital" was planned. "A First Aid Squad and a Demolition Squad" were formed, and the Red Cross "prepared a sufficient number of bandages for an emergency." No civilians were to bear arms during an alert, but the Defense Council requested from Governor Gruening "seventy-five rifles and sufficient ammunition." Air raid wardens were appointed and patrols organized for around-the-clock watches. The city needed more gas masks, but its food supply in the middle of June was "sufficient for about eight weeks." In spite of these preparations, the Council recommended to the governor "that all women, children, and overage males be evacuated."[29]

Naturally, the Japanese attack created more problems for the military. Matters were uncertain. The navy was concerned about further enemy strikes. One navy officer, the commander of the Western Sea Frontier Staff at San Francisco, admitted to Thirteenth Naval District Headquarters that "we are still pretty much in the fog" about Japanese movements in the Aleutians. A civilian at Dutch Harbor reported that "everything at the base was in a chaotic condition, disorganized, and construction paralyzed. No one seemed to know what to do and there was no definite program to follow."[30]

Unalaska city suffered a continuation of long-standing problems. Workmen fired from construction jobs at Dutch Harbor were "escorted by armed guards to Unalaska city to arrange their trip home." Many were left stranded in high-cost Unalaska with already inadequate housing. This practice by contractors inflicted an "intolerable burden" on "residents of an otherwise respected municipality." These discharged workers, "involuntarily dumped and stranded," resorted to "petty crimes" and panhandling. Unalaska, according to one worker's report, was unable to care for such people.[31]

In addition, Unalaska Aleuts, in the words of Philemon Tutiakoff, "felt the brunt of the travesty." By "travesty" he primarily meant the bombing. But he referred also to the inroads the military had made into Unalaskan life. "We were cut off from the rest of our home island by a barb wire fence erected by the United States military," he recalled. "We had to conform to curfews, blackouts, respond to alerts and establish foxholes near every home." The air raid alerts "disrupted our school life" and the city was disfigured "with machine gun nests and anti-aircraft guns," Tutiakoff, an artist, remembered. "Our health facilities were inadequate. . . . We were cut off from this food supply and had to make do with what we could buy from the stores. Our first taste of inflation came. Our church . . . was strafed. It was only after a very long lengthy struggle with the military that the leaders of Unalaska were able to have holes dug to store furnishings of the church."[32] Heavy-equipment roads that had been built across streams restricted instream flow and destroyed salmon spawns. Pollution of Unalaska's bays affected marine life, including waterfowl used by Aleuts for food. After the Dutch Harbor "travesty," things looked bleak indeed for the Aleut people of Unalaska.

5

Contemplating Aleut Evacuation

> Before the evacuation our family of six . . . spent the last night
> in the underground shelters we had made months earlier by the
> command of the United States Army platoon stationed here.
> We were not expecting to be evacuated.
> —Dorofey Chercasen, Nikolski Aleut Evacuee
> Commission on Wartime Relocation Hearings

The question of Aleut safety had become more urgent after Pearl Harbor, when it seemed inevitable that war would carry into the Aleutians. Military and civilian authorities ultimately would have to deal with it. To some, Aleut evacuation appeared a certainty, with only the details to be worked out. But planning was needed. The previous evacuation of nonresident military and construction worker dependents, plus the removal of residents of Japanese ancestry, provided convenient models. Based on these cases, evacuating Aleuts might be a relatively simple matter, or so it seemed.

But to Aleuts evacuation would mean more than a physical move. They were attached to their island homes, and to leave would be traumatic. These were the only homes most of them had ever known. Mainland Alaska—or anywhere else—would be alien. Anyone concerned with Aleut well-being would have to consider the effects of uprooting them.

Authorities contemplating evacuation faced other difficult problems. There were no available safe havens, and the logistics were staggering. Transportation, supplies, food, and health care would have to be provided. Personal and community property left behind would need protection. Approximately nine hundred people would be involved. If they were to be moved, careful planning would be necessary.

Military and government officials were uncertain whether evacuation would be more harmful than leaving Aleuts on their islands. They appreciated the fact that they would not escape condemnation should they do nothing and have Aleut casualties mount up in an enemy attack. Certainly, caring for the Aleuts would be easier outside an active military zone, but no one had any idea where that might be. Consequently, inertia, plus the weight of other wartime problems, precluded Aleuts' evacuation soon after Pearl Harbor, even though the area was vulnerable to enemy attack.

There was also ambiguity about the military's obligations concerning civilian safety. Its responsibilities for the safety of dependents and military post employees had been clear. Army and navy commanders were less certain, however, about resident civilians. The Fletcher case had validated Governor Gruening's position that Alaska residents were responsible for their own safety. They should enjoy freedom of choice in their movements. This incident suggested that Alaska's military did not have responsibility for or control over civilians. Without a declaration of martial law or the use of Executive Order 9066 or actual combat, the military was hesitant about the evacuation of civilians.

The same hesitancy was shared by government officials. Whereas the military had considerable experience in moving and provisioning large numbers of people, the Alaska Indian Service had essentially none. Fish and Wildlife Service personnel on the Pribilof Islands had engaged in supplying two Aleut communities, but their transportation had to be supplemented even in normal times by the navy. A mass movement of Aleuts would pose formidable challenges for both the Office of Indian Affairs and the Fish and Wildlife Service. Transportation, lack of personnel available for the task, and, above all, overwhelming costs not heretofore budgeted dampened enthusiasm for evacuation. Discussions, then, ended in deadlock for these and several other reasons. Alaska military command was not unified, leaving the army and navy to operate independently. Furthermore, although Aleuts were citizens of the United States and the Territory, only the Department of the Interior took responsibility for them, and that was split between two divisions. As a consequence, no chief planner was designated to determine whether evacuation was necessary. If it were, there was nobody to decide which Aleuts were in greater danger and should be evacuated first. Nobody was appointed to prepare relocation facilities. And so nothing definite evolved. There were only ruminations.

Immediately after Pearl Harbor, Captain William N. Updegraff of the naval air station at Dutch Harbor pressed for some answers to the evacuation question. He wired Claude Hirst, superintendent of the Alaska Indian Service, asking for the destination of Unalaska's "native women and children . . . if and when evacuated and any plans you have on this subject." In reply, Fred Geeslin, acting general superintendent in Claude Hirst's absence, stated he knew nothing of any plan. He deferred to Hirst, who would be returning from a field trip the next day. Geeslin suggested that Updegraff contact Unalaska's school principal, Homer I. Stockdale, about "the possibility of destinations of Natives at neighboring villages where relatives may assist in providing temporary housing facilities."[1]

After eighteen days, Superintendent Hirst finally announced a policy that he apparently developed through consultations with several parties. His position closely resembled Governor Gruening's concerning the non-Native population. "This Office would have no control over the removal of Natives," Hirst stipulated. "They are at liberty as citizens to go where they wish." He further emphasized, "We have no funds appropriated for paying the expenses of their removal." He suggested that Unalaska Aleuts "go to other villages on the Alaskan Peninsula or nearby islands and that none . . . go to Seattle unless they have funds to pay their own transportation and subsistence after reaching the states."[2] Hirst feared that these Aleut wards of the federal government would produce an unwarranted strain on the budget of their trustees even if leaving voluntarily.

In the meantime, teacher Stockdale had polled Aleuts about their desire to leave and where they would like to go. Not surprisingly, nearly one-third expressed "no choice" since they had never been away from their island homes. Some eventually did leave on their own, perhaps upward of twenty who had the means to pay their own costs.[3]

Those staying in Unalaska understandably suffered a case of war jitters. Alerts sounded when enemy aircraft were heard approaching the island. "Temporary plans were made for the evacuation of . . . citizens" by trucks "to nearby places of safety." Unalaska city's "proximity to the Base places us in a very uncompromising position," lamented teacher Stockdale, "and I hope that plans are made to relieve the nervous tension."[4]

In Stockdale's mind, relieving the nervous tension meant evacuation. If plans were progressing, they could not be forthcoming fast enough for him. Unalaska was definitely an undesirable place. Water mains had been ruptured by heavy construction equipment, cutting water supplies to the community for over a week. Rumors circulated that heating oil supplies would not be replenished. Hospital and government property next to the school had become a storage yard for the army. The Indian Service physician's living quarters in the hospital were taken by the army, forcing him to rent accommodations in town.

Worse than this, Stockdale lamented, in case of attack, "it seems very probable that all lives in Unalaska would be in great peril." He argued that Aleuts should be evacuated because "not only would they be a problem to care for during an attack," there would soon be food shortages. "Aleuts would be safer placed upon other islands remote from the Base," Stockdale told his superiors, "where they can live by hunting and fishing and in canneries rather than be left here as a menace to military maneuvering and victims of starvation in case of a siege." As for himself and colleagues, he argued, we "should be transferred to places of safety even if the natives are not moved rather than force us to resign to escape the increasing danger."[5]

As Stockdale saw it, Unalaska's grim situation was caused by more than the Japanese threat and U.S. military encroachment. He felt Aleuts were as much, if not more of a menace to the community than the Japanese and the military. In reports to Juneau in January and February 1942, he complained that Aleuts inherently are inferior and immoral. "Some of the native men are employed but it will no doubt be temporary because of their nature," he said. "Their unmoral nature makes them a menace to soldiers and imported workers at the Base." These "unmoral propensities," moreover, express themselves especially in Aleut women. "The adolescent period of the natives seems to begin very early in life," he observed; "then apparently solicitation begins." Soldiers consider young Aleut women "exotic," making it "unsafe for any female to appear on the street after dark." The "natural unmoral propensities of the native Aleuts" lead to "moral problems that are beyond the Federal law to express through the United States mails." He added that another hazard was caused by truck traffic on Unalaska's streets, where the lives of children were jeopardized. "We try to teach them safety," Stockdale claimed, "but of course they have very primitive tendencies and forget the teachings when convenient to do otherwise."[6]

Given these conditions in Unalaska, Stockdale became impatient. He surmised that evacuation was imminent and anxiously waited for it. But Unalaska's physician, Dr. Corthell, did not wait for military action or Indian Service plans. By February 1942 he was gone, and Stockdale bemoaned his loss. In March, Mr. and Mrs. Stockdale were recalled to Juneau for "temporary assignment," leaving at Unalaska a lone teacher, Aileen M. Dammasch, who "asked to remain."[7]

Although Unalaska city was in a precarious situation, the villages of Atka and Attu lay in even more dangerous paths. Evacuation for their residents was fast becoming a crucial matter. Shortly after December 7, 1941, Atka's teacher Ruby Magee and her husband, Charles, made plans to leave the island. Canceling school after war was declared, the Magees and the Aleuts packed their belongings for departure. They had been told they would be evacuated. When they were not, the Magees announced in January 1942 that they intended to leave Atka on their own, feeling "keenly the insecurity of this location." Believing that the navy would not "defend this long stretch of islands on which so few people live," they concluded that "a place not worth defending is not worth living in."[8] But their plan came to no avail. They were stranded on Atka until June, when the Japanese occupied neighboring Attu and Kiska.

Least fortunate in the timing of events were Attuan Aleuts, who never were rescued, either by the military or the government. Don Pichard and his wife, Giner, who were boat operators, visited the island in April 1942 and could have evacuated the residents. They had, however, been given no orders to do so. Expecting a rescue ship, the Attuans were ready to go. In May, the navy attempted to evacuate them but were turned back by foul weather. One Attuan observed that "before the Japs came to Attu in 1942, the Navy was going to take us away . . . but they didn't . . . because it was too stormy."[9]

Recognizing the possible need for civilian government officials to be involved in evacuation procedures, the Federal Security Administration provided a bulletin with certain guidelines. This document was sent to Governor Gruening's office. It emphasized that planning for "evacuation of civilians from places of danger to places of relative safety" required two procedures. One was "the actual removal"; the other, evacuee "reception and care." The removal process, the document indicated, would be difficult, but "planning and carrying out the procedures of reception and care" would be "more difficult and complex" and would "require careful preliminary organization." The Security Administration stressed that planning should not be restricted to providing "emergency shelter on the day of a sudden disaster." Needed instead was the appointment of a "director of evacuation to cooperate with the Federal agency," then "at least one month to undertake the many phases of organization" before the order for evacuation would be given.[10]

If applied in Alaska these suggestions would have given direction to civilian agencies. However, about six weeks after Pearl Harbor, rescue by the military seemed to be in the offing. Interior Department officials received word that the army and navy were in accord on several important principles. First, if and when Caucasian civilians were evacuated, the navy would also "furnish transportation to native women and children." Significantly, "the activities of the Army and Navy connected with evacuation" would "be coordinated with the activities of the Governor's office." This military involvement and civilian coordination were agreed to by Paul W. Gordon, the Alaska director in the Interior Department's Division of Territories and Island Possessions. He expected "that appropriate instructions" about this arrangement would be issued.[11] None, however, came.

At the same time, inertia prevailed at other bureaucratic levels. Between the end of January 1942 and the middle of March, civilian officials failed to act. Then, in Governor Gruening's absence and at the suggestion of "welfare agencies," Acting Governor Bartlett, on March 18, 1942, convened a meeting in Juneau to plan "for transferring people from one section of the Territory to another or from the Territory to the States, should the emergencies of war demand." Bartlett had requested that the National Resources Planning Board draft "an evacuation plan" that would be blended with the Territory's. This was to be a marriage of its proposals with Federal plans. Such arrangement would assure efficiency and cooperation by all parties.[12]

For government officials, the topic was far from trifling. Those who met with Bartlett on evacuation plans were top-rank. Only two, Edna Wright of the Social Security Board and George W. Sundborg of the National Resources Planning Board, appeared to have non-supervisory positions. The others, Hugh J. Wade, director of the Social Security Board; Claude M. Hirst, general superintendent of the Alaska Indian Service, and his director of education, Virgil Farrell; Russell G. Maynard, director of the Territorial Department of Public Welfare; and the supervisor of the Child Welfare Department, Kenneth R. Forsman, were an eminent group.[13] As it turned out, this meeting was their first and the last to consider evacuation.

In preparing, Bartlett had written "a statement of problems" as a "basis for discussion." Before evacuation was "necessitated by defense developments," agencies would have to determine "lines of administrative responsibility" and "financial participation" to coordinate functions and utilize "the full resources of the Territory." Planning should include the following fields: "health, welfare, transportation, communication, education and recreation." All procedures would have to be developed "in close cooperation with military authorities," and plans "be formulated and preliminary organization set up well in advance of any emergency."[14]

Meetings of disparate bureaus like this are notorious for lack of harmony, but this one was different. The conferees agreed that "no general attempt should be made even in case of actual enemy attack, to evacuate Eskimos or other primitive natives from Alaska." They reasoned that "these people could never adjust themselves to life outside of their present environment." Furthermore, they "could 'take to the hills' in case of danger and be practically self-sufficient for a considerable period." Exception to this general policy might be made in moving "some natives from Seward" on the Kenai Peninsula and from Yakutat on the Gulf of Alaska. The plan did call for the evacuation of "approximately 150 Aleut women and children at Unalaska who should be moved to other villages less exposed (to both military and social dangers)." The other villages included "King Cove, Akutan, Sand Point, Squaw Harbor, Belkofsky, Kanatak, Karluk, Chignik, Perryville and False Pass." At three of these locations to the east, "there are living quarters available at canneries not to be operated this year." With the evacuation of 150 Unalaska Aleuts, "three teachers from the Unalaska Government school could be assigned to Alaska Peninsula or Aleutian Island villages which would gain most markedly in population."[15]

Responding to humanitarian concerns in a besieged Alaska, Bartlett's group determined that a six months' "supply of staple food should be widely distributed for natives as well as whites." Nearly forty tons of food already obtained by the Indian Service had been sent by the navy to Unalaska for distribution to Aleut villages. Furthermore, the committee decided that a $2-million share of the $15 million appropriated for United States territorial emergency supplies be allocated to "a food stock for Alaska." Liaison between an Alaska Railroad official and Indian Service supply headquarters in Seattle was established for distribution purposes. Problems in supplying the interior might be solved by using Skagway as a depot and moving food on the White Pass and Yukon Railroad and the Yukon River system.[16]

Other deliberations touched on the extremely important matters of finances and transportation, the two constant problems in evacuation planning. Concerning finances, Hugh J. Wade of the Social Security Agency was notified he would have twenty thousand dollars to spend for the evacuation of persons not able to pay their own passage from Alaska. He was given no instructions, however, about how the money was to be disbursed. Concerning transportation, everyone present agreed that it "is the sine qua non . . . and that vessels" necessary for evacuation "would have to be made available by the Navy."[17]

Before adjourning, the group identified further needs. "Basic thinking and definite decisions on matters of broad policy relating to evacuation" were necessary, "beyond what has been evidenced to date." For example, the question of whether people should "be encouraged to leave Alaska in advance of actual crisis" must be answered. By whom? "These decisions . . . must be made by the military authorities: the sooner the better." Also, government agencies should issue "a joint declaration . . . stating evacuation problems and recommending lines of procedure." To whom? "This should be addressed to the Army and Navy commands in Alaska and the Governor."[18]

This was the sum of Alaska evacuation planning as of March 1942. The group concluded that "further development of plans" and another meeting "in the very near future" would be "desirable."[19] What they had really done, however, was to make another meeting irrelevant since they had in fact just capitulated to military leadership in the matter of evacuation. The committee's plans in reality had about as much effect as a whisper against a williwaw.

But at least this conference attempted to develop policy: Natives in critical areas were not to be evacuated except possibly at Seward, Yakutat, and Unalaska. Only Aleut women and children from Unalaska were slated to leave. Deference in all these matters, however, was given to the military. Forearmed with these agreements, Bartlett wrote to General Buckner about reports that "nonessential civilians" were being urged by the army to leave Anchorage. He told Buckner that a "study was being made by the National Resources Planning Board" that would be helpful "if the time should come when the Army and the Navy determine . . . evacuation advisable." Bartlett emphasized that "this study will not go to the point of whether evacuation should . . . be ordered since that is a strictly military problem." The general did not take the bait. He responded by branding the reports "rumors." The army had no intention to evacuate civilians. Life in Alaska, he felt, "should go ahead in normal fashion with as little disturbance due to war as possible." Nevertheless, there might "come a time," Buckner admitted, "when evacuation will be necessary as the result of enemy action."[20]

In spite of Bartlett's concern with evacuation planning, Juneau ultimately would not be the arbiter of policy. Washington, D.C., where stronger bureaucratic power resided, would. Hitherto silent about these matters, Interior Department officials were drawn into discussion partly as a result of the Juneau conference. Hugh J. Wade told his Social Security Administration superior in the capital what he had learned about Aleutian conditions from these talks. In the area "are numerous villages populated principally by Aleut Indians," he reported. "They are a class of people that do little or no thinking for themselves . . . and are dependent upon the Government" for economic maintenance. They should be supplied but not evacuated except for the Unalaskans, who faced the most danger of attack, he opined, and "are creating a major social problem, and the sooner" their women and children "are removed from that area, the better it will be for everybody."[21]

In Wade's estimation, two serious problems blocked Unalaska evacuation. Indifference was one; transportation was the other, perhaps the key. "Money won't help," he concluded. "What they need is shipping facilities," and the whole "area is under complete control of the Navy." The navy had even "taken over the boats of the Office of Indian Affairs." Wade said that Alaska officials had explained these factors to the commissioner of Indian Affairs. Yet "for one reason or another, no action is being taken." Action was essential, Wade felt, and the matter should "be brought forcefully to the attention of the Navy Department. I think it would be a crime to leave these Native persons in a spot . . . as vulnerable as Unalaska is any longer than is absolutely necessary."[22]

Benefits to be gained from stockpiling supplies in scattered Aleut villages and evacuating Unalaska women and children were obvious to Wade. If the Navy would do that, it would "rid itself of a very serious problem and protect itself against having to care for these natives . . . when and if" the military is "engaged in warfare in that area." Removing the Unalaskans, moreover, would avoid possible criticism of the government like that leveled at the British when they "left the natives of the Malay Peninsula on their own" and the Japanese attacked.[23]

The need to avoid criticism in this situation awakened Assistant Commissioner of Indian Affairs William Zimmerman, Jr. He wired Admiral Freeman in Seattle on April 1 asking about navy evacuation plans for the Aleutians. Freeman thought that Aleuts might be vulnerable to enemy attack. Their removal, however, was "desirable but not mandatory." The navy could do nothing about the situation, anyway. There is, he argued, "no Navy transportation available." Freeman suggested that should the Office of Indian Affairs decide to act, it could charter the SS *Cordova* for evacuation of Aleuts.[24] Thus Freeman tossed the hot potato back into the Interior Department's lap.

On April 10, 1942, Commissioner of Indian Affairs John Collier asserted that the time for decision on evacuation was at hand. He explained the Aleutian situation to Secretary Harold Ickes and noted that informal discussions with the navy, army, Red Cross, and Federal Security Agency had produced no agreement and no action. Alaska officials and the Department of Indian Services were split, he told Ickes; Superintendent Hirst supported evacuation of Unalaska's women and children, but Governor Gruening opposed any Aleut removal. Collier outlined other, more serious considerations for Ickes. The navy would "provide no protection west of Dutch Harbor." Admiral Freeman's claim that navy ships were unavailable also suggested that other sources of transportation were unavailable, even though funding was in place "for the cost of evacuation." There was a risk, too, according to Collier, "that we might be criticized if Dutch Harbor were bombed with incidental loss or death at Unalaska." In addition, Aleuts varied in their own opinions about relocation, and their wishes, according to Collier, should be considered. "The residents of the western islands show no inclination to move," he reported, "but those at Unalaska have indicated that they are willing to move eastward to other islands or perhaps even to the mainland."[25]

Collier told Ickes that after weighing all factors, he felt "inclined to leave the Natives where they are, unless the Navy insists that they be moved out." This "no evacuation" policy with its navy corollary replaced the one recommended by Bartlett's Juneau meeting. That policy had recommended that Unalaska women and children be moved, but that the actual decision be left to the military. Collier told Ickes that he was more inclined to agree with Gruening's opposition to any evacuation. Such removal, Collier felt, would inflict more harm on Aleuts than would be visited upon them in a Japanese attack. But there was a problem with Collier's terminology. Did his use of the term *the Navy* really mean *the military*, which would include the army? It is not clear. To muddle it even more, Secretary Ickes answered Collier in a handwritten addendum on the bottom of this memo: "I concur," he declared, "unless they [Aleuts] want to move."[26] Now the Department of the Interior had both a navy and an Aleut corollary. Evacuation would take place only if the navy (or army?) insisted or Aleuts requested it.

The question of evacuation seemed to be answered by Ickes's "I concur" of April 15, 1942. The matter was laid to rest. It might have stayed that way had it not been for Donald W. Hagerty, an Interior Department employee. A former Alaska Indian Service field agent with experience in the Aleutians, he was on special assignment in the Indian Service's Seattle purchasing and shipping unit. This gave him access to Admiral Freeman's office in the course of arranging shipment of supplies to Alaska Native villages. Hagerty became an interested party—a self-appointed one—in the evacuation issue. He sent information about the Aleutian situation gleaned from navy sources to Superintendent Hirst and Assistant Commissioner Zimmerman. He also offered them his own policy suggestions. Hagerty's efforts covered the gamut. He addressed questions of whether there should be evacuation, who should implement it, which Aleuts should be moved, and to what locations. His suggestions made him a middleman among Hirst and Zimmerman, the navy, and the Department of the Interior.

Early in April 1942, before the Interior Department's decision not to evacuate Aleuts, Hagerty had already begun operating. He telegraphed Zimmerman's office, for instance, indicating that he had opened negotiations with Alaska salmon packers to aquire housing if it became necessary to move Aleuts. He suggested that he would need official certification for his role when dealing with the navy. Then he wired Hirst about Washington's interest in "evacuation of natives from Attu, Atka, Nikolski, Kashega and Unalaska." Hagerty had contacted Admiral Freeman about evacuating these people and was told by the Admiral that from a "humanitarian standpoint" it should be undertaken soon. In his earlier contact with packing companies on Kodiak Island and the Alaska Peninsula, Hagerty had learned that jobs and living accommodations for the Aleuts would be available in August. Sensing urgency, Hagerty next found a "splendid location on Tulalip Indian Reservation" near Marysville, Washington, thirty-three miles north of Seattle. He informed Hirst that he expected approval soon for army transportation to move Aleuts to that locale.[27]

Hirst reacted defensively to Hagerty's activities. He resented being bypassed. Hirst claimed that his office had been working with Governor Gruening and the military toward evacuating Aleuts to the Alaska Peninsula. The Tulalip idea was "bad policy" because it would be difficult for Natives to adjust to that region, he insisted. Furthermore, "we have no funds to transfer or construct houses." If Hagerty were to continue with this business, he ought to be in Juneau, according to Hirst, "where information is available." As it was, Hagerty's work in Seattle added "confusion to an already difficult job." In a subsequent letter to Hagerty, Hirst bolstered these points, doubting the advantages of Hagerty's Seattle base. Seemingly intimidated, Hirst felt that "matters can get into the records that will be embarrassing to us here" in Juneau. Relocation to the Tulalip Reservation "would be a great mistake." Aleuts, he claimed, are "asking to go to places on the Alaska Peninsula where they have always lived." If moved elsewhere, they would become "quite homesick within a very short time." Worse yet, "welfare problems would be coming from that group to this office for at least 15 years," Hirst predicted.[28]

Hagerty boldly maintained his stand. He had the benefit of information from Thirteenth Naval District headquarters and Assistant Commissioner Zimmerman's ear. In letters to Zimmerman, Hagerty reiterated Admiral Freeman's belief that Natives on Unalaska and westward islands should be evacuated because they were unprotected. Because navy transportation was not available, Hagerty felt the Alaska Office of Indian Affairs should find ships on their own. Admiral Freeman had referred him to the federal shipping coordinator, who "worked out a means of transportation if the Department deems it advisable." Tulalip, Hagerty emphasized, had land available and both subsistence and commercial fishing opportunities. "Natives could be housed in tents having board floors and walls." In a postscript, Hagerty asserted that "the people of Attu and Atka are the ones that will need immediate attention."[29]

Hagerty also refuted Hirst's contention that Juneau officials were better informed about Aleutian realities. "It is very evident," he wrote Zimmerman, that Hirst "does not have recent information about the area." The place to be was Seattle, he asserted, because information must be obtained through Freeman's office. The Tulalip Reservation idea made sense to Hagerty because it was the only place available where proper care could be given Aleuts collectively rather than to scattering them in other Alaska villages where accommodations would worsen through overcrowding.[30]

By the time Interior Department officials developed their hands-off policy, Hagerty's efforts to locate ships for evacuation had paid off. Captain Parker of the navy's Alaska Sector suggested that the Indian Service recommission and fit the *Boxer* for an evacuation transport and enlist the Fish and Wildlife Service's supply ship, the *Penguin*. Hagerty identified another ship, the *Western Trader*, for the removal of Attu and Atka people. It appeared the transportation problem could be solved without navy ships. Still, Hirst was reluctant. Funding the evacuation and finding relocation sites were problems still not settled. Hirst had a difficult task, and rumors made it even more difficult. An official of the Social Security Board in Seattle, Henry W. Clark, wrote to Hirst that he understood the "evacuation of all villages west of Unalaska" had been approved, and Aleuts from there would be carried to Marysville, Washington. The question of Unalaska's evacuation, however, was still not decided.[31]

Hagerty next assigned himself to determine whether Aleuts wanted to be moved. Wiring the teachers at Attu, Atka, and Nikolski, Hagerty directed, "Confer with natives and advise immediately if agreeable to evacuate. . . . Necessary food and transportation will be arranged." A communiqué from Assistant Commissioner Zimmerman may have prompted Hagerty to take this action. In any case, he kept Zimmerman informed, claiming that the Aleuts were not aware of the misfortune that might befall them. The teacher at Nikolski, Pauline Whitefield, and her husband apparently were aware because they "wanted an immediate transfer."[32]

Hagerty's attempts to alert Interior Department personnel to the dangers faced by western Aleuts took on a crisis tone in letters to Zimmerman. They also reflected the influence of Admiral Freeman, whose concern for Aleut safety impressed Hagerty. He saw in Freeman a model of humanitarianism and was flattered, too, when the Admiral confided in him sensitive military matters concerning the Aleutians. Informed of Japanese brutality to "helpless natives," some of whom were "liquidated" in the Philippines, Hagerty was swept by a sense of duty. He wanted to help Aleuts escape such a fate. Admiral Freeman even "designated one of his official staff to work directly with Hagerty" to this end. The issue, so far as the Admiral was concerned, "was not a question of whether natives wanted to evacuate, it was a question of the proper thing to do for them." At least it was possible to do something to avert a tragedy. Navy officials told Hagerty if the Office of Indian Affairs chose to evacuate the western "Aleutian people . . . they could be transported" on an Army ship "free of cost other than food." After informing Zimmerman of this on April 20 and sending Hirst a copy of the letter, Hagerty awaited instructions.[33]

Instead of receiving instructions to move ahead, Hagerty received disquieting signals from Zimmerman that dampened his enthusiasm. Nothing Zimmerman had been told by Hagerty about Admiral Free-man's fears would change departmental policy. Zimmerman further-more indicated that the Washington, D.C., office opposed evacuating Aleuts to Tulalip. Distance was a drawback and "their presence at Tulalip would give rise to various problems" not likely to occur in Alaska. Zimmerman was pleased that Hagerty had kept Hirst informed and apologized for not doing so himself. He was, however, upset over Hagerty's direct inquiries to Aleut communities about evacuation with-out working through the Juneau headquarters. "If you communicate directly with people in Alaska," he warned, "you will inevitably cause confusion." Zimmerman himself must have caused some confusion for officials considering evacuation, because he asked Hagerty: "Have you considered the possibility of moving any of these people to Bristol Bay?"[34] This locale had not been mentioned before, and Zimmerman's suggestion of it only added another element to a clouded picture.

Unappreciated and frustrated, Hagerty was defeated. Zimmerman even resolved to move him out of his position. "I have some doubts as to the propriety of paying you a per diem there," he complained to Hagerty. "Alaska travel money is running short." Zimmerman had in mind a different assignment for Hagerty. "Could you finish your work next week?" Hirst is "much disturbed," he wrote, about your activities in Seattle.[35]

This chastening was taken to heart. Although a subdued Hagerty stayed on at Seattle, Zimmerman now handed evacuation matters directly to Hirst in Juneau.

It now appeared that navy and Indian Service officials would evacuate all Aleuts and Indian Service personnel from Attu and Atka in May. Assuming this was about to happen, Captain Parker of the Alaska Sector wired Hirst that the navy intended to replace the two Indian Service radio operators on Attu and Atka with navy aerological personnel. Parker asked Hirst for permission for the military to use government buildings and equipment already there. Because Hirst was on a field trip to Nome, Assistant Geeslin replied. Authority for the use of property would have to come from Commissioner Collier, but the Juneau office approved of teacher and Native evacuation. Geeslin directed that Attu's Indian Service employees should be transported to Squaw Harbor on Unga Island near the Alaska Peninsula, and Atka's to Port Graham on the tip of the Kenai Peninsula. He asked Parker to keep him informed "of final plans for evacuation" of both "natives and our personnel." The same day, Geeslin wrote to Zimmerman requesting advice about these plans. "To date," he admitted, "we have not received any information from our teachers at these stations indicating whether . . . the Natives desire to be evacuated" or where "they should be taken should it be desired that they be evacuated." So far, it appeared, Geeslin knew only that the Interior Department was not convinced that Aleuts should be evacuated and if they were they should not go to Tulalip.[36]

But in the middle of May, evacuation planning was still muddled by conflicting information. Geeslin, for instance, asserted to Zimmerman that the navy had decided to evacuate Attu and Atka. "But details are not yet known," he wrote. "It is my understanding that those from Attu will be evacuated by a Naval vessel and those from Atka by the Bureau." If this were true, Hirst knew nothing about it. Hagerty, still advising from Seattle, knew nothing about it, either. During the same week, Hagerty wrote Hirst that Captain Luker of the Thirteenth Naval District, acting on Parker's command, asked for the destination of Attu and Atka Natives and "who had authority" to decide. Hagerty showed Captain Luker Interior Department correspondence that contained no answers. Luker responded by asserting that the "Navy considered it very advisable to get these groups out of there immediately," although it was not their "responsibility."[37]

Pursuing the matter, Hagerty suggested to Hirst that discussions should end. Because, as far as Hagerty knew, the navy would not order evacuation, the responsibility rested on Alaska Indian Service shoulders. Hagerty urged Hirst to request that the navy use the *Western Trader* to evacuate Attu and Atka. The ship was already lined up in Seattle for supplying the Aleutians. These natives should then be taken to Juneau's

Peterson Creek area where a Civilian Conservation Corps camp could be built. Frank Heintzleman of the Alaska Civilian Conservation Corps had already agreed to undertake the project, which would be composed of buildings like the government built to house "Japanese evacuees" near Seattle. "We must act," Hagerty pleaded, "within the next few days."[38]

But nothing happened. Hirst did not act, adhering instead to department policy. Summing up Captain Parker's position of April 15 and Hagerty's of May 14, Hirst explained to Zimmerman again that the navy claimed they had no transportation available. He repeated the Ickes formula: "We are in favor of moving these people . . . provided they request the same, or the Defense Authorities so order." In either case, Hirst knew he needed approval of funding before pursuing evacuation. Under no circumstance, he insisted, should Aleuts be moved to "Juneau or its vicinity." A better location "might be secured for them either in Cook's Inlet or Prince William Sound." He apparently had abandoned his earlier preference for Alaska Peninsula sites. Old unused canneries, some of them in Southeast Alaska, might also be rented or purchased. But again, without approval for funding, the possibilities remained only possibilities.[39]

The vacuum in which Hirst and Hagerty operated extended all the way to Washington, D.C. Grasping for some indication of the latest developments in Alaska, Assistant Commissioner Zimmerman wired Hagerty on May 19, "Henry Clark says Freeman decided evacuate islands west of Unalaska. Ultimate destination Marysville. Is this correct. Wire." Hagerty responded, "Evacuation matters being decided by Hirst and Captain Parker." He stated that the problem of destinations was not yet solved, and that Freeman still insisted on an Indian Service decision. Juneau, Hagerty claimed, had been kept fully informed about all of these suggestions. Zimmerman immediately telegraphed Hirst: "Hagerty wires you and Captain Parker will decide question evacuation of natives. Wire new developments, if any."[40] There were no new developments.

It might have been true that Hirst was slow to understand the perils facing Aleuts, that Hagerty was too much under the sway of Admiral Freeman, and that Zimmerman was too isolated from the scene. But the result was obvious: inertia. Hirst, although he was the chief Interior Department officer in the region, adamantly refused to act. When Zimmerman finally pressed him to make a decision, Hirst shot back, "Will make no decision . . . have referred all communications from Captain Parker to you." Also, Hirst now thought Hagerty should accompany the evacuation ship, since it seemed military authorities had already decided to undertake the Attu and Atka removal. Ever compliant, however, Hirst promised, "Will continue forwarding any information to you and Hagerty." Zimmerman was not ready to make a decision, either. In response to Hirst's concern for funding, Zimmerman reported that a total of twenty million dollars was available for evacuation. It could cover "expenses . . . even temporary shelter or housing." Yet the Interior Department's position on evacuation had not changed. Zimmerman again urged Hirst to decide: "I assume that the Natives themselves have less information on which to base a decision than you have, and I feel that we here must be guided largely by recommendations coming from you and Hagerty and others in Seattle."[41]

In early June, when it was too late (although he did not know it), Governor Gruening joined the debate with his own ruminations. Based on discussions he had had with Hirst and General Buckner, Gruening supported the do-nothing position for Attu and Atka. "There seems to be considerable doubt as to the desirability of this evacuation," he wrote to Ickes. He also doubted that evacuation was feasible "with the presence of Japanese vessels off Dutch Harbor." From the onset, Gruening had recommended no evacuation of Aleuts. Hoping for Aleut support for his stand, he suggested to Ickes that the problem be presented to the Natives "understandingly, sympathetically and clearly. It would be a question whether they would understand fully the implications of being moved." Gruening added that General Buckner believed that evacuating the western Aleuts would come "pretty close to destroying them," since they would have trouble adjusting to new circumstances. The general warned: "If they were removed they would be subject to the deterioration of contact with the white man, would likely fall prey to drink and disease, and probably would never get back to their historic habitat."[42]

Likewise too late, but not realizing it, the relentless Hagerty tried again to help the Aleuts. He had participated in the debate longer and more persistently than most. Even as the Japanese were invading the Aleutians, Hagerty, a veteran of the Indian Service in the Aleutians for many years, tired of the impasse. He wrote to Zimmerman:

> Some of our Alaska Natives are in for some serious trouble. . . . Had an off-the-record report this morning . . . that things were happening in the Aleutians. . . . Now if anytime you feel that we should have some one on the ground out there, I would make arrangements to go. . . . All the Natives out there need is a wire placing the teacher in charge of the evacuation and for them to get aboard ship. Those groups will do anything we ask them within reason.[43]

6

Aleut Evacuations

> I was about twelve years old in June of 1942. . . . When we
> got to the ship, we were told that we had to come aboard
> . . . . They were going to take us away. They did not tell us
> where they were going to take us. . . . Some people
> requested permission to go ashore . . . but they were
> not allowed to leave the ship. They just took their boats
> and destroyed them, they chopped holes in them.
> —Alice Snigaroff Petrivelli, Atka Aleut Evacuee
> Commission on Wartime Relocation Hearings

To most Alaskans, war brought discomfort and sacrifice, but very few anticipated what it would bring to Aleuts. Evacuated for safety's sake, they were often thrown in harm's way and deprived of home, health, and even life itself. Unprepared to be uprooted and given little advance warning, Aleuts were surprised and shocked by the urgency of evacuation and relocation. Although many had never before left their islands, they were moved about to unfamiliar places where danger lurked and deprivation struck. Pathos and irony are linked in their evacuation stories. Although a video documentary concludes that Aleuts were simply "at the wrong place at the wrong time," their poignant odysseys will forever be etched in Aleut history.[1]

Nobody can say what would have happened had Aleuts been left on the islands. Surely their experiences could have been devastating. Attuans might have perished in the battle to retake Attu. The others might have suffered by being cut off for the duration from necessary supplies. The crush of military presence might have destroyed their villages and made their lives miserable. But what might have been is only idle specualtion.

As it turned out, evacuation of the Aleuts happened quickly, with little preparation or planning. Executing evacuation sooner might have made it less hectic. But the removal was a reaction forced on authorities faced with Japanese military moves. It came as an emergency.

When it came, moreover, it came in bursts, not as a comprehensive simultaneous move. The experience of each Aleut group varied. At Atka, some Aleuts were taken in early June. Others were left to be rescued at some undetermined later time. Shortly thereafter, St. George and St. Paul people were removed from the Pribilofs. In early July, Aleuts from Akutan, Biorka, Kashega, Mukushin, and Nikolski were evacuated. Several weeks later, most but not all Unalaskans were taken. Attu's people, never reached by U.S. rescue efforts, were captured by the Japanese. They were carried to Japan in September 1942, where they were incarcerated and pressed into labor.

In retrospect, the evacuations were distinctive responses to particular situations. Timing and reasons varied according to circumstances. To be sure, there was a humanitarian concern for Aleut safety, to prevent their death or suffering in a combat zone. But the evacuations were more complex than this, the motives mixed.

The military thought it highly possible that the Japanese would move eastward across the Aleutian Chain. In that event, it would be more convenient for battle if the Aleutians were unencumbered by civilians. Also, for pragmatic reasons, the military would not want to assume the burden of safety and care of Aleuts—that should be the responsibility of civilian officials. The principle of military gain was at work.

Both military and government officials realized it would be risky to keep Aleuts on the islands. Transportation and supply would be severely tested if battles erupted, not to mention movement of equipment and troops. Even if fighting did not materialize, Aleuts could become involved in social problems with troops stationed in or close to their villages. Contagious disease would be a problem for both. Alcohol and sexual activity could entice military personnel away from duty. Moreover, it would be diversionary for military police to patrol Aleut villages. Finally, if Aleuts were evacuated, their houses and lands would be open for military use.

The picture was further clouded by racial motivation. Interior Department paternalism and condescension had been a complaint of Aleuts for a long time. Aleuts, who had no political clout, had been stigmatized as "wards" or "breeds." Natives in Alaska had always been considered genetically inferior. Traditionally, they had been set apart from white Alaska. Race had hovered there like a specter.

This Alaska then, and its similarly biased military, provided a context for anti-Aleut prejudice. Evacuation was a subtext. Unalaska was an example of racial discrimination as an underlying motive in the convoluted Aleut removal. Aleuts were evacuated after danger to Dutch Harbor had passed. Causcasians were allowed to stay. The commanding general of Fort Mears thought Aleuts were degenerates and wanted them removed in part to cleanse the area.

After the war, Aleuts asserted that the evacuation—especially the way they had been treated in the relocation camps—had been racially discriminatory.

The first Aleut evacuations began after the invasion and occupation of Attu and Kiska in early June 1942. It was feared that the American retaliatory blitz of Kiska would lead to a Japanese blitz of Atka. With Japan still in control at Kiska, Atka might be the recipient of the next Japanese strike. Consequently, the navy ordered Atka's eighty-three Aleuts out of their homes. They were to seek safety in their summer camps. One officer was struck by the scene. "They were evacuated while eating breakfast," he noticed, "and the eggs were still on the table— coffee in the cups. A lot of their personal clothing and stuff was still hanging in closets," and "the village was declared off-limits for all but medical personnel."[2]

At 8:30 P.M. on June 12, 1942, Navy Lieutenant Commander J. P. Heath, captain of the USS *Gillis,* dispatched a demolition crew led by Lieutenant W. W. Fitts to burn down Atka village. By 10:30 P.M. the village was in flames, and the razing party had returned to the ship.[3] If the enemy came, they would find ashes in this ancient Aleut village.

The USS *Hulbert,* a companion seaplane tender, relieved the *Gillis* to refuel the remaining pontoon planes in Nazan Bay close to Atka. Having spent its aviation fuel, the *Gillis* took aboard Ruby and Charles Magee, the Caucasian teacher and her husband, just before the Fitts torching detail returned to the ship. In the early morning of July 13, the *Gillis* was underway to Dutch Harbor carrying these two, the first of Atka's evacuees.[4]

Late in the night of June 12th and early the next day, a parcel of Atka's Aleuts were rounded up to board the *Hulbert.* They saw their "village burning," its glare visible from far away. Not all of them got the word that a ship, signaling in the bay with a searchlight, was waiting for them to board. Among those who did was the Andrew Snigaroff family, with a one-year-old daughter. At 11:00 P.M. they took a hazardous dory trip to the *Hulbert.* Once on the ship, Snigaroff requested that others ashore be notified about the impending evacuation; his request was denied. His dory was destroyed by the navy. At 5:22 A.M., June 13, the *Hulbert* hauled up anchor and headed for Nikolski on Umnak Island, a journey of some ten hours. Sixty-two Aleuts were aboard, leaving twenty-one still on Atka Island.[5]

In the evening of June 13, the *Hulbert's* evacuees were discharged to U.S. Army authorities at Nikolski. They stayed there for three days with little more than the clothes on their backs. "During my stay in Nikolski," Poda Snigaroff recalled, "I was starving." The military failed to feed them and there were no groceries for them in the Native store. Showing compassion, Nikolski Aleuts befriended the hapless Atkans, fed them, and allowed them to sleep in their homes. In the early morning of June 16, these Atka Aleuts were taken on an army transport to Dutch Harbor. There they were put in military barracks and reunited with the last of Atka's evacuees. The twenty-one remaining Aleuts had been beckoned by signal flares on June 15. They sneaked out of hiding and were flown to Dutch Harbor on two seaplanes, arriving the day before the *Hulbert* discharged their Atka relatives from Nikolski. Relieved, Poda Snigaroff exclaimed, "I was glad to see them again!"[6]

Within days of the navy's evacuation of Atka, the army moved into the Pribilofs. General Simon B. Buckner, Jr., who once advised against evacuating Aleuts of the western Aleutians for fear it would threaten their survival, organized a nine-man volunteer unit to evacuate St. Paul. Afterward, they were to lay land mines and then "sit there and wait." The group was to be led by Sergeant Lyman R. Ellsworth. Should the Japanese appear, Ellsworth wrote, "we were to give Dutch Harbor the warning and keep the enemy from getting" St. Paul "by blowing it up." At his Fort Richardson headquarters Buckner told these men, "You'll be on your own. . . . If you get in trouble we won't be able to give you any help."[7]

Sergeant Ellsworth and his army detachment steamed from Dutch Harbor toward St. Paul on the USS *Oriole* (AT 136). The *Oriole* also had been ordered by the commander of the Alaska Sector, Captain Parker, to evacuate St. Paul's residents. On their way, they stopped at St. George village, where the ship's captain, a lieutenant commander, "bellowed through his megaphone." He ordered everyone there to "get ready to leave the island in the next twelve hours." Ellsworth thought the skipper sounded "a hell of a note for the poor devils. Their faces showed bewilderment, anxiety, fear." Then the ship continued to St. Paul.[8]

Anchoring off St. Paul on June 14, the *Oriole* was joined by the United States Army Transport *Delarof,* also ordered by General Buckner for this evacuation. St. Paul Aleuts were told to prepare for leaving, and on the afternoon of June 15, the loading began. Crews from both ships lent a hand to this army-navy operation. The Orthodox priest, his wife, and thirteen Fish and Wildlife Service employees joined 294 Aleuts on the transport.[9]

The evacuation was not a pretty scene. "Excitement and confusion stepped up," Ellsworth conceded. One sailor grabbed a "beautiful set of chinaware," an heirloom, from an elderly Aleut woman and "heaved the carton overside into the water." A look of mingled horror and misery came over the woman's face; a faint moan could be heard coming through her sunken lips. Ellsworth "felt sorry for her."[10]

This evacuation completed, the *Delarof* sailed south at 3:10 A.M. on June 16, for its next destination, St. George village. There, starting at 5:30 A.M., it took aboard six Fish and Wildlife Service personnel and one Orthodox priest along with St. George's 183 Aleuts.[11]

Throughout, the people of both islands sustained indignities. Each passenger was allowed to carry only one package of belongings aboard, although St. George people took a bidar, a handy boat representing an ancient Aleut tradition. On the short notice they had been given, they had to kill livestock and leave behind their subsistence equipment and family keepsakes. They were not told of their final destination.[12]

As a precautionary measure, the navy assigned a United States Coast Guard cutter, the *Onandaga*, to escort the *Delarof* and ordered her to head for Dutch Harbor "by devious course," zigzagging to avoid any enemy submarines lurking below. Packed into her hold was a frightened human cargo. The ship was extremely crowded, so most had to eat standing up. Only one bathroom was available. There was no privacy. The hold of the ship was cold and drafty.[13] Unbeknownst to the Aleuts, there would be little improvement ahead.

The next day, June 17, the *Delarof* picked up the evacuated Atkans held over at Dutch Harbor, adding to the ship's overcrowding. It now carried 83 Atka Aleuts and 477 from the Pribilofs, a total of 560 men, women, and children. Owned by the Alaska Salmon Packers and chartered under wartime procedures to the army through the War Shipping Administration, the *Delarof* had a passenger capacity of 376. Counting Caucasian passengers, it was overloaded by more than 200 people. On June 18, it departed for an "unknown destination" rumored to be Seattle or Alaska's Cook Inlet or Wrangell village in Southeast Alaska.[14]

What would be done with this human cargo? Where would these uprooted Aleuts finally be taken?

What followed this military action became a quagmire of events so confusing and contradictory that it is extremely difficult to clarify them. Orders were issued by one command only to be countermanded by another. It is evident that planning for evacuation and leadership in implementing it were lacking.

The Atka and Pribilof evacuations shocked Department of the Interior officials. The military had suddenly obligated Interior with the care of hundreds of evacuees. The unsoundness of the department's policy was now demonstrated. Its officials had only talked of plans for evacuation.

There had been no consensus about what would be done if the military suddenly evacuated the Aleuts and, consequently, there were no prearranged maneuvers ready to put into action. Contingency plans were nonexistent. Civilian authorities were forced into hasty improvisation. Captain Parker, commander of the navy's Alaska Sector, had contacted the Juneau headquarters of the Alaska Indian Service on June 14. "What Alaskan port should be first used" for "Natives and Whites from Atka and the Pribilofs?" he wanted to know. Superintendent Hirst, who no doubt was unprepared for the question, wired back "Port Graham" on the southern tip of Alaska's Kenai Penninsula. Since Port Graham had not figured prominently as a relocation site before, this response came as a shot out of the blue. Not satisfied with Hirst's response, the navy command telephoned Thirteenth Naval District headquarters in Seattle for confirmation.

By chance, Indian Service field agent Donald Hagerty was in Admiral Freeman's office and took this message. Hagerty may have confused the issue by telling Captain Parker to take the Aleuts to his favored location, Tulalip Indian Reservation, for that same day Alaskan Sector headquarters at Kodiak telephoned the navy office in Juneau: "Atka and Pribilof Natives to be evacuated Marysville, Washington. Notify Indian Affairs Agent." Then, however, in a telegram to Assistant Commissioner William Zimmerman, Jr., in Washington, D.C., Hagerty claimed that Hirst was working directly on evacuation plans with Captain Parker but nothing was definite yet. According to Hagerty, Hirst's choice "probably" would be "Killisnoo Bay Herring Village." Hagerty said he was trying to locate in Seattle the owner of the Killisnoo facility.[15]

In the meantime, the army, too, was putting pressure on Hirst. It wanted "immediate and definite instructions as to where these refugees can disembark and receive adequate care." Probably to Hirst's relief, a decision soon came from Washington, D.C. A Department of the Interior conference on June 16 finally settled it officially. "All Indians now aboard ship," it determined, "should be kept in Southeastern Alaska." The best arrangement, the conferees decided, would be to relocate each village separately in "abandoned canneries or other canneries after season." Unless Hirst had "definite designation to furnish Navy," Zimmerman telegraphed, "Wrangell Institute is to be used as temporary location . . . or at any convenient point Fish and Wildlife Boats" could supply. Zimmerman indicated that expenses were provided for and that supplies would be forthcoming. Hirst would have to coordinate matters with both Edward Johnston of the Fish and Wildlife Service and Hagerty. He would also have to notify the navy and keep Zimmerman informed.[16]

In Seattle, Hagerty continued to play his hand. On June 16, the day of Interior's decision to send the Aleuts to Southeast and the *Delarof's* departure from St. George, Hagerty consulted with Admiral Freeman and Commissioner Zimmerman. He then talked to Superintendent Edward Johnston about loading supplies on the Fish and Wildlife Service ship *Penguin*. The U.S. Forest Service would be contacted for tents to be set up as living quarters. That done, Hagerty completed rental arrangements with A. J. Hatlund, the owner of the Killisnoo plant where the Atka people could stay. Further, he thought that another location might be obtained for St. George Aleuts. He told Zimmerman that Hirst was also investigating relocation sites.[17]

When the *Delarof* left Dutch Harbor on June 17 with 560 Aleuts, the frantic search for a destination was still under way. Hirst wired to Hagerty, "Please rush . . . re use Funter Bay Cannery," which was on Admiralty Island. Hagerty replied: "Agreeable to use plant. . . . P. E. Harris Company will not assume any responsibility for injuries sustained." Always concerned about department spending, Hirst must have been overjoyed to learn that "no rental will be charged but any damage resulting from native occupancy must be assumed by the department." For the time being, this relieved one of Hirst's major concerns. Yet both Fish and Wildlife and Indian Service personnel thought the *Delarof* might bypass Funter Bay and put in at Wrangell. Hagerty notified Hirst, for instance, that evacuation supplies would arrive at Wrangell Institute, the Indian Service's vocational school, before the evacuees landed. The dock at Funter Bay was reported to be in disrepair.[18]

Other suggestions rolled in from various agencies. The Alaska regional forester, B. Frank Heintzleman, pledged his cooperation and proposed sites at Wrangell Institute, Funter Bay, and the Excursion Inlet cannery on Alaska's mainland northwest of Juneau. These facilities needed repairs, and he intended to employ Aleuts in the Civilian Conservation Corps for this work. The Washington, D.C., Office of Indian Affairs proposed the cannery at "Big Port Walters" on the southern tip of Baranof Island. Hagerty concluded after conferring with its owner, however, that it was not suitable. Then, on June 18, Hirst claimed he had found satisfactory sites. He wired Zimmerman, "Have now completed arrangements . . . have notified authorities re: their destination."[19] His telegram, however, was no more specific than that; he did not name the sites.

It was now Governor Gruening's turn to muddy the waters. He intervened on behalf of the Alaska War Council, of which he was chairman. Gruening, who was out of the Territory much of the time promoting

Alaska causes, had opposed evacuation from the start. He had not changed his mind about that when the military suddenly moved. Now Gruening asked many questions and issued numerous directives, only to cause more confusion.[20]

Gruening asked General Buckner if there would be other Aleuts coming toward Southeast, as Alaskans call the panhandle. He complained about news coming "through various channels in casual and indirect manner which makes adequate preparation difficult." Did the general, he asked, "contemplate evacuating Nunivak and any other places in addition to Atka and Pribilofs?" Avoiding a direct answer to the question, Buckner told Gruening that the "Natives of Atka and Pribilofs [were] evacuated at their own volition." Two days later, Buckner's adjutant general told Gruening the evacuations so far were "a Navy undertaking." Of course, the Ellsworth mission alone contradicted these assertions.[21]

Attempting to play a role in evacuation, Gruening wrote to Secretary Ickes that the army had evacuated "the natives of Atka." Then, on the day after the *Delarof* departed Dutch Harbor, he called a meeting of concerned agencies for evacuation "planning and forethought." The Alaska Indian Service was represented at this meeting because of "possible future evacuees from such places as Nunivak, St. Lawrence Island, Umnak Island and Unalaska." The army sent a representative to the meeting, as did the navy, "because the Army did not know whether the evacuees would come on Army or Navy vessels."[22]

The Governor thought the convened officials would take responsibility for Aleut well-being. Because employment for Alaskans was one of Gruening's constant concerns, the Social Security Board would help them find work. The United States Marshal's Office would bring "these new colonies . . . law enforcement, particularly in regard to liquor." Both the Territorial Health Department and the United States Public Health Service would be concerned about "health problems particularly with a view to avoiding epidemics" and should be "involved in the selection of these new sites." The U.S. Forest Service would be an interested party because the "localities planned for resettlement are within the Tongass National forest." The conferees developed one recommendation: that the dual jurisdiction of the Fish and Wildlife Service over Pribilovians and the Alaska Indian Service over other Aleuts would be abolished. The Indian Service would be responsible for the care of all evacuated Aleuts.[23] This proposal made sense, but as events unfolded, it had no real impact. To add to the confusion, Gruening's conferees proposed that the plan to land the Aleuts on the *Delarof* at Wrangell must be changed. Funter Bay and Killisnoo were better destinations. As chairman of the Alaska War

Council, Gruening flexed his muscles. When Hirst received a telegram from the Coast Guard indicating that the *Delarof* would anchor at Wrangell, ironically Gruening complained to the Department of the Interior, to Buckner, and to the Coast Guard about the "confusion." Plans were "being fully worked out in Juneau," he insisted, and "I recommended that these matters henceforth be cleared through" the "Governor's Office . . . so that we may have effective coordinations." Military authorities at Juneau confessed to not knowing the origin of the Wrangell directive but said they would correct it.[24]

If a fog of confusion blanketed Alaska, it reached all the way to Washington, D.C. Officials there had never designated a port of disembarkation, stipulating only that Aleuts should be evacuated to Southeast. Although the decision to land at Wrangell came from a special Interior Department conference, this destination was chosen only because other sites were not yet available. Bypassing the Governor, Interior finally instructed Superintendent Hirst in Juneau to coordinate all evacuation moves.[25]

Hirst was alarmed by Interior's intent to place the Aleuts at Wrangell. It "will be inadequate, inconvenient and expensive," he told Zimmerman. He wanted to know, "When will funds be alloted for evacuation purposes?" Although he admitted confusion was caused by "messages from the Navy at Seattle and Kodiak, and from the Alaska Defense Command at Anchorage," Hirst insisted that "no one is at all frantic. . . . We are getting fairly well organized." Although the governor "feels somewhat provoked that all evacuation matters have not come to him direct," cooperation would be forthcoming. "I am only interested in getting this job well done," Hirst claimed, "and to take care of the people."[26] He said all of that only one day before the Aleuts were scheduled to arrive.

Government officials hoped they were ready to care for the passengers arriving on the *Delarof*. But before they could heave a sigh of relief, they received more disconcerting news. On June 22, Hagerty informed both Hirst and Zimmerman that he had learned from Admiral Freeman's office that "two more villages must evacuate." Surprised, Hirst wired back: "Governor received . . . radio from Buckner advising no more evacuations . . . which is contrary information Freeman gave you." But, if more should come this way, Hirst decided, "we will . . . take care of them at Killisnoo temporarily." Hagerty said because of security he could not disclose which two villages would be moved, but indicated that the navy had confirmed that the two villages "will be delivered per your instructions. Will keep you advised," Hagerty promised.[27]

In the meantime, on June 24, the first of the Aleut evacuees arrived at Funter Bay, Admiralty Island, in Southeast's Tongass National Forest.

It turned out that not two but six villages were targeted for the next evacuations. By the end of July, Akutan, Biorka, Kashega, Makushin, Nikolski, and Unalaska Aleuts were removed and relocated to Southeast. Not much is known about some of these evacuations, but what emerged later was similar to the Atka and Pribilof stories. Attu's Aleuts, who had been left on the chain, were evacuated by the Japanese as prisoners of war. Their story was told years later.

When the Atkans were held over temporarily at Nikolski Village, the Aleuts there were already facing serious food shortages. Both military supplies and civilian stores were inadequate or unavailable. Confirming this emergency, the Indian Service schoolteacher at Nikolski, Pauline A. T. Whitfield, sent a call to Hirst for help on June 16, the day Atkans had been moved on to Dutch Harbor. "Food supply almost exhausted," she warned. The commanding general in the area, Edgar B. Colladay, at Dutch Harbor's Fort Mears, was also contacted by the frightened teacher. She "requested either evacuation for the Nikolski natives and civilians or food." Not responding directly to the appeal, Hirst wired Whitfield: "Army and Navy to use any supplies [at Unalaska] belonging to Indian Service." No emergency supplies were available for Nikolski. "We will advise destination," Hirst continued, "and provide further care in case Army Navy decides evacuation."[28] Hirst apparently assumed that Whitfield's cry for help was not an Aleut request to leave Nikolski. Still operating under Interior's policy of not moving Aleuts unless they themselves or the military demanded it, Hirst characteristically made no move.

At Unalaska, the anticipated arrival of Aleuts on the *Delarof* was looked to with alarm. Food and housing there were already scarce. The Indian Service head nurse, Margaret Quinn, sounded an alarm when she airmailed Hirst a gloomy message. "Due to four hundred natives arriving here from Atka and Pribilofs a difficult situation arises." Besides the scarcity of food and housing, there was a "lack of ships dry provisions"—only three days' worth "at hand." She reiterated the obvious, that the area "is subject to air raids." Nurse Quinn wanted a commitment from Hirst. "Request you advise immediately steps being taken to remove all natives this area or to adequately take care of them," she implored. "It is absolutely essential that a decision be made immediately. If you are not able to make this decision, will wire Washington. Request rush reply." Hirst replied, holding firm to Interior policy. "Use any supplies belonging to Indian Service," he directed, but "other matters subject to recommendation and decision your local Army Navy officials."[29] The Department of the Interior would make no decision on evacuation from Nikolski or Unalaska city.

Government officials in Juneau did not interpret these requests for help as petitions for removal. But did the military think they were calls for action? Did they interpret the warning pleas as bona fide agency requests for evacuation? Whether they did or not, government officials remained passive. If what Hagerty had learned on June 22 from Admiral Freeman's office was true, that more villages were slated soon for evacuation, it would have to be a military decision.

Governor Gruening, wanting to avert the confusion involved in the Atka and Pribilof moves, implored Admiral Freeman on June 26 to keep his office informed about the Navy's intentions. "Adequate preparations can be made," he argued, and a muddled situation avoided. Gruening smarted over "contradictory messages sent to miscellaneous individuals and different agencies" during the first evacuation.[30]

But to the consternation of all parties involved, the same pattern was repeated. In an undated communiqué to the navy office in Juneau, Alaska Sector Commander Parker wired these directions: "Notify interested parties that natives of Unalaska on one vessel and natives of Makushin, Akutan, Chernofski, Nikolski, Kashega on another vessel. Date of arrival sent later."

As one of the interested parties, Hirst must have been surprised. He and other officials, based on Hagerty's information, had expected more evacuation from only two villages. Also, according to the 1940 census, no Aleuts lived at Chernofski, and those at Biorka on Sedanka Island were not mentioned in this wire. In a June 30 letter, Hirst wrote to Zimmerman, "Last week we had indications that something might be done about Akutan and Nikolski, but to date we have heard nothing further." However, he assured Zimmerman, "We have made preparations for them in Southeastern Alaska should they come."[31]

Some Aleuts indeed were soon to come, but Hirst and his staff were not prepared for them. A few days before the second wave of evacuations began, Hagerty asked Hirst for the destination of the estimated 110 Aleuts at Unalaska city. He said the navy wanted to know and also indicated that the navy had decided to evacuate Aleuts from surrounding islands. Hirst was still searching for sites. "If you must answer immediately," he told Hagerty, Unalaskans were to be sent to Wrangell, and the rest to Killisnoo. Wrangell Institute principal George T. Barrett, at Hirst's request, was investigating Burnett Inlet on Etolin Island and sites in the vicinity of Comma Lake Bay. Hirst also asked the Coast

Guard at Ketchikan for help in locating "abandoned canneries and other places" near Boca De Quadra Inlet on the southeastern tip of the Alaska panhandle.[32]

Although principal Barrett continued the search at Cholmondeley Sound on Prince of Wales Island, he informed Hirst that Wrangell would take "at least two days" to prepare, that the "Lake Bay site" could not be used, and that supplies should "be landed" at Burnett Inlet on Etolin Island.[33]

On July 6, the Alaska Steamship Company's SS *Columbia* sailed for Southeast with the July evacuees. Another emergency was at hand. More panic. More confusion. More misinformation. Hirst wired Barrett: "Have been notified that seventy Akutan and ninety Nikolski natives on one vessel and one hundred ten natives on another." Hirst wanted the Nikolski people landed in the "vicinity of Hood Bay," just south of Killisnoo on Admiralty Island. He instructed Barrett to "proceed there immediately" and "arrange for tents to be taken from Funter Bay." The Unalaska people, Hirst commanded, should be taken to Burnett Inlet. Then Hirst asked Leonard C. Allen, principal of the Ketchikan Indian School, and Coast Guard Commander Frederich A. Zeusler, to try to obtain a site at Ketchikan for the people of Akutan and perhaps other Aleuts later. Getting back to Barrett, he advised, "You should come to Juneau and let us know what arrangements you have made at Hood Bay before you return to Wrangell."[34]

When Governor Gruening heard of the July 6 evacuation, he felt bypassed again. As chairman of the Alaska War Council, he telegraphed Commander Parker of the Alaska Sector. He complained that Southeast was becoming overloaded. "If subsequently it is planned to evacuate natives of Nunivak and St. Lawrence Island," Gruening said, "Office of Indian Affairs advises it can take better care of them on mainland of western Alaska. I concur."[35] Gruening was anticipating evacuations not yet undertaken. His advice offered no solution for the problem at hand. Where would the present evacuees be landed or taken for longer-term care?

The search for relocation sites continued even as the *Columbia* bore down on Southeast. Hirst had authorized a chartered boat to help Leonard Allen explore Kasaan or the vicinity of Prince of Wales Island north of Cholmondeley Sound. George Barrett, working on the Hood Bay site, was relieved to hear from Hagerty that further evacuation could be delayed. In the meantime, Hirst reported to Hagerty that some otherwise promising facilities were not available and that one particular fish saltery was not large enough. Three days before the

Aleuts were scheduled to arrive, Hirst was forced into a decision, his searches a failure. "Advise authorities," he told Hagerty, to land all evacuees at Wrangell Institute. Stores would have to be transferred there from Killisnoo.[36] Wrangell would be a staging area for buying time, with subsequent removal to other Southeast points.

To handle matters from closer to the scene, Hirst left Juneau on July 11 for Wrangell Institute. He wired Zimmerman that he would greet 280 Aleuts from Nikolski, Unalaska, and Akutan who would be held there until abandoned canneries could be readied. The superintendent told Wrangell's captain of the port of his plans and indicated that both he and Barrett would be there with tents and bedding. Wooden floors would be built immediately for more than twenty large tents. If the evacuees arrived sooner, they should be temporarily housed in the school building. While Hirst was under way, Leonard Allen recommended yet another site, a cannery at Skowl Arm on Prince of Wales Island. It had few conveniences and no electricity, but, he wired Hirst, accommodations were "adequate."[37]

While the *Columbia* was heading toward Wrangell, the commander of the Alaska Sector directed the Ketchikan District Coast Guard to land the ship at Killisnoo and discharge its Aleuts. Just in time, Gruening's office intervened. He wired the Commander on June 11 to divert the ship to Wrangell because there was no room at Killisnoo.[38]

When the *Columbia* arrived at Wrangell, Indian Service officials were surprised that the numbers aboard did not correspond to figures given by the navy. There were fewer Aleuts, but they came from more diverse and scattered communities than expected. Six communities were represented: Akutan had 41, Biorka 18, Kashega 20, Makushin 8, Nikolski 72, and Unalaska 1, a total of 160 Aleuts.[39]

These evacuations were not carried out under emergency conditions as the Atka and Pribilof removals had been. But there were similarities. Again, the military gave scant notice, allowed Aleuts only a few possessions, and told them nothing about their destination. Compared with the journey of Atkans and Privilovians packed on the *Delarof,* however, this one was not nearly as crowded. The *Columbia* had room for 481 passengers.[40]

The journey from the villages to the relocation site was not direct; there were many starts and stops along the way. On July 5, when army officials told the Nikolski people to pack only essential clothing and await evacuation, they deposited their personal belongings before darkness in a village store building. Then, one Aleut remembered, they waited for a ship to arrive. When it failed to arrive that night, some of them slept in an underground bomb shelter outside their homes. Early the next morning, they were loaded on several small navy vessels and taken to Chernofski, an army supply depot on the northwestern shore of Unalaska Island. There they found Aleuts from Kashega and Makushin also awaiting evacuation, some of whom had been staying in army tents.[41]

Embarked on the *Columbia* at Chernofski, these Aleuts were taken north to Akutan Island, where its Aleuts, only one suitcase in hand, boarded at the whaling station. None of them had wanted to be evacuated. Some of those aboard the *Columbia* remembered that it stopped at night at several places before arriving at Wrangell. Probably one stop had been at Dutch Harbor to pick up eighteen Aleuts from Biorka and one from Unalaska city. Those from Biorka on nearby Sedanka Island might have been taken to Dutch Harbor on a small navy vessel like the patrol boat used in the Nikolski, Kashega, and Makushin transfers.[42] In any case, the *Columbia* landed its 160 Aleuts at Wrangell Institute on July 13, their accommodations and care in Southeast now in the hands of Alaska Indian Service personnel.

The only Aleuts left on the chain were at Unalaska city and Attu village. Paradoxically, it seemed they should have been the first people evacuated because of dangers they faced; the one because they were near the only worthwhile Aleutian military facility the enemy could attack, and the other because their village was closest to Japanese military forces in the North Pacific. Yet these two Aleut communities were the last to be removed—Unalaska under United States supervision, Attu under the Japanese.

Of all the evacuations, Unalaska city's was the most bizarre. In previous removals, military decision alone was the propelling force. But in the case of Unalaska city, others—Secretary Ickes and the city's mayor, John W. Fletcher—played a role, along with the army and navy.

Fully a month before Unalaska Aleuts were evacuated, the commanding general of Fort Mears, Edgar B. Colladay, had taken the first step in their removal. He perceived Aleuts as serious problems interfering with the area's two-year military buildup. The army had been using buildings in Unalaska for hospital facilities and had garrisoned troops on its perimeter. General Colladay still needed room for further expansion. On June 14, he wired Buckner "for authority to evacuate all natives of Unalaska." Although no Aleut had been injured in the Japanese attack, he thought that they might be in another one. "The possibility of women and children being wounded would make the medical problems difficult," wrote Colladay. He felt that "from a humanitarian point of view," the army "would have to take care of them while they are in our midst, to the detriment" of soldiers. The general announced a plan:

> I would like to clean out and evacuate the entire town. Most of the white women left on a recent transport. The Navy evacuated the natives from Attu [sic] and dropped them at Nikolski, from there they will come in here today or tomorrow, which means I will have to take care of them until we can get them out on a boat, which I do not like. I will in a day or two, submit official recommendations covering in general what I have told you in this letter. The speed at which the above can be accomplished, of course will depend a lot on the ability of the Navy to help us. However, due to the fact that they are particularly anxious for housing for their construction battalions, I think we will have little difficulty along that line.[43]

Colladay was right about the navy. In Aleut evacuation so far there had been cooperation between the two military services. It would continue. In recalling the events of Unalaska evacuation, Army Captain Hobart W. Copeland wrote, "On or about 29 June 1942, Post Headquarters received an information copy" of a navy communiqué from the commander of the Alaskan Sector to the naval air station at Dutch Harbor "directing the evacuation of all natives from the Aleutian Islands." Concerning this, Copeland was told by General Colladay to consult with Captain William N. Updegraf, commander of the naval station, "on plans for evacuation of Unalaska and to offer the services of my office in that evacuation." That he did. "It was agreed that the Navy furnish the transportation at the Unalaska Dock and my office carry out the actual evacuation."[44]

Department of the Interior officials, consistent with the adopted policy, had made no moves. When Unalaska's chief nurse, Margaret Quinn, on June 23, had appealed over Hirst to Washington, D.C., nothing had resulted. She had been alarmed over the area's "vulnerability." Telegraphing Commissioner of Indian Affairs John Collier, Quinn had reported "serious unrest" among the Aleuts and had recommended "immediate evacuation" because the "Juneau office states decision must be made locally."[45] This could have conformed to the principle adopted by Interior. It could have been taken as a request by Aleuts to be evacuated. But Interior had not moved.

Soon, however, political activity was at work in Unalaska. Its evacuation was consequently somewhat different from the others. Unalaska's Caucasian mayor, John Fletcher, visited Donald Hagerty in Seattle and was told that the decision to evacuate Unalaska city Aleuts had already been made. Both he and Hagerty assumed that Unalaska's people were to be moved immediately. Zimmerman, in the capital, assumed the same. In fact, he was quoted as having confirmed it in a newspaper article. But when Fletcher returned to Unalaska, he was shocked to find his city's Aleuts still there. Nurse Quinn "denounced" him "as neglecting natives who are desperate to be taken out." In a telegram on July 7 to Secretary Ickes, Fletcher wrote, "I wish to register vigorous protest in behalf of natives. . . . Transportation denied Unalaska natives and statement that they had been offered opportunity to leave since attack is false."[46] Again, civilian authorities obviously had not been informed of military intentions.

This finally jolted Department of the Interior officials off dead center. Ever sensitive to political flak, Ickes discussed the problem with James V. Forrestal, under secretary of the navy, and the next day, on July 9, wrote to Forrestal officially of his desire that the navy would "do something about this matter." Ickes depicted this statement in his reply to Mayor Fletcher as "an urgent request that some measures be taken to evacuate the natives of Unalaska." Forrestal responded to Ickes claiming that the Commander of the Thirteenth Naval District assured him that Unalaskans "will be removed on a ship departing from Dutch Harbor in late July."[47] This revealed that the navy had been awaiting an available ship.

The evacuation vessel began boarding Unalaska city Aleuts on July 19. They had been told only the day before that they would definitely be evacuated. The ship was the SS *Alaska,* owned and operated by the Alaska Steamship Company as a 382-passenger capacity troopship. There were problems with the loading. "Several natives, due to the U.S. Commissioner, refused to go." Jack Martin had favorites whom he did not want evacuated. Army Captain Copeland, who was placed in charge of this evacuation by General Colladay, called Navy Commander Updegraff "for authority to compel them," but "he refused to assume the responsibility for this compulsion." Not wanting a fight, Copeland allowed them to stay. Who then should leave? Updegraff, in spite of the fact that Aleuts there had intermarried with many Caucasian groups for two centuries, adopted a blood quantum principle. "All natives, or persons as much as one eighth (⅛) native blood were compelled to go." Updegraff was probably unaware that the Alaska Indian Service previously had set a one-quarter blood quantum test to determine who their "wards" were. Those who were allowed to stay, "native or white," were workers employed by the Siems-Drake-Puget Sound Company. John Yatchmeneff qualified to stay under this rule and because of his connection with Commissioner

Jack Martin. In the end, both William Zaharoff, the Aleut leader, and Yatchmeneff aided Copeland in identifying Aleuts and otherwise cooperated in the evacuation. As before, "only such portable baggage as the people could carry was permitted."[48]

The evacuation of Unalaska took place later than it had actually been expected. Hagerty wired Zimmerman that the navy had been "unavoidably delayed . . . since early June," indicating they had been planning it all along. Indeed, on June 18 in a telephone conversation between General DeWitt and Admiral Freeman, evacuation of a "few other Aleutian Islands" was mentioned as if it were imminent. Although Hagerty had been keeping up with the situation at Admiral Freeman's office, he mistakenly informed Zimmerman on July 22, the day of departure, that 110 Aleuts were heading toward Wrangell Institute on the *Alaska*. When the ship arrived there on August 1, it actually carried 137 Aleuts.[49]

Perceptions of Aleuts as social problems and obstructions to routine military activity were major factors contributing to their removal from Unalaska. Race was undoubtedly another. The army officer in charge of evacuation claimed that they "seemed to have no conception of cleanliness or orderliness and the majority of their homes had little value as buildings or contained little furniture."[50] It seems fair to say the Aleuts were looked down upon not only by the military but by Caucasian citizens of the city who were allowed to remain for the duration of the war. Only a few Aleuts who worked in defense construction and Yatchmeneff were allowed to stay.

The July evacuations from Unalaska and surrounding islands ended in arguments about who made the decision. When billed by the Alaska Steamship Company for the removal of Aleuts from Akutan, Biorka, Kashega, Makushin, and Nikolski, Navy Captain Charles S. Kerrick, the port director of the Thirteenth Naval District Transport Service, claimed that "the decision . . . was made by someone in the Department of the Interior. . . . The Navy did not have any part in this." He would not pay for transportation, even when provided a citation of the navy order. Some years later, the commander of the Alaskan Sector admitted in connection with a damage claim by the Caucasian owner of Nikolski's sheep ranch "that such evacuation was on Naval order."[51]

Captain Kerrick also steadfastly refused to authorize payment for the *Alaska*'s cost in the evacuation of Unalaska city. Department of the Interior personnel were surprised, having "nothing of record" in their files . . . that would substantiate "the Navy's charge that evacuation was on civilian authority."[52] Nevertheless, the Interior Department paid $35,468.93 for these two evacuations. Yet in connection with restoring the villages after the war, the Secretary of the Navy took responsibility for the evacuation of Atka and Akutan; the Secretary of War for the rest, except Attu.

In August 1942, the people of Attu village were the only Aleuts still in their island homes. Nobody outside knew what had happened to them. Captain Parker best expressed the extent of this lacuna ten days after Attu was invaded. "What disposition was made of them, whether they have been detained at Attu or on board some Japanese naval vessel, or have been taken back to Japan for confinement . . . I cannot say."[53] Much later it was learned that Attu Aleuts had been the last removed— by the Japanese. They were also the last to be returned.

Attu's people were the only Aleuts taken out of United States territory. While still captives on Attu, they had lost some of their freedom but were otherwise not treated harshly. Aleut children and a few of the soldiers even became friends. The youngsters taught the Japanese "how to live there" by catching sea urchins for food. But this relatively bucolic situation did not last long. The Japanese decided Attuans must be taken from the island. Parascovia Lokanin Wright remembered that "they rushed us," even though they were allowed to take food and items which would help them survive in Japan. Some of the children were frightened and cried when forced aboard the evacuation ship.[54] At least the Attuans were told their destination.

There were several motives for the evacuation. The Japanese military, fearing a harsh winter, at first had planned to withdraw. They thought Aleuts left at Attu "would have been a source of invaluable enemy intelligence to the Americans." Then, when the Japanese changed their minds and decided to stay, they reasoned that Aleuts represented "the possibility of guerilla activities, particularly in the event of an American counter-attack."[55] In the end, they were removed not for their safety but for Japanese security. Mike Lokanin recalled that the long journey to Japan started on September 14 and ended about two weeks later.

Forty-two of them were loaded on a Japanese merchant ship, the *Yoko Maru*. Aleuts remembered that it was "dark and dirty." It had been a coal carrier and was now used as a troop ship. Aleuts were taken to Kiska and then transferred to another merchant ship, *Osada Maru*. The military officer who had been in charge of them at Attu complained about living conditions aboard the ship and prevailed on the civilian captain to make the Aleuts more comfortable.[56]

As the ship headed for Japan, some of the Aleuts feared it would make an appealing target for American submarines or fighter planes. Other concerns weighed heavily upon them. "All we had is rice" to eat "and salted vegetables" but "not enough water," claimed Mike Lokanin. His friend Alex Prossoff recounts the journey and landing: "We could go on deck once a day for fresh air but if we were going by any cities we had to stay in the hold. . . . One night about 11:00 P.M. we landed at the city of Otaru on the island of Hokkaido. . . . When morning came some . . . soldiers, some policemen and some . . . doctors came on board. They examined all of us but did not find any disease. . . . I was just wondering where they will take us."[57]

7

In Strange New Lands

We slept like sardines. . . . We ate a lot of starchy foods
. . . . My sister, Irene . . . caught double pneumonia. . . .
When we got to our destination, she . . . because of
unsanitary water and the conditions . . . died and I
have two grandmothers that died during that time. . . .
This whole story has left a scar in my life.
—Anatoly Lekanof, St. George Aleut Evacuee
Commission on Wartime Relocation Hearings

Aleuts who were evacuated to scattered island sites in southeast Alaska and northern Japan faced overwhelming obstacles. Threat of impending death tested their perseverance from the beginning. Two died while en route to relocation camps. The first, a St. Paul infant girl, died of pneumonia on the *Delarof* between Dutch Harbor and Funter Bay. She was buried at sea in the Gulf of Alaska with Orthodox rites. The other, a fifty-six-year-old Attu woman, died on the *Yoko Maru* between Attu and Kiska and was cast into the North Pacific. The Japanese forced the Aleuts to throw her body overboard without religious ceremony.[1]

Except for the Otaru site in Japan, the other relocation camps were described as temporary—for the duration of the war. However, nobody knew when the war would end or who the victors would be. How long would temporary be? Aleuts must have been haunted by the fear that these makeshift camps might become their permanent homes.

As it turned out, the Pribilof people had the shortest stay, not quite two years. The Atkans and the eastern Aleut communities were returned after nearly three years. The Attuans were prisoners in Japan for three years and were relocated again in the Aleutians, but not on Attu. They and the people of Biorka, Kashega, and Makushin were resettled elsewhere because the Department of the Interior declined to rebuild their home villages and provide schools and other support systems.

Forced to travel to unfamiliar places, Aleuts looked back to their island homes and felt deep sadness. At once, they became homesick for the villages they had left behind. William Ermeloff from Nikolski was asked to remember when it was that he first wanted to return. He answered, "As soon as I got to Wrangell."[2] Everything in the new environment was different. It was also inferior. It was too hot in summer, too cold in winter. The rain fell strangely downward without being windblown. Vision was obstructed by many thick, tall trees. The air was heavy, and the sea gave off an unusal odor. For Aleuts, there could be no adequate replacement for life in the Aleutians. This was not home.

Furthermore, they were sent to places not fit to accommodate them. One was a temporary camp for itinerant government workers. The rest were seasonal facilities, long since abandoned, for housing gold mine laborers and fish cannery employees. They were old, ramshackle places—one of them having once been damaged by fire. Disrepair, decay, and rot greeted Aleuts at the camps. They were dangerous places not suitable for human habitation.

Evacuation to these hastily acquired sites created yet another stigma for Aleuts. To be certain, it was not as first-class citizens that they entered the camps. They had been wards; they were now wards and evacuees. Technically, they were not internees. The Attuans in Japan, of course, were prisoners of war. One Japanese observer euphemistically called them "captive guests."[3]

All the evacuated Aleuts had one thing in common—they were not allowed to return home during the war. But there the comparison ends. Aleuts who were taken to Alaska's Southeast faced a different set of conditions from those forced to Otaru. In the camps, there were no barbed wire fences, security guards, forced labor, or house arrest. The Aleuts were, however, treated to the harshest of environments and the most irritating neglect. In spite of this, they defied authorities' attempts to limit their rights.

Because Aleuts were wards, officials wanted them to live in intact camp communities. That way, they would be easier to care for and would cause fewer problems. They could be put to work rebuilding the camps. The Pribilovians would be a ready workforce when the seal harvest was resumed. But as it turned out, some Aleuts left the camps and worked elsewhere. Some even chose not to return to the islands after the war.

A few Aleuts, moreover, enjoyed certain aspects of their relocation. Some children were fascinated by the new environment and explored its "exotic" nature. While most elders regarded trees as obstructions, youngsters used them for hiding and climbing. Good wages in the wartime economy also benefited some Aleuts. But the majority hated the camps and could hardly wait to go home.

When the first Aleuts arrived from their fifteen-hundred-mile journey, the beauty of Admiralty Island, with its towering green Sitka spruce, western hemlock, and colorful flowers, appeared soothing after the arduous journey. The *Delarof* put in at Funter Bay on June 24, 1942. The 560 Aleuts packed aboard did not realize that the ship's overcrowding would be matched by the living conditions ashore. Funter Bay would soon come to replace in their minds the "ugly grimy gray" vessel now ready to disgorge them.[4]

The hurry-scurry searching of the Alaska Indian Service had located two sites at Funter Bay, an abandoned cannery and a gold mine camp. The Pribilovians would be settled there. The area was close to the Indian Service headquarters at Juneau, only twenty miles as the raven flies, fifty by water. Fish and Wildlife Service personnel headquartered in distant Seattle had not investigated the sites for lack of time. Upon arrival, what they and the Aleuts discovered was shocking. The camp's problems had already been detected by Indian Service officals, who nevertheless tabbed it for Aleut occupation. In a report to Superintendent Claude Hirst the day before the *Delarof* arrived, a three-member team led by Hirst's assistant Fred Geeslin made clear the grim reality that Funter Bay was not habitable. Yet, bowing to the emergency at hand, most of which had resulted from their lack of forethought and planning, investigators recommended the place for Pribilovians to live.[5]

Geeslin's report indicated that some conditions at Funter Bay could be improved, but not at once and not without Herculean effort. There was no outside help available, and supplies were few or nonexistent. The residents would need a boat to maneuver around the bay and haul firewood. Coal could be used for heat and for cook stoves, but it was unclear if and when it could be acquired.

At the cannery site, the water system not only was inadequate for fighting fires but would provide drinking water in summer only. In the winter, the mains would freeze, and residents would have to carry water from beneath the ice on frozen streams. Worse, there was "no sewage disposal system. Three large outdoor toilets" sat "on piles slightly below high tide mark." They depended "on the action of the tide to remove the sewage." This primitive arrangement would be a health hazard.[6] The electrical generator at the cannery was inadequate to light dwellings or the mess hall. Laundry would have to be done by hand in buckets or streams, because there were no laundry rooms. Bathing facilities did not exist. In the mess hall, there were few dishes or utensils.[7]

The cannery had identical two-story wood-framed dormitory buildings named the China House and the Filipino House after the nationalities of cannery workers kept segregated by their origins. In addition, there were fifteen cottages of assorted sizes and small sleeping rooms for twenty families. The China House had been stripped of all electrical wiring and plumbing fixtures. It had no furniture. Its kitchen ranges were without tops, grates, draft doors, or venting pipes. A small wash-room originally piped for cold water was missing its plumbing; another one had never been completed. There were no utilities for heating water. The outside toilet mounted on pilings was in need of repair and should be avoided. The Filipino House was no better. The cottages, referred to as "shacks," had sleeping rooms with assorted ills: no doors, "studding stripped of plaster board," no plumbing, no stove, no flues, no heating units. An old warehouse that might be used in an emergency had broken windows or none.[8]

Three miles away, the gold mine looked no better than the cannery. According to the report, many dangers lurked there, such as bare electri-cal wires and too many electrical drop cords. Drinking water would have to be carried from two small streams, and "a large number of people in these facilities would immediately create danger of water pollution unless adequate precautions were taken to prevent contamina-tion." The Indian Service did not know if water there had ever been tested. The sewage system consisted of two pit toilets situated on pil-ings over the beach.[9]

The gold mine dwellings were in somewhat better shape than those across the bay at the cannery. Two cottages had cots, heaters, and cook-ing ranges, but no plumbing. An old two-story bunkhouse was in fairly good condition except that its inside was unfinished and the sleeping cots were damaged. The old mess hall contained usable equipment, as did a newer mess hall, which nonetheless lacked a range and heating unit. Unlike the cannery, the gold mine had a bath house, a small unit containing one shower. This facility had a hot water system that could be repaired and expanded. A bunkhouse had been started but was only a shell with roof and flooring. Both an assay office and a mill building contained "corrosive and poisonous chemicals" used in "a cyanide pro-cess" for extracting gold from ore. These buildings would have to be locked and security measures taken to keep children from the toxic substances. There was a private residence, a good four-room house. If this should become available, the report judged, "it would make an excellent teacher's residence."[10]

The Aleuts brought to Admiralty Island numbered 477 Pribilovians representing over one-half of all evacuees. They were initially placed at the cannery. It was situated on a clearing of about five acres dominated by muskeg and covered with heavy underbrush. Its buildings were "located on low, well-drained ridges," but "the swampy area surrounding them . . . necessitated the construction of wooden sidewalks." Some of the area was already covered by "dilapidated plank sidewalk." Cottages were nearly covered by "a dense growth of alder and underbrush . . . making them very dark and damp." The Indian Service report "estimated 100 man days of work" would be needed for clearing brush, repairing walks, and getting the facilities in shape for occupancy. At the gold mine, buildings were "located on a very narrow beach extending from high tide line to the foot of a high mountain." There, "dense underbrush" crowded "the buildings on the side toward the mountain."[11]

The June 24 unloading of the *Delarof* was witnessed by a journalist, Joseph Driscoll of the New York *Herald Tribune*. He was invited there by Governor Ernest Gruening, himself a former newspaper reporter. The governor and his Juneau party arrived on a Fish and Wildlife Service ship, the *Brant*. Superintendent Claude Hirst of the Alaska Indian Service was also aboard. Driscoll interviewed Aleuts who, as was obvious to him, had been on "no pleasure cruise." He was fascinated by this "strange cargo" of people being transferred to the cannery. They "perspired freely" in the unaccustomed heat as they helped unload the ship. Their first reaction was dislike for the heat, the second a complaint about "too many trees" leaving "no room to walk around."[12]

To Driscoll, Aleuts were exotic curiosities like those at carnivals. He liked them. "They are cousins to the Eskimo and there is an Oriental strain in them." Over the years, "tuberculosis and the white man's burden, venereal disease," were given them by Russians and Americans, he wrote. Also, "many of them are pock-marked." Strong in some respects, they have "a weakness for candy as for alcohol." Drinking sends them "to the dogs and gutters." If they step out of line, "their white guardians discipline them by cutting down on their allowance of sugar and candy." Driscoll thought they had other disabilities. They "lean too heavily and too often upon the government." All this reliance on "Uncle Sam" and rejection of their ancient ways made them spoiled takers of handouts. These, "our Pribilof wards," Driscoll claimed, "lived on a scale denied to millions" in Europe and Asia.[13]

This news reporter from sophisticated New York felt that he stood above Aleuts. He condescendingly asked "a dirty-faced" Aleut boy whether he knew what a tree was. Giving up their traditional skin-boat technology, the Aleuts now were "casting envious glances at the white man's launches" equipped with "outboard motors." He asked one young Aleut, "Are you all pure breeds?" Driscoll knew the answer all along. "On the islands there is some promiscuity in sexual relations, and many a native has had unknown Americans, Russians and Orientals for fathers." Aleut "morals" are not "the same as ours," he claimed, and concluded, "Yes, there is quite a mixture of breeds."[14]

When comparing the Atka and Pribilof people, Driscoll favored the "Atka natives, who had scratched for a meager living out in the middle of the ocean." In contrast, "the Pribilofs were pampered." Government officials called them "steam-heated Indians." After the annual sealing, the government "lavished on the Pribilof natives" monetary "bonuses" and "all other necessities." Mrs. Daniel Benson, wife of the St. George agent and caretaker, agreed. She argued that "the Pribilof natives tended to be extravagant and to throw away goods that less fortunate aborigines would envy."[15]

Pampered or not, the Pribilovians were shocked by Funter Bay. One of them called it "a nightmare." Almost immediately, said another, "we were dreadfully homesick." They slept on the floor, mattress along side of mattress and "head-to-foot." Some of them remember being able to "see through the roof." Bunkhouses were described as "not fit for humans." What little privacy there was, Aleuts created by using blankets as makeshift partitions to create ten-foot-square cubicles.[16]

They were not well fed. Fish and Wildlife records testify that "when the food was low we were only able to give one good meal per day." Its quality was questionable. "You could feed it to the rats for all I cared," protested one evacuee. They complained about having no fresh meat or vegetables, but plenty of powdered eggs and "clams, clams, clams." Eating facilities were "very inadequate, unsanitary and unorganized." Hunger stalked them. We "had nothing to eat."[17]

The effect on the Aleuts was immediate. Mike Lekanof remembered that "people were in very depressed moods." Their observations confirmed what Geeslin and others had already reported—conditions were deplorable. On June 26, Fish and Wildlife personnel moved the St. George people to the gold mine site because the cannery was so overcrowded. But one Aleut thought conditions there were no better. The buildings were "damp, drafty, cold." A pregnant woman was given no medical checkup or help. "Nothing was sanitary." Their health was threatened, and when people died there they had to be buried in the soggy marsh close by.[18]

In the remaining months of 1942, government officials were confronted with more problems. At one point the Fish and Wildlife Service planned "to take all of the white personnel to Seattle and leave the natives to shift for themselves." Not all of them left, however; eight Caucasians were temporarily left in charge. But both medical doctors resigned on the spot. Five of the most severely ill Aleuts were taken to Juneau for medical care. Dr. Langdon R. White, Alaska Indian Service medical director, said that one of them "had only a few days to live."

Superintendent Hirst told Governor Gruening of the dangers faced by the ninety-five Pribilovian families. "Housing facilities at the Funter Bay cannery are inadequate for such a large group." Crowded conditions posed a threat to health, especially, he claimed, because "facilities are lacking for bathing and sewage disposal." Existing "privies certainly constitute a menace to health as well as a nuisance," Hirst concluded. There were no sanitary facilities for dishwashing and no equipped medical facility. His recommendation was that "dormitory . . . living for this group should be discontinued at the earliest possible date."[19]

At the gold mine facility, Fish and Wildlife agent Daniel Benson and the St. George Aleuts were no better off. Benson saw ominous problems ahead. Because he felt especially that dwellings for the white employees were inadequate, he decided to construct new buildings for them. "The crowded, dark, and unheated quarters for the natives are definitely out of the question" for white people to live in with winter approaching. "Water and sanitation," he predicted, "are also going to be problems of a serious nature."[20]

Benson's counterpart, agent Lee C. McMillin at the cannery with the St. Paul people, was less sanguine. He forecast disaster unless immediate action be taken to relieve the situation. The Territorial Department of Public Health had condemned the entire operation. The water system could not "under any conditions be made usable for winter." Portable houses with stoves, flush toilets, and hot water should be acquired. The sewage and garbage dumped into the bay made it necessary to dig clams for food at least a mile away. No open pit privies should be allowed, "even though they empty into the water at high tide. The sewage still washes back onto the beach for the flies to walk on and the children to track around." By mid-July, according to McMillin, "the novelty has worn off." Aleuts were beginning to protest, and rightfully so. They have "no brooms, soap or mops or brushes to keep the place suitable for pigs to stay in." He wanted help. "It seems funny," he wryly complained, "that our government can drop so many people in a place like this, then forget about them altogether."[21]

At the end of July, McMillin was still waiting for supplies and building materials to improve the cannery. A heated storage area had to be built to protect stores from freezing. Leaking roofs needed repair. Very apprehensive, McMillin even suggested moving the Aleuts from Funter Bay to temporary winter quarters elsewhere. "Otherwise," he counseled, "the only thing I can see is extreme hardships and possible deaths."

To solve some of these problems, the Fish and Wildlife Service headquarters in Seattle turned to the Fisheries Division in Juneau for help.

The Division, a part of the Fish and Wildlife Service, was not up to the task. Its supervisor, Clarence L. Olson, argued that Fisheries Division operations had always been "completely separated" from the Sealing Division. "When the present emergency arose, we were almost totally unprepared to meet it." Olsen nevertheless tried, but admitted that some problems in the "camps . . . are beyond our power to cope with," especially when health officials demanded the rebuilding of water supply lines to insure against contamination. Asking the Fisheries Division to help the Sealing Division was indication of dire emergency. It did not help the situation, and strained relations between the two divisions. "We are," Olson claimed, "under the gun here at all times."[22]

On August 9, much-needed supplies arrived aboard the *Penguin*, with the superintendent of the Seal Division, Edward C. Johnston, overseeing the unloading. "Plenty of work for the whole gang," he wrote in the report of his brief stay. Cottages and a "combination shower, laundry and toilet" would be built at the cannery and the gold mine. The water supply would be improved and prepared for winter. For St. George people, a new bunkhouse could be put up. Johnston said that the "large percent of . . . severe colds" suffered by Aleuts had been "cleared up and the general health is good." In a few days more supplies obtained from Juneau would be arriving, and, convinced that progress would be made, Johnston sailed south.[23]

A letter from St. Paul agent Lee McMillin described a serious problem for Johnston. There was dissension in the ranks at Funter Bay! In a stinging protest, McMillin charged that talk of construction for improving facilities was unrealistic. Not only were materials scarce, but water supply and pressure were inadequate. "What will we flush these toilets with?" McMillin wondered. There was no sand or gravel for concrete. Moreover, the recently announced policy allowing Aleuts to leave the camps would result in chaos. McMillin predicted they would leave in droves. He was doing his best to keep the community intact, but Aleuts were leaving, not responding to his claims that they were duty-bound to stay. Some of them promised to return, but "they are very good at dishing out the bull to get sympathy." It was all "a very good opportunity to embarrass this office." He was fed up. Superintendent Johnston had overlooked Funter Bay's real conditions. "Best do your building in Juneau to take care of them there," McMillin wrote. Actually, he warned, "we can be criticized or prosecuted for criminal negligence."[24] Here it was, the middle of September, McMillin charged, and Aleuts "are still sleeping on the floor with only a blanket under them." Not all are able to "hover around the few stoves furnished." Water for cooking and drinking was in short supply. Aleuts deserved better. The govern-

ment had "many dollars" invested in them, and now came this shocking
treatment. He rebuked Johnston:

> To change from an absolute meat to a fish diet worked for a few days.
> Sleeping the way they do, eating and living in present set up and we are
> going to build them a nice toilet! Is it any wonder they remark so much.
> "You don't understand, Mr. McMillin, you are no Christian" when I try
> to explain to them that the country is at war and they should make the
> best of the conditions. . . . A warm office in Seattle . . . does not in any
> way effect the temperature in Alaska.

Furthermore, a distressed McMillin asked, "What shall we do here in case
of death?" There is no "place large enough for burial ground," and "we
do not have material here for coffins unless we use salvaged lumber."[25]
   Johnston attacked McMillin's letter as "careless, or even disrespectful,
and lacking . . . cooperative spirit." It was not constructive; and "carp-
ing criticism is not desirable," wrote the wounded Johnston. However,
he did not refute a single McMillin allegation. Another official called
the letter "unfair," but he was nevertheless pessimistic about Funter Bay.
No wood had been cut for winter, no fish had been salted, no repairs
done on the water line. In October, at wit's end, McMillin submitted his
letter of resignation.[26] It was not accepted.

Soon after the Pribilovian arrival, Department of the Interior officials in
Washington, D.C., learned of the conditions at Funter Bay. Secretary of
the Interior Harold Ickes assigned his roving field representative for
Alaska, Ruth Gruber, to investigate the camp. She visited the cannery
and gold mine in October. Gruber thought Funter Bay was the worst of
all evacuation camps. "It has accommodations for about 250 people;
500 are living there," she reported. Overcrowding was made worse by
"difficulties of transportation and priorities. Building materials were
held up. Fresh meat, vegetables and fruit were almost unknown." Characteristically, Fish and Wildlife personnel were apprehensive that Aleuts
would leave and never again help in sealing. But, "the immediate problem is a human one," Gruber said, "and more urgent than that of
slaughtering seals." Her recommendations were to send a "trained and
highly skilled worker" to help Aleuts adjust and find jobs elsewhere; to
send sawmill equipment from Oregon for an Aleut lumbering business;
and to "ship in good and adequate food, commensurate with maintaining the simplest nutritional requirements."[27]
   Superintendent Hirst was contacted for his opinion of these proposals. He flatly stated that no social worker was available. The Forest

Service opposed the lumbering suggestion, and moreover the money for it was not available. The food problem had to be solved by the Fish and Wildlife Service; it was not an Indian Service responsibility. In the face of all the denial that was taking place, one Interior Department official was pleased, ironically, that the Fish and Wildlife Service would now have to be "concerned about the fate of the *sealers* and not merely the seals."[28]

But Secretary Ickes was very concerned about the fate of seals and the United States Treasury. In November 1942 he wrote to Secretary of War Henry L. Stimson requesting that Pribilof Aleuts be returned in the spring for sealing operations. He complained that Aleuts were evacuated by "our armed forces" and neither he nor "any official of this Department" had been consulted. "This action caused great inconvenience and hardship, and resulted in the loss of more than a million dollars" in seal skin harvest and by-products revenues. As for the Aleuts, the return would release them "from their present unsatisfactory status as refugees, improve their health, enable them to earn a livelihood." It would also "produce revenue for the government."[29]

For the remainder of 1942, however, Aleuts suffered daily in the neglected, unimproved camps at Funter Bay. In the first six months of evacuation, two Pribilovians died, even though both had been taken to the Indian Service hospital in Juneau. One was a victim of chronic pulmonary tuberculosis, the other of premature birth.[30]

The last of the *Delarof*'s passengers, the Atka Aleuts, were removed from the ship anchored in Funter Bay on June 25, 1942. At 4:00 A.M., they were packed on a "hulking red scow," a "fish-stinking scow," borrowed from the Hood Bay cannery. Alongside was the *Brant,* with Governor Gruening, Superintendent Hirst, and reporter Joseph Driscoll aboard. To entertain these dignitaries, Ruby Magee, the Atka teacher, led Aleut children in singing songs like *Cheer for Old Atka,* capped by *God Bless America.* To Driscoll, "it was rather touching to hear little aborigines singing their heads off before breakfast to prove that they were just as patriotic, just as Rotarian, as the rest of us." In appreciation, they tossed the children "some coppers." By mid-morning that day, the Atka Aleuts had been discharged from the scow at Killisnoo.[31]

Joseph Driscoll, the eastern journalist, had a pleasant time with the Aleuts. "These little yellow-skinned barbarians were much better mannered than many children back home," he wrote. He seemed relieved that "a paternalistic government decided to transport the natives to a safer home, for the duration of the war, if not forever." They had been on a long journey, had not been able to shower, and were dressed for cooler weather. This inspired Driscoll to use a saying from Alaskan sourdough lore: Atka men, he said, were "dirty as dogs" and "loaded for bear." Nevertheless, they were eager "for Americanization."[32]

The old village at Killisnoo had a whaling and herring saltery built in the 1880s, which went out of business around 1930. Killisnoo was located on the "northwestern side of Kenasnow Island, close to the western shore of Admiralty Island, about three miles south of the entrance to Kootznahoo Inlet." The village name was probably derived from this inlet's name, a Tlingit Indian term meaning "bear's rectum," descriptive of "its geographical formation." Legend has it that the stench from the plant's fish oil and fertilizer wafted north with such potency that bears who inhaled it grew to gigantic size.[33]

The facility was first noted as a potential site for evacuees by Virgil R. Farrell, Alaska Indian Service director of education. His report to Hirst on May 13, 1942, apparently was to be the first and only one of its kind before the evacuations began. The site was about fifty miles south of Funter Bay and three miles from Angoon, a Tlingit community. Kenasnow Island was only six square miles in size. Its herring saltery buildings had been abandoned about a decade earlier. Before that, around 1928, the entire village had burned and was not rebuilt. Its people had resettled at Angoon. Farrell was told that Killisnoo's water supply system needed repairs and would have to be more closely inspected. Also, there were no sewage disposal facilities "other than 3 outdoor pit toilets." Buildings were wired for electricity, "But it is very doubtful whether the present wiring could be utilized without encountering great fire hazards." Although there was a small laundry, no bathing facilities existed except for a bathtub.[34]

Director of Education Farrell estimated that Killisnoo "would accommodate approximately 75 to 80 people." One house was to be the teacher's quarters. That left two houses for one large family each. There were five cabins, some without furniture, one with only a single room, for small families. The only bunkhouse had room for two large families. Other facilities included a warehouse, a shed, a store, and machine shops.[35]

When the nineteen Atka families arrived, a total of eighty-three people, they were virtually empty-handed. The Navy had prevented them from retrieving their belongings at Atka village. They were described in Hirst's report as "indeed very poorly provided for." As an angel of mercy, Captain Downy, skipper of the *Delarof*, "furnished these people from his ship's stores a four-day supply of food, a mattress for each adult, and blankets . . . to ensure each person protection against suffering." Ruby and Charles Magee were left in charge, with authority "to proceed at once with the rehabilitation of the buildings." They were to purchase "necessary supplies . . . from the traders at Angoon."[36]

Immediately, Aleuts detected the flaws in their Killisnoo accommodations. One of the elder men made an inspection that was very disappointing. Heating equipment and fresh water were conspicuously absent. "No stove pipe, no water pipe," he grumbled. "No place to walk" was added to the list. For sanitation measures, Dr. Langdon White, who was to leave that day for Juneau aboard the *Brant,* instructed Aleuts how to "dig wells and latrines." He warned the company watchman there to begin boiling his drinking water.[37]

The Magees remembered vividly the Aleut reaction to this site. They never found consolation at Killisnoo for the Atka homes that had been ravished. They were told to "fix over the very old flimsy buildings" as they would have nothing more to do in the first months. But they grew restless, nevertheless. "Discontentment was very noticeable among them," the Magees recalled. "The people hated this tiny tree-covered island with poor, rocky beaches. There was no place to go hiking as on large, grassy Atka."[38]

This discontent was based on more than the Magees included in their analysis. Nadesta Golley, who was twelve years old at the time, later recounted the harsh living conditions at Killisnoo: "My mother, Jenny, couldn't get over how rough that first winter was. We lived in an old herring cannery and those buildings were never meant for winter. We had to boil our water. We were left to gather our own food. There were no boats to fish. We were just dumped off with the clothes on our backs. Later they dumped off a pile of winter clothing."[39]

Recalling her experience there, Vera Snigaroff resented having to live with her family "in one bedroom for three years." One elder, Henry Dirks, remembered using army surplus clothes handed down to them. They got little in addition. "We starved, sure we starved," he complained, "except in the summertime when we used to go down to the beach and pick up what we could." The water supply he described as "a dead lake."[40]

Humanitarian relief for the Atkans and Pribilovians was offered by the mayor of nearby Sitka, Walter R. Hanlon. He wired Governor Gruening in July informing him that the Salvation Army and the Women's Club of Sitka's American Legion had gathered clothing for the evacuees. The Governor curtly elbowed the mayor aside. "Indian Office and Bureau of Fisheries under direction of Governor are handling situation satisfactorily," he telegraphed back, cutting short this attempt to help.[41]

Similarly, teacher Magee was frustrated in an attempt to replace radios, guitars, mandolins, banjos, and accordions destroyed when the navy burned Atka village. Something was needed for "entertainment . . . contentment and pleasure" in leisure time, playing "instead of idly sitting around." Superintendent Hirst sent the request to the commissioner of Indian Affairs, asking that it be paid out of the emergency evacuation fund. It was rejected. "We question seriously the legal applicability of the fund in question for the purchase of these instruments." Instead, the commissioner's office suggested contacting the American Red Cross.[42]

Life in the Killisnoo camp was seldom described accurately by high government officials. Superintendent Hirst telegraphed to the commissioner's office, for instance, that the Atka people were "splendidly adjusted." Such cheerfulness was wishful thinking. The Territorial medical director's report to Hirst about Killisnoo indicated that any adjustment there would be made in difficult conditions. Although Dr. White thought living space and furnishings were reasonably adequate, there were no lights or water in the dwellings. Repairs were necessary to make them "weather-proof and to prevent injury." Porches and stairs were rotted. Chimneys and flues presented fire hazards. Some of the sources of water were likely "to be contaminated by pollution of the watershed" from human occupancy. "Privies . . . were in various stages of deterioration." They would have to be removed and "the pits filled." Aleuts would remain at Killisnoo, so "plans should . . . be made to enable them to establish satisfactory homes."[43]

To assure some measure of health, Dr. White determined that evacuees be immunized against diphtheria, smallpox, and typhoid fever "at the earliest practicable date." By the end of 1942, one Aleut at Killisnoo, a nine-year-old child, had died of acute pulmonary pneumonia with tuberculosis complications.[44]

On July 13, 1942, a second ship carrying the Aleuts from Akutan, Biorka, Kashega, Makushin, Nikolski, and Unalaska arrived in Southeast. It landed at Wrangell, a small incorporated city on the northern tip of Wrangell Island. One-half of Wrangell's 950 residents were Natives. Rich in history, the city could boast a Tlingit Indian background and past occupancy by British and Russians. A little over one hundred years before the evacuees arrived, its namesake, Ferdinand Petrovich von Wrangell, had been the governor of Russian America. The area's strategic position and Russian linkage were gone except in name and memory. Although it had briefly been a U.S. Army outpost after 1867, only shrimp canneries, a cold-storage plant, and a faltering lumber mill now helped support the city's three churches and the staff of a one-physician hospital.[45]

On the shores of Shoemaker Bay, nearly two miles from the city's center, stood Wrangell Institute, an Alaska Indian Service "coeducational vocational boarding school for Native children." This was the stopping-off place for 160 Aleuts aboard the S.S. *Columbia*. The two-story Institute building, with separate boys' and girls' wings, was built in 1932 and housed over one hundred students. Summer vacation conveniently made space available for the evacuees.[46] The move to Wrangell, however, was a stopgap measure to buy time while other sites could be found.

Hirst sent Assistant Superintendent Fred R. Geeslin to Wrangell to make arrangements. Geeslin admitted that the Service lacked "time to find other locations." In this emergency, and because the Institute could not hold all 160 Aleuts, Army tents with wooden floors were set up in front of the building to house Aleuts who could not be fit into the dormitory. Then Service officials began final surveys and plans for suitable sites in Southeast.[47]

The already overloaded facilities of the Institute were further taxed by the arrival of 137 Aleuts from Unalaska city. They arrived August 1 aboard the S.S. *Alaska*. They, too, were housed in temporary tents. Combined, 297 Aleuts waited on the ground of Wrangell Institute for other living facilities.[48] They knew nothing about where they were to be taken, when, or for how long. Uprooted Aleuts remained that way in Alaska's Southeast.

The stay at the Institute had to be brief, for fall instruction was slated to begin soon. Some of the evacuees were destitute, some with "babes in arms." Government officials had a difficult time, according to one newspaper report, in obtaining mattresses, bedding, dishes, and assorted items. Another news item claimed that Aleuts there had "practically nothing but the clothing they wear." Affording them a measure of protection, however, the Wrangell physician administered innoculations for typhoid and smallpox.[49]

Never having seen Aleuts before, some of Wrangell's residents were pleasantly surprised. The local newspaper quoted a letter published in the Portland *Oregonian* about them. "Nobody gave these hapless original proprietors a thought," claimed the author, "not to mention a second thought. If we have pictured them at all . . . it has been as a primitive people, well greased with blubber, offering otter pelts for fishhooks." Now Wrangell's citizens could develop a more realistic view. Doris Ann Plummer of Wrangell wrote, "We are enabled to see them as a people quite different from our smug conceit." Visiting them at the Institute, she and her mother, both insurance brokers, touted "war risk" policies for Aleut property left behind. "Their first concern" was "for their churches . . . and the treaure of art objects" in them. The two also learned that Aleuts were excellent musicians, even being able to "rattle off the classics." Mrs. Plummer admitted that she never thought these "quite distinguished looking" Aleuts from "way up there" could be "quite so cultured."[50]

But Aleuts were not enamored of Wrangell Insitute. Living hand to mouth grated on them. Philemon Tutiakoff remembered that Unalaska "mothers and children were placed in tents," while men and boys occupied dormitory rooms. Some tent dwellers were crammed into tents for several weeks, eight people to the unit. "Only mother had a bed," the rest slept on the floor. An impressionable youngster, Tutiakoff was reminded of Aleut ancestors who were taken from their homes by the Russians and, eating "some sea foods," were poisoned by "red tide. They died there on those narrow beaches." Although no Aleut died at Wrangell, their food left much to be desired. "We started eating dog salmon, tea and bread, day in and day out," was one description of the new diet. "The food was not fit to eat." Some had to cook outside the tents. One complained that when it rained, "we couldn't cook."[51]

Some remembered unaccustomed treatment at Wrangell. The sick were not given medical attention, and children had their heads shaven to eradicate "lice and such." The kerosene rubbed on their scalps for disinfectant "could not be removed," Laverna Dushkin recalled, "for half a day."[52] Aleuts were relieved when they left, although they did not know what would face them elsewhere.

The last Aleut group to arrive at Wrangell—the Unalaska city people— were the first to leave. They had been there nearly a fortnight. Assistant Superintendent Geeslin's strategy for this move was to split them into two clusters. The first was an advance party of sixteen Aleuts, which Geeslin accompanied. They left on August 12 with building supplies on a barge towed by the *Wrangell Institute I,* an Indian Service boat. An open space in the middle of the barge held the Aleuts, a tarpaulin over them; they were surrounded by lumber and supplies. Their destination, about forty-five miles away, was Burnett Inlet on the western side of nearby Etolin Island, named after a famous explorer and governor of Russian America. This work detail was to repair buildings at a long-unoccupied cannery facility. Encountering blustery weather, they were forced to lay over for the night. The next morning tired Aleuts were discharged at Burnett Inlet to start work. Geeslin returned to Wrangell to load the remaining Unalaska city people. In the late afternoon of August 14, these 122 Aleuts disembarked from the *Penguin* at Burnett Inlet, where they were introduced to their new island habitat.[53]

They found there "an isolated . . . burned out cannery site." Phil

Tutiakoff observed that the only buildings left had housed cannery workers. According to Superintendent Hirst, "considerable repairs were necessary to the cannery buildings being occupied." In all, there were eleven cottages and one large bunkhouse. New cottages would have to be built by Aleuts. Until the cabins were completed, however, evacuees were crowded into decrepit dwellings where they slept on the floor for lack of beds. Other essentials were lacking. "There was no school, church, hospital, or store . . . no electricity, no plumbing."[54] Fortunately, some of the Aleuts were skilled carpenters.

As it was, they had to serve in many roles. "Each had to fend" for himself sometimes, Gertrude Hope Svarny claimed, but there was cooperation and community support. Her mother, for example, helped care for cuts, bruises, "any sort of injury." She cared for her fellow Aleuts also in sickness, the camp having no doctor or nurse. Soon after they arrrived, "everyone got boils," and "some people were covered with them." They were told later by a visiting physician that they were merely adjusting "to a new atmosphere."[55]

This strange island frightened some Aleuts not familiar with its wildlife. If Admiralty Island was impacted with brown bears, Etolin Island apparently was home to numerous wolves. Blood-chilling mournful howling replaced soothing familiar sounds of Aleutian winds in Aleut ears. In the early days after arrival, one Aleut remembered "looking off through the rafters and seeing the moon and listening to a wolf howl." It was very "frightening." Even after many months at Burnett Inlet, Aleuts were filled "with dread" by "the eerie howl of the wolves."[56]

Unalaska city Aleuts had been the least isolated before evacuation. At Burnett Inlet this was reversed, and they became the most isolated of all evacuated Aleuts. They had been branded by government and military authorities at Dutch Harbor as troublemakers, "social problems." This charge had grown in shrillness as military activities there encroached on their lives. Remote Burnett Inlet eliminated that problem by establishing a kind of quarantine. Superintendent Hirst felt that the Unalaska people should go to Burnett Inlet because "we do not have with them teachers who know the drinking habits of the various individuals." He and George T. Barrett, principal of Wrangell Institute, were warned by Coast Guard Captain Frederick A. Zeusler that "it would be a serious mistake to send the Unalaska group to Ketchikan on account of the liquor problem."[57]

In less than ten days, Aleuts at Burnett Inlet had their fill of it and wanted to leave. Their leader, William Zaharoff, wired Hirst from Wrangell on behalf of the "Unalaska Community people." It was the first of several protests from various relocation communities. "The wa-

ter is low and not fit to drink." Illness had struck. There is "no game or
fish anywhere," bemoaned Zaharoff, and the "houses are not fit to live
in." Aleuts wanted a "better place."[58]

Better places in the Southeast came at high premium; and the Indian
Service had neither time nor will to find them. This Burnett Inlet crisis
came when the other Aleuts still at Wrangell had not yet been dispatched. Assistant Superintendent Fred Geeslin and Director of Education George Barrett, confirmed the emergency situation. Aleuts are
"dissatisfied," Geeslin wired Hirst, "and insist they will not stay." Moreover, the teachers at Burnett Inlet "question advisability of proceeding
with construction of living quarters." Again, Hirst resisted another
move. He sent a telegram back with his plan to retain the Burnett Inlet
locale. First, the weak-willed teachers would be replaced by Edythe and
Elmer Long. Next, a practical nurse and Indian Service physician from
Juneau would be sent to the camp. Then the question of whether to
move these Aleuts again would depend on the advice of this medical
team.[59]

In a week, Superintendent Hirst received news from Burnett Inlet
that the doctor was leaving, but the nurse would remain. "Everything
OK at Burnett," telegraphed Geeslin. Barrett reported that "people
there satisfied and believe main difficulty was due to delay in getting
lumber to them." The report was extremely upbeat. The Longs were
"making excellent adjustment at Burnett," and "everything in camps
[*sic*] coming along fine."[60]

At the same time, Mary Zaharoff, the fifty-three-year-old wife of the
Unalaska leader, had been hospitalized in Ketchikan on recommendation of the visiting physician at Burnett Inlet. The only other afflictions
were a "dozen cases of furunculosis," or boils. Aleuts there were "fairly
satisfied," the physician informed Superintendent Hirst, contradicting
William Zaharoff. The water supply was being improved, and immunizations had been completed except for whooping cough shots. Contrary to the wishes of the Unalaska city Aleuts, Burnett Inlet would
remain their relocation camp. The people were especially saddened to
learn that on November 4, 1942, Mary Zaharoff died. She was buried
in Ketchikan's Bayview Cemetery.[61]

Now the only transient Aleuts remaining in Southeast were the five
groups at Wrangell from Akutan, Biorka, Kashega, Makushin, and
Nikolski. They were slated to be placed in an abandoned Civilian Conservation Corps (CCC) work camp about eight miles northwest of
Ketchikan. An exception was made for a Makushin family who wanted to
take up residence in Wrangell. All but approximately twenty-five of the

rest were taken to the Ward Lake CCC camp by Army transport on August 23, 1942. The remainder left a few days later with Geeslin on the *Penguin*, which towed an Aleut-built barge full of building supplies.[62]

Arranging transportation had been a problem. The captain of a Canadian cruise ship refused to take the evacuees aboard even for a per-passenger "steerage rate" of $8.00. No cooperation was given to Geeslin by the army until Coast Guard Captain Fred Zeusler intervened and had transportation directed to Wrangell. The tents were dismantled and the flooring planks sent to Ward Lake for the new cabins to be constructed there.[63]

Except for the Attu people, these Aleuts were located closest of all evacuees to a major population center. True to its chamber of commerce moniker, Ketchikan was a gateway city—providing an introduction to big city life for the Aleuts settled at Ward Lake. With a population of five thousand, Ketchikan was, after Juneau, Alaska's second largest city according to the 1940 U.S. Census. It was an important port and busy fishing center. Unlike most Southeast communities, it had twenty-four miles of highway plied by 450 automobiles. Ketchikan dominated Revillagigedo Island, named by the British explorer George Vancouver after the Viceroy of Mexico, Revilla Gigedo. The name *Ketchikan* was supposed to have had a Northwest Coast Indian derivation meaning "spread wings of prostrate eagle," but "prostrate" probably referred to the splayed style in Tlingit art. Both Ward Lake and nearby Ward Cove are misnomers, Ward being a degenerative misspelling of W. W. Waud, "who established a saltery here . . . and was drowned nearby in 1892."[64]

Aleuts lived on neither the shores of Ward Cove nor those of Ward Lake. The CCC camp did not even have a view of water that might have been reminiscent of their Aleutian homes. It was instead buried deep in thick forest. Ward Lake was a public recreation area administered by the Department of Agriculture's Forest Service. The lake's fifty-seven scenic acres drew Ketchikan's people to swim and picnic. Before the New Deal's CCC camp was established, the area was "virgin wilderness."[65]

Completing the hundred-mile journey from Wrangell to Ketchikan, Aleuts in the first group arrived in the city at 2:00 A.M. They were discharged at the camp, where they were told, "Find your house." There would be 157 Aleuts at this site. There was a shortage of dwellings. The camp consisted of a mess hall, a "toilet-lavatory and urinal building, . . . two bunk houses and two cabins." Aleuts had "to sleep in the limited buildings on the floor in their bedrolls and blankets." Some had to stay in tents brought from Wrangell. According to Geeslin, the evacuees experienced there "a sense of oppression and suffocation." Food preparation was at first chaotic but improved when a regular system was established by Geeslin and Leonard Allen, principal of the Ketchikan Indian Service school. Pauline Whitfield, the Nikolski teacher, and her husband, Sam, were put in charge.[66]

A plan was adopted to enlist Aleuts to build livable residences before they took on work at local canneries. Everybody pitched in, some as cooks and mess hall helpers. One skilled Akutan Aleut installed electrical wiring for the sixteen newly constructed cabins and became the camp's chief electrician. "Much scrubbing and cleaning" of the "restaurant-type kitchen range" required considerable elbow grease. The first two days were the worst. "All were glum," Geeslin noticed. It was the only time he saw signs of distress in them.[67]

Yet the Aleuts crowded into this makeshift camp complained about its conditions. Especially objectionable was the "outhouse," a kind of "village toilet" with "no seats whatever," only a "long trough." It was "not sanitary or healthy," one recalled, and "it made bugs a problem." The dwellings had no running water, hot or cold. No regular transportation into the city was available to the Aleuts, and they had no telephone. Dorofey Chercasen of Nikolski had a first impression: he was "being put in prison." He acutely felt a deep separation from his "home which was far away."[68]

The most serious deprivation at Ward Lake was lack of medical help. "No doctor was available when a person got sick," said Leonty Savoroff from Nikolski. Based on examination by a visiting Indian Service physician and a nurse, five Aleuts were sent for tuberculosis treatment to the Indian hospital at Tacoma, Washington, about two months after they had arrived at Ward Lake. Others, too, eventually were sent. Before Aleuts arrived at Ward Lake, the Alaska Territorial medical director had proposed that the camp be used "for detention of persons infected with venereal diseases who fail to take treatment."[69]

For the several weeks Geeslin was there, no liquor was allowed in camp. He was proud of this ban and even impounded a taxicab bearing the hated booze. Then he faced down a possible lawsuit over the impounding and the arrest of the driver. Geeslin contacted Captain Fred A. Zeusler of the Ketchikan Coast Guard station, arranging for "surveillance of the camp with a guard at the entrance" if it should become necessary. Zeusler was enthusiastic over mitigating what he saw as burgeoning vice in Ketchikan. Before the evacuees arrived, he had complained to the governor's office about such problems. Acting Governor Bartlett agreed that "vigorous action" had to be taken "to correct evils." He would instruct government officials "to put an end to flagrant vice conditions." Ketchikan apparently was a sin city full of prostitution, venereal disease, and drunkenness.[70]

In spite of Assistant Superintendent Geeslin's policy and the wishes of Captain Zeusler, Aleuts could not be shielded. Unsavory gates were open to them in the gateway city. Steps were taken, however, to curb abuses. Ketchikan's mayor, Harry G. McCain, warned in October "that selling of liquor to drunken servicemen and Aleuts and natives has got to stop, with the Police force so instructed." Captain Zeusler wrote to Acting Governor Bartlett about Aleuts who were offenders. Bartlett was alarmed about "the mounting delinquency of the natives brought to Ketchikan from the Aleutian Islands." It "distresses me exceedingly," he mourned. "We must act and act soon to prevent their total demoralization." Bartlett promised that Governor Gruening would be heard from soon addressing this problem. "It will never do to allow these people who . . . are a particularly high type to acquire all the sins the white man has to offer."[71]

When Governor Gruening telegraphed Mayor McCain about Zeusler's complaint against Aleut abuse of liquor, the mayor adopted a get-tough policy. Although he acted vigorously, he still felt that Zeusler's "complaint" was "largely a tempest in a teapot." After a conference with Zeusler, the mayor concluded that there was no evidence of Aleut violations. But the Coast Guard claimed they "had received instructions from somebody to see that the Aleut evacuees were protected."[72] That "somebody" was no doubt Geeslin.

The ensuing police crackdown hurt Aleuts. They regarded it as unfair discrimination and harassment. "The Ketchikan City Police many times picked us up," Dorofey Chercasen claimed, "for no reason." Once when carrying bakery goods without having "a single drink," he was arrested, jailed, and fined. Before this new policy, only two Aleuts had been charged with drunkenness. In November through December 1942, arrests rose to six, still not a large proportion of Ketchikan's or Ward Lake's population.[73] It was a preview, however, of later unfounded allegations about the Aleut visitors.

For the time being, more important challenges faced the Aleuts in camp. Their first to die was a thirteen-year-old boy who had been ill for a year. This was in September 1942. Three others died by the end of the year. Worse was yet to come, for the death rate would more than double.[74]

The Aleuts' introductions to Alaska's Southeast had been a shocking surprise for most of them. But by far the most severe hardships in evacuation were faced by Attu's people, who landed at Otaru city around the end of September 1942. For them it was a forlorn place 1,600 miles from home. It was located on the western coast of

Hokkaido Island, once called Yezo, the northernmost of Japan's four major islands. Some think that its aboriginal people, the Ainu, are related to Aleuts. But the hospitality there left much to be desired. Emblematic of their stay, the docking of the ship carrying them was extremely rough. Olean Prokopeuff remembered that the skipper of the *Osada Maru* "collided with the dock, and . . . we were thrown from our seated position right on to the deck. . . . This was a scary experience."[75]

Having landed at night, Aleuts were moved the next morning to their quarters in the Wakatakecho district of Otaru. They were "all getting hungry," and the children wanted milk. Late in the evening they had their first Japanese food, some of which they found inedible, describing it as "jelly stuff." They refused to eat "an unusual looking cooked bird with its feathers still on it." At first they were nourished somewhat by the food brought with them from Attu. When Japanese rice became the major fare, said Alex Prossoff, "we began to get very hungry."[76]

Although Hokkaido Island was known for its Asiatic brown bears and food production, Aleuts saw no bear and little nourishing food. To Alex Prossoff, Otaru city, with a population of around twenty-five hundred, looked ragged, its houses unpainted. All forty Aleuts were crammed into one house, a five-room two-story structure "that looked like nobody had lived in" it for perhaps ten to fifteen years. "It was very dirty" and crowded. As is the custom, the Japanese placed "mattresses and blankets on the floor." The house was cold in the winter. Mike Lokanin thought the abandoned building was meant for chickens and pigs. One called it a "shack," but it did have electric lights.[77]

After cleaning up this house, Aleuts were pressed into work elsewhere. Whether at the dwelling or going to work and returning, they were under civilian guards, and their freedom of movement was strictly limited. When they were able to cook, they had to do it outside. Necessities were scarce. Alex Prossoff enjoyed only "one pair of pants, two shirts, one pair of socks and one towel in two years." In 1942, however, none of the evacuees died.[78]

For three years this foreign country's strangeness confronted Attu's Aleuts, the most unusual situation experienced by any of the evacuees. Alex Prossoff reported a few of the unfamiliar practices: "I saw many statues of the gods they pray to. Most were of Buddha, though. They had a funny custom of taking a dragon-like piece of wood into their houses and talking while they open and shut its big fiery mouth. . . . Another custom was to send men with big umbrella-like hats and dressed in white to our camp. They . . . begged for money. Finally, guards told them it's no use; we did not have any."[79]

8

Matters of Death and Life

I was thinking . . . why they didn't bring up the conditions . . .
at Funter Bay—the two winters—the biggest loss we ever had. . . .
I am one of the men who was working on the cemetery . . .
fencing it around . . . and putting up the crosses. . . . Bill Merculief
from St. George and myself made a sign and called it Pribilof Islands . . .
out of twigs. . . . Tried to make the sign look like it was a floating sign.
—Michael Lestenkof, St. George Aleut Evacuee
Commission on Wartime Relocation Hearings

Aleut evacuation had few scenes more poignant that the one described above. The sign was a marker, rigged by Merculief and Lestenkof, to point out this dreadful place which, of course, could never substitute for their real homes, the Pribilof Islands. The twigs were symbols of privation and death. This "floating sign" would be necessary, they thought, when tides at Funter Bay inundated the Aleut cemetery where they had to bury their dead.

The shock and pain of being uprooted was felt by Pribilovians from the start. On the ship that took them away from home, St. George people faced their island, knelt down, and prayed. "Everybody," Martha Krukoff said, "was crying."[1]

Evacuation was the beginning of a long journey with many hardships for all Aleuts. They were strangers in unfamiliar, dangerous places, and the loss of what had been left behind was made more acute by their never knowing what would happen to them next. Cast abroad, they found their cohesive, communal life threatened with extinction. Could they ever really be themselves again? Would they ever again be Aleutian and Pribilovian islanders at home?

There was little consolation for Aleuts in the relocation camps. They missed the soothing sound of intimate bays, the winds rushing from rugged mountains, the abundant and varied marine life, the colorful birds of their home islands. To make matters worse, they suffered lack of food, clothing, and shelter in the camps. Simple endurance became a way of life. No wonder they remembered the camps as their worst of

108

trials. In those inhospitable places, Aleuts were grounded in a routine of destitute anxiety. For the elders and women left to mind children and fend for themselves when others found work outside, life became frighteningly empty. Overcrowding, poor sanitation, and lack of adequate food and warm shelters culminated in deadly situations. The Horseman of Pestilence rode into the camps and struck with vengeance.

But somehow, with little help from the government or the military, most Aleuts survived. In Southeast, they worked hard to improve buildings they had found in disrepair and ruin. With skill and effort, they gradually improved their accommodations. Those who left for military service or employment elsewhere sent money back to their relatives in the camps. This relieved the overcrowding somewhat, and decreased strain on the budget of the Department of the Interior. Those left at Southeast camps were provided minimal food and even a weekly maintenance wage for certain camp employment. Those in Japan, however, all but starved and were forced to labor for a pittance.

Work to rebuild or erect housing in the camps was, in the words of a newspaper article, a "low cost job." Cabins were built for an estimated $150, and the four projects—Funter Bay, Killisnoo, Burnett Inlet, and Ward Lake—were appropriately dubbed "duration villages." Some units were "built from foundation to roof in a single day." The projects were finished in three weeks or less, and the stronger, more able-bodied Aleuts were eventually allowed to look for jobs outside the camps. Assistant Superintendent Geeslin wanted evacuees to "be able to pay their way" as soon as the cabins were completed.[2]

Ironically, during the evacuation period, the Interior Department in Washington, D.C.,was reorganized and a part sent to Chicago, Illinois, its "duration village." Offices for both the Department of Indian Affairs and the Fish and Wildlife Service were placed in empty offices in the Merchandise Mart. This move, made to provide space in Washington, D.C., for more important wartime agencies, was a burden for Commissioner Collier and Assistant Commissioner Zimmerman, who told their boss, Secretary Harold Ickes, that "they were puzzled over the problem of their own personal locations." Told to proceed by "trial and error," Director Gabrielson of the Fish and Wildlife Service was especially dejected because he had to sell his house in the capital. Others, including "most of his staff" were "downhearted too." So distraught was Gabrielson that he asked Ickes if he could retreat to his summer home on a small island near Quebec, Canada, for healing. He hoped in this idyllic setting to "recover some equanimity of spirit."[3] Wartime evacuation was no respecter of persons.

However, the "war effort" or "sacrifice" fell hardest on Aleuts, and especially so on the Attu people in Japan. All Aleuts were tested, and what happened to them was ennobled not so much by sympathy but by their resilience in overcoming an unfortunate fate. Such would be a matter of pride to any people.

When Pribilof Aleuts were deposited at Funter Bay, Fish and Wildlife personnel hurriedly attempted to develop some kind of camp policy. St. Paul Agent Lee McMillin suggested to Superintendent Edward Johnston that Aleuts be paid minimally for work in the camps. Evacuees learned, however, that good wages were available outside the bay. Several told McMillin they would move their families and take up employment elsewhere.[4]

Thinking ahead, McMillin feared this would result in a lost work force when sealing resumed. Also, if Aleuts moved they would have access to liquor, and if they were allowed "to roam at will," the Fish and Wildlife Service would have a "terrific expense to pick them up." McMillin, therefore, recommended paying between ten and twenty-five dollars a month to men who had been drawing top pay of sixty dollars a month on the Pribilofs. In the meantime, he informed Johnston, he had "denied all Aleut requests to leave" for work.[5]

Johnston, however, saw things differently. Although he indicated to a representative of the United States Employment Service that "it is our desire to keep our native organization as nearly intact as possible," he allowed that small units could leave camp. Those who stayed should be paid "in a lump sum through the Agents in charge of each island contingent." This would replicate former Pribilof procedure according to which communities shared proceeds from the seal harvest. But McMillin bristled when U.S. Employment Service personnel attempted to employ St. Paul people. "You will have them scattered all over the territory," he complained to Johnston, and then will have "to pick them up and bring them back here." Aleuts would not be able to hold jobs, McMillin felt, because "they will be so badly outclassed no one will keep them."[6]

Such argument seemed to sway Johnston, who informed his superior, Ward T. Bower, about the problem with the hope of getting a policy decision from above. Some Aleuts, he reported, "have the idea that the Government has to take care for them no matter where they go." Unfortunately, "in their contacts with fishermen and other white people," he complained, Aleuts heard they could command higher wages outside camp. He now endorsed trying to keep them at Funter Bay. Johnston agreed with McMillin that skilled workmen would be lost and it would be costly to round up Aleuts who left. Furthermore, wage earners might not share their wages with those not working, which would cause more dissatisfaction among evacuees. Johnston worried that "the social setup . . . applied on the isolated Pribilof Islands does not seem practicable . . . where there are so many new factors to consider." He recommended cash payments to hold Aleuts in the camps.[7]

At first, military travel restrictions helped Fish and Wildlife Service personnel contain the evacuees. After fifty-five Aleuts had been dispatched to fish for the two camps, the Coast Guard issued identification cards and fingerprinted the remaining Funter Bay evacuees. For security reasons, the Coast Guard wanted no one to leave the beach unless they were sent fishing. McMillin did obtain permission for visits across the bay between St. Paul and St. George people, but no other travel was allowed. Yet strict military travel prohibitions failed. By the middle of July, six Aleuts had obtained employment away from the two evacuation sites.[8]

At the end of July, policy was handed down from Washington, D.C., and the McMillin-Johnston approach was abandoned. There would be no large sums spent to keep Aleuts in place or to pay them for camp work. Only a small emergency fund of twenty-five thousand dollars would be tapped. A conference on the subject determined that the Department of the Interior had "no definite hold on the Pribilof natives." Only if they stayed at Funter Bay would they be "subject to the jurisdiction, care, and support of the Government." They would be free to go and there would be nothing placed in their way. The Fish and Wildlife budget was the deciding factor. "While they are away they are earning money," Bower concluded, and that would "at least relieve the Government of the expense of their maintenance."[9]

Many Aleuts chose to support themselves. Within the first six months, there were 135 Pribilof people working outside Funter Bay, mostly in Juneau. By Johnston's calculation, this was "28% of the total population" and included 8 women. He estimated a year later that as many as 200 Pribilof Aleuts, nearly one-half of the evacuees, were employed outside the camps.[10]

Now that agents and caretakers had no restraining authority, Aleuts sought better wages and a better life elsewhere. The Funter Bay encampments were riddled by departures. Early in 1943, the twenty-dollar monthly payments for camp work were halted because they had failed to keep Aleuts in camp. When the Fish and Wildlife Service recruited workers for the seal harvest in the summer of 1943, Johnston was told that "pupils at Wrangell Institute have an opportunity to make more wages than you will be able to pay" the sealers. At Excursion Inlet, some

Aleuts were employed in a defense project and were "making from $50 to over $100 weekly plus allowances."[11] It would be difficult for the Sealing Division to compete.

For those who found no way out, the camps were dreadful places. Aleuts who did not forget what they experienced there later testified to it. A deep mood of depression, according to Anatoly Lekanof of St. George, overtook the camp as Aleuts saw many of their loved ones die. Stefan Lekanof of St. George felt "terrible" about life at Funter Bay. He tried to improve conditions but had little success. Another evacuee, Natalie Misikian, remembered ever-present "honey buckets," portable chamber pots, that the children had to tend. "We kids used to have to add water to it and dump it out. . . . We had to do it. We learned how to survive." Vermin and germs flourished. A young mother recounted that she and her children "got head lice, diarrhea and were sick from we don't know what. The living conditions were horrible."[12]

Survivors also testified that the best accommodations in the camps went to Fish and Wildlife Service personnel. "They had real good houses," noticed one Aleut, and "the white people . . . got much better food than the native people."[13] Before evacuation, such conditions also had prevailed at some of the Aleut villages.

Reacting to their hard lot and the discrimination they perceived, Aleuts at Funter Bay protested, led by the St. Paul women at the cannery. In a signed petition sent to Superintendent Johnston in October 1942, forty-nine protestors asked for "a better place than this to live." In a meeting with Johnston and McMillin, they requested that the document be sent to Fish and Wildlife Service headquarters.[14]

These Aleut women were direct and they were angry. Funter Bay was "no place for a living creature," they charged. "Skin disease" plagued the children, and many others were ill. The water was contaminated, the mess house was too close to the outhouse, and, they charged, we have to "eat the filth that is flying around." There were no bathing facilities, "no place to wash our clothes or dry them when it rains." Women were "always lugging water up stairs" where they had to "take turns warming it up" on undersized stoves. Families were cramped with hardly room to "turn around." Blankets substituted for walls. Privacy was practically nonexistent.[15]

In addition, the women complained that other basic needs were not fulfilled. "We need clothes and shoes for our children." The twenty-dollar monthly salaries were used to provide supplemental food for the children and were spent well before the next payment. Both men and women wanted to work, but there was no work at Funter Bay. They warned that dire consequences lay ahead if nothing changed. Aleuts should be moved "to a better place to live and work." The women predicted that the onset of winter would bring frozen water pipes and more food shortages. They said they would "see our children suffer." The document ended on a defiant note: "We all have rights to speak for ourselves."[16]

Johnston and McMillin discussed each of the petition's points—they called them "complaints"—with the Aleut women and reported to Chief Ward T. Bower, now located in Chicago. Johnston agreed about camp overcrowding and lack of privacy. He told the women, however, "that under war conditions they could not expect to enjoy the comforts and conditions as they existed" at home. He said they could not be moved again because there "was no other place in Southeastern Alaska where so many people could live at one locality." To help the situation, six "tent houses" were being built and at the St. George camp a refurbished house was nearly finished.[17]

As for health conditions, Johnston said steps were being taken to protect Aleuts. He admitted that the water, with its "reddish brown vegetable coloring," had been tested and found "potentially unsafe." Chlorination equipment would be obtained as soon as possible. The water pipes were being prepared to prevent freezing in winter. "Fish poisoning," which was afflicting children, "will clear up when the salmon runs are over," and the "impetigo . . . is under control." There were fewer colds than "would normally be expected," Johnston pointed out, "but that is no indication that colds will not increase." Johnston argued that the cannery toilet hanging "over tide water" was farther from living and eating quarters than any at home on the Pribilofs. Nonetheless, Johnston announced a plan for building a "combination toilet, shower, and laundry house" which would "provide sanitary toilets."[18]

According to the superintendent, supplies that would bring immediate benefits were being requisitioned. Wallboard for privacy, clothing and shoes for protection were on the way. Only rubber boots could not be obtained. He predicted, therefore, that it would "be impossible to keep feet dry" given the area's climate. The men were "satisfied with the food furnished," but women hated the "community mess. They refuse to help with the cooking." Some fresh meat had been secured. For the health of children, canteen supplies of candy, he felt, ought to be curtailed, thereby reducing the risk of dental caries.[19]

According to Johnston's report, improvement at Funter Bay was imminent. He even detected two safety valves which would further ease the situation. Nineteen St. Paul workmen were in Juneau, seven of whom "have their whole families with them." In addition, the principal at

Wrangell Institute would take children, "all we can send between the ages of 14 and 21." Johnston recommended taking advantage of this "because the children sent there would be living in better quarters during the winter, as well as making our camp a little less crowded." At Wrangell they could continue their schoolwork "much more efficiently."[20]

Chief Bower in Chicago was quite satisfied with Johnston's work and the way he handled the petition. "Your presence at Funter Bay has gone a long way toward improving conditions at that place," he wrote. Everything that was possible had been done, and no other "particular action was necessary to answer the complaints mentioned in the petition." The women signers should be informed that headquarters received it. They should be told "the document . . . has had careful consideration." Bower and Gabrielson had discussed it. "Let them know," Bower wrote from the Merchandise Mart, "that we are all called upon to make sacrifices in connection with the war program."[21]

The sacrifices Bower had in mind ostensibly did not include death. Nevertheless, Aleuts at Funter Bay did die, and in far greater numbers than they would have had they been living on the Pribilofs. Between September 1941 and their evacuation in June 1942, only two died. Their physician at St. Paul determined the mortality rate for 1941 to be 10.5 deaths per 1000 people. Based on this, the deaths at Funter Bay should have totaled five per year, ten for the nearly two-year stay. Instead, thirty-two died, none of whom were accident victims. On the Pribilofs, the major killer was tuberculosis; in Southeast, it was pneumonia. Tuberculosis claimed two victims at Funter Bay, whereas eleven died of pneumonia. Age distribution created a significant pattern. Fourteen aged ten or under, and ten aged fifty years or older, died. The worst year was 1943. Twenty-four Aleuts, from newborns to seventy-three-year-olds, died that year—75 percent of all the Funter Bay Aleut deaths.[22]

Chronic health problems before the evacuation do not explain this high rate of mortality. Death rates at Funter Bay were three times higher than they should have been. Just before 1943, the year of highest death rates, Aleut women protestors had warned that living conditions at Funter Bay were deadly. The large number of camp deaths were not attributable only to the measles and influenza epidemic that hit in 1943; only four of the twenty-four who died succumbed to measles, and none to influenza.[23] Funter Bay camps themselves were the problem.

The warnings of Aleut women and others about camp conditions brought about no major changes. However, after less than a month from the time of arrival, Lee McMillin also sounded an ominous note.

He catalogued major camp disabilities based on an inspection in July 1942 by Richard S. Green, director of sanitary engineering in the Territorial Department of Health. "Many changes will have to be made," Green insisted, "to safeguard the health of the people and to prevent the contamination of the clam beaches and the other sources of the local food supply." Facilities would have to be "improved to the point where it will pass a sanitary inspection." Provision of adequate living quarters was necessary, and "the water supply must be protected from freezing in the winter months."[24]

Government officials failed to complete even these minimal safeguards. To make matters worse, the winter of 1942 was unusually cold, so nasty that schoolteachers from the cannery could not venture across the bay for classes at the gold mine site. Daniel Benson reported to Johnston, who had flown like a migrating bird to warm Seattle, that "the weather here has been so bad for so long that all of our water finally froze up." Aleuts had to resort to "digging holes in the ice and getting it in pails for the whole camp." He claimed it was "the worst winter they've ever had here." Superintendent Johnston was lucky, Benson sighed. "You left just in time." A week later bad news came about the water. Laboratory samples "contain large numbers of coliform organisms," wrote the sanitary engineer. "This water is unsafe for human consumption unless properly sterilized."[25]

In the spring of 1943, following the harsh winter of deprivation and death, 116 able-bodied men were taken for seal pruning operations in the Pribilofs. Benson worried about the effect of these departures. "It's going to be tough on us here," he reflected, "losing so many men all at once—work will progress quite slowly with only about enough to cook and saw wood." The sealers, who set a record for pelts taken in the operation, could have helped fellow Aleuts at Funter Bay.[26]

Measles struck hard, as did the flu. "At one time there were 140 natives sick in bed," a report in July 1943 stated. "The older men are still in a weakened condition," and a few of them "lost as much as 20" pounds during their illness.[27] Word soon spread about illness at Funter Bay.

A report in early September 1942 by Public Health Engineer John Hall confirmed what Aleuts already knew. Hall's office "registered sharp criticism of sanitary conditions there." In response, Director Ira Gabrielson invited Hall to inspect the camps again. He found most aspects of life at Funter Bay bad: housing, drinking water, food, stoves, kitchens, shower and laundry facilities, privies, sanitation and refuse, even boardwalks. Everything at the cannery was hazardous. The mining site across the bay, according to Hall, was somewhat better because management there had a more positive attitude. Although agents and caretakers were gone on the sealing expedition, they left a storekeeper in charge of the St. Paul camp and the husband of the schoolteacher to supervise the St. George site. Hall thought that storekeeper Carl M. Hoverson, in charge at the cannery, was negative toward Aleuts, projecting an attitude of "helplessness and pessimism." Hoverson said, "Many of the people have no sense of cleanliness, will not follow instructions and cannot be taught." Children were unruly, he added. But the real problem, as far as Hall was concerned, was the absence of agents and caretakers who had taken "all the able-bodied men" sealing, leaving the camps bereft of responsible supervision.[28]

Hall also faulted Fish and Wildlife Service officials for sending a physician with the sealers who could have served the Aleuts better at Funter Bay. Also, "someone to organize recreation and other morale-building activities would . . . have been helpful." The sanitary engineer turned social engineer complained that no system had been developed to signal passing boats for help in emergencies. Hall felt it was "bad administration" not to have a two-way radio or to install a signaling device that had been prepared for months.[29]

Soon politicians became concerned about Funter Bay conditions. The Territory's attorney general, Henry Roden, an officer of the company that owned the gold mine site, wrote to Governor Gruening about the camps. "I have no language at my command which can adequately describe what I saw; if I had I am confident you would not believe my statements." He mentioned "hanging blankets" that gave "absolutely no privacy." Aleuts were "huddled together" in a room heated by a "100 gallon gasoline drum," a jerry-built heater without a damper. "Large burning cinders escape from this pipe and the Lord only knows why these have not set the place on fire." There was only one exit in case of a conflagration. The situation was "shocking. I have seen some tough places in my days in Alaska, but nothing to equal the situation at Funter." Roden could not believe that public authorities would allow these conditions.[30]

Governor Gruening was rather unconcerned about this volley from a political opponent. He did admit that the camps were undesirable and said he would contact the real man in charge, Director Gabrielson. Gruening wrote to the director expressing "hope that these natives can be sent back to the Pribilofs at the earliest possible moment."[31] That was his response. He marshaled no resources to provide material aid. Instead, Gruening was defensive. He took no steps to improve Funter Bay camps.

The reports of health engineer Hall and Attorney General Roden led to a later investigation by Dr. N. Berneta Block, director of the Division of Maternal and Child Health and Crippled Children's Services in the Territorial Department of Health. She was invited to Funter Bay by a fellow physician in response to sanitarian Hall's alarm about the measles epidemic. Her report, based on a four-day visit, was full of criticism. She found a dangerous environment, dark and overcrowded buildings, and inadequate health facilities in a community struck by disease, with "118 or so patients." She claimed conditions were "beyond description." Shocked and disappointed, Dr. Block surmised that lack of "civil pride" and "low morale" were caused by "degrading conditions." Above all, she argued, "conditions such as these should not have existed at the beginning of this epidemic."[32]

According to Dr. Block, if improvements were not made, disaster lay ahead. The "discolored, contaminated and unattractive" water made it difficult "to get people to force fluids." The men returning from Pribilof sealing "will be exposed to measles," and many could become seriously ill. Health care workers were desperately needed, as was a radio system for obtaining help. Dr. Block was told that Gabrielson and McMillin "wish for permission and materials . . . to better the health and welfare of the wards under their jurisdiction." Dr. Block was beyond wishing. She implored "that all who were responsible" would "immediately work together to change the picture."[33]

Many concerned observers were in agreement about conditions at Funter Bay. It lacked "a safe water supply and sanitary disposal of garbage and human excreta." There was no "proper refrigeration," no "proper methods of dishwashing and bathing." Many worried about the "precarious condition of the slippery sidewalks which are not lighted at night." Whose fault was it? And what could be done? The chief of the Division of Alaska Fisheries, Ward T. Bower, had some explanations. Needed materials "under priority requirements" had been "very difficult to obtain." However, this situation was changing, he wrote to Dr. Block, and now was "better than it was some time ago." Edward Johnston had been issued "definite and positive instructions . . . to leave nothing undone . . . to see to it that the natives are maintained in much better shape than they were last winter," he alleged. He added that a physician was soon to be sent to Funter Bay.[34]

Bower further explained that "supervisory officials have looked upon it as a temporary situation that would be relieved with their return before too long to the Pribilof Islands." If the camps at Funter Bay were in fact temporary, there was not much incentive to improve the facilities at further cost. Aleuts, too, argued Bower, were part of the problem. "It may well be that the natives of the Pribilof Islands have been coddled too much and the time has come to bring home to them forcefully the need to look after themselves in more decent ways." Bower warned, "If they do not respond to ordinary instructions and suggestions along this line, more drastic measures will be necessary."[35]

Bower's excuses and assertions, however, were not shared by those closer to the scene. The Juneau office's assistant supervisor of Alaska fisheries, Frank W. Hynes, described the situation in late October 1943 as "growing more and more tense." He told Bower that because there would be no return to the Pribilofs that year, Funter Bay camps would have to be put "on a workable basis before another winter sets in." There was "no longer any point in waiting and hoping for the end of a bad situation." If there were no improvement, Hynes felt, there was "more than a possibility that the death toll from tuberculosis, pneumonia, influenza and other diseases" would "so decimate the ranks of the natives that few will survive to return to the islands." So far, Sealing Division officials had been lucky, he asserted. Wartime censorship of the press limited news about Alaska from getting out. But reports by medical people, one of whom described Aleuts "being herded into quarters unfit for pigs," were now likely to be made public. The resulting exposé would be damaging to the Department of the Interior.[36]

Bower seemed to take this red flag seriously. Reacting to Hynes's analysis, he called Edward Johnston's attention to the "extremely urgent necessity of drastic and positive action to improve conditions." The task was Johnston's responsibility, he charged. "There has been altogether too much leniency" at Funter Bay, and if change was not forthcoming, "inefficiency certainly will lie against those who are responsible." To threaten and get tough with Aleuts might be the solution, Bower thought. Both Bower and Gabrielson were favorably impressed with reports that a recalcitrant, "impudent" Aleut was disciplined by a St. George supervisor, Homer Merriott, who "laid hold of him and shook him up. Thereafter, he behaved himself."[37]

Aleut impudence, however, was not the cause of problems at Funter Bay. When Aleuts working outside the camps returned, overcrowding was bound to get worse, although steps were subsequently taken to obtain military Quonset huts from the Juneau area. Thirty-two men returning with the sealing crew were known to be ill with measles. As Lee McMillin was being replaced and nurse Beatrice Porter was leaving, a physician temporarily caring for Aleuts reported "a multiplicity of diseases" prevailing in camp. He treated 143 sick Aleuts in a one-day visit. He explained the root cause: "The resistance of the Pribilof people is rather low due especially to the crowded, unsanitary conditions. . . .

Efforts have been made to improve conditions, but they are by and large insufficient."[38]

Between January 1944 and May, when the Aleuts finally left, six more had died at Funter Bay, more than double the expected yearly mortality rate. Four, including the youngest at three months and the oldest at seventy-three, were victims of pneumonia. Measles and tuberculosis were the other killers.[39]

Aleut determination to survive at Funter Bay overshadowed much of the adversity. Their "Pribilof Islands" graveyard sign was an amulet of hope for returning home someday. When conditions did not improve, many Aleuts defied authorities who tried to keep them in the camps. Those who stayed pitched in as best they could. The women vigorously protested the unhealthy environment. Anatoly Lekanof praised one Aleut, Peter T. Kochergin of St. George, for care that helped to save lives. Anne S. McGlashen worked to aid her people in the absence of a nurse or physician at the gold mine site.[40] They and others like them did the best they could to ease life in the camps,

Evacuation challenged every Aleut, including the children who were sent to Wrangell Institute. Saddened by separation from their families, some of the children plotted to stow away on the Fish and Wildlife Service supply ship "to get immediate passage home." Their daring plan was discovered, however, before it could be executed. Adult Aleuts displayed a similar spirit. Contrary to suppositions by agent and care-taker McMillin that because they were "classed as wards" they had "no voting privileges," Aleuts voted anyway. They cast ballots in the election to replace Territorial Delegate Anthony Dimond. Sixty-two Aleut votes at Funter Bay were cast against Alaska's secretary and sometimes acting governor, Bob Bartlett, in the political camp of Governor Gruening. These two were targeted for opposition by the Tlingit political activist in the area, William Paul. Aleuts delivered their votes accordingly.[41]

The other Southeast evacuation camps were no better than Funter Bay. Aleuts in these camps were under the care of the Alaska Indian Service, which, like the Fish and Wildlife Service, was ill-equipped to handle the situation. Nevertheless, Commissioner of Indian Affairs John Collier saw possibilities and potential in evacuation. In his 1942 annual report, he claimed that "prior to the attack on Dutch Harbor, plans were being developed in cooperation with the Naval authorities for the possible evacuation of the Aleutians." Actually there was no planning, but in Collier's mind, evacuation was a golden opportunity for Aleut advancement. Besides tiding them over the war emergency, evacuation experience would gear Aleuts for "future self-support."[42]

When the smallest group of Aleuts on the *Delaraf*, Atka's eighty-three people, were unloaded from the fish-stinking skow that brought them from Funter Bay to Killisnoo, newspaper reporter Joseph Driscoll echoed Collier's optimism. Aleuts, he wrote, "were promised all the guns and fishing lines necessary to provide a good living, with some canned groceries thrown in for good measure." They would set about with the greatest of gusto to "repair the ramshackle cottages and dormitories" which once "had sheltered Chinese and Filipino workers." When Driscoll returned some months later, he found Atka Aleuts "happy at Killisnoo and busy as bees."[43]

But Atka Aleuts were never happy at Killisnoo. Contrary to Driscoll, they were distressed. Seventeen died there. Excluding two accidental drownings, the Atka mortality rate, 18 percent, was the highest of Southeast evacuees. The cause of death in four cases is unknown; tuberculosis took four, and pneumonia, five. The mortality age distribution was particularly harsh. Death all but eliminated the elderly, the repository of community honor and wisdom. Four above age seventy died, along with six who were over fifty. Four newborns and three who were age ten or younger also died. Unlike at Funter Bay, where 1943 was the worst year, the majority of Atka deaths, nine, came in 1944. Measles was not listed as the cause of any deaths at Killisnoo.[44]

Although it is difficult to weigh accurately the factors leading to such high mortality, evacuation itself was understandably very stressful to Atka's older people. The substandard living conditions at Killisnoo obviously, also contributed to the causes of death.

Atka's Aleuts began their stay at Killisnoo with the barest of necessities, which did not include fit drinking water. Bill Dirks's daughter died at Killisnoo, a "sad place," while he was away working. He and others attributed their diseases to the water—"dead water," as they called the stagnant pond where they drew it. Henry Dirks, Bill's adopted son, remembered it as a "dead lake" with "bugs in it." No fresh running water was available, so rainwater and water from a more pure source were hauled across the Bay, having to be boiled before being used for drinking or cooking. The "brown water" at Killisnoo was symbolic of the whole place. Vera and John Nevzaroff testified, "Just about everything was poor."[45]

Upon arrival at Killisnoo, the Atkans were given old army surplus clothing. Alice Petrivelli recalled that they were provided neither guns nor boats for subsistence harvesting. The Tlingits of Angoon village, about three miles to the north, befriended them and donated blankets and mattresses. Sympathetic fishermen gave them salmon. In spite of this, Aleuts were cold and hungry. Alice Petrivelli said the camp's "icy cold" winters were made even worse by "no indoor plumbing" and cramped living quarters.[46]

"Poor drinking water, lack of food and poor living conditions," according to Petrivelli, caused Killisnoo's high death rate. Her sister, Vera Snigaroff, almost died "from double pneumonia the first year." Aleuts also were afflicted with "epidemics of head lice and red measles." Although not fatal, they were nevertheless "awful." Killisnoo was burned into the memory of six-year-old Henry Dirks, who had never before seen anybody die. In the camp, he remembered "going to funerals"; and "nobody knew why" Aleuts were dying.[47]

Aleuts asked for help and were joined by teacher Ruby Magee who told Acting Superintendent Fred Geeslin of problems in the camp. Thirteen Atka men who left to work at Excursion Inlet were sorely missed because they had helped haul wood for cooking and heating. This, she wrote, was "serious." Atka people were finding it "difficult to adjust themselves to this locality." They missed most the fresh reindeer and sea lion meat they harvested at home. Canned meat was practically unobtainable, explained Magee, "and it would be much too expensive anyway." Fishing was curtailed by lack of good equipment. They could rely on only "one outboard motor," and it was "often out of commission." Hence, "one can hardly blame them for being dissatisfied."[48]

The weather in the winter of 1943, Magee reported, was called by local people "the worst in fifty years." Atka Aleuts "were not very comfortable in their poor houses. Food froze solid during the coldest weather," and "meat was scarce." No wonder "the people were plenty homesick for Atka."[49]

Teacher Magee admitted that, to her dismay, some Aleuts at Killisnoo went astray. Liquor, she wrote, "is the curse of this village," especially since money spent on it was lost for purchasing necessities like clothing and supplies. Ironically, she felt Aleuts also should have invested what little money they earned in war bonds! Magee's preachments, not surprisingly, fell on deaf ears. "Nothing we say seems to have any influence on them at all." Instead, "they like the influence of their new Angoon friends better." Some Aleut young women, Magee noted with disdain, were promiscuous; they "went 'wild.' "[50]

The Magees had not wanted to accompany Atkans to Southeast. In June 1943 they were granted a transfer to Port Graham on the Kenai Peninsula. They fled from Killisnoo and its many problems. "Our work will be less strenuous than at Atka," the Magees predicted. Consequently, Atka's Aleuts were temporarily isolated. Few on the outside learned of the camp's conditions. Ruth Gruber, the roving investigator for Secretary of the Interior Harold Ickes, visited Funter Bay but not Killisnoo.[51]

In spite of the adverse conditions, Atka's people did not submit to defeat. "These people," Hirst reported to headquarters in October 1942 "have worked very industriously to make . . . necessary repairs and get settled." Some men found jobs, and the rest were "arranging to start their cooperative store." They would pay "for the supplies they use." They worked in canneries and for the Forest Service near Juneau. Some worked in Sitka. Happily for Hirst this arrangement paid off. "All families have been self-supporting since October," wrote their new teacher. Superintendent Hirst was pleased that the Aleuts were self-sufficient and not a burden on the Alaska Indian Service budget. "Co-operative" Aleuts "constructed their new cottages without wages being paid them."[52]

This policy was in contrast to the six-hundred-dollar bonus paid to Charles Magee for "additional work above that ordinarily required of Special Assistants in managing these Evacuation Camps." In addition, the Magees had taken the only house at Killisnoo with a cooking stove.

The successful Atka Native store at Killisnoo became a model for other camps. Geeslin was especially proud of it because, he boasted, it kept "the evacuation costs to a minimum." The store was supported by the $6,661.65 proceeds from the pre-evacuation fur harvest of 1942.[53] When "a widow with six children needed help," she was provided "credit in the store for her needs."

John Nevzaroff expressed what sustained Atka's people in difficult times when he said, "We all work together." Carpentry skills came in handy at Killisnoo, where many buildings needed repairs. Some women found babysitting jobs for fishermen at Chatham across Chatham Strait on Chichagof Island. Others used hand-sewing skills to fashion clothing from castaway garments. Many shared the work and the rewards of these endeavors. Also, keeping to an ancient tradition of self-governance, Atkans elected a new leader, William Dirks, when Steven Gardner was drowned.[54] The women in the camp especially missed having their own kitchens and their own cooking stoves. These women were proud of a tradition of turning out satisfying meals. They resented having to cook and eat meals in the "cannery mess hall," a feeling that was exacerbated by the fact that the Magees had a furnished kitchen. To mollify the women, Andrew Snigaroff "scrounged up a stove for heat and cooking."[55]

Undergirding all, Atkans held a persistent hope to see a rebuilt Atka someday. A few of the men refused to join the Pribilof summer sealing crew, staying with Southeast employment instead. Only after Atka lived again would "they be willing to go to the Pribilofs." Other resistance surfaced in 1943, when young Atkan women protested after they learned that an Indian Service physician, Dr. Bauer, claimed that they "all had venereal disease." They testified that his immunizations were unnecessary and that he had taken advantage of them when the camp's men were away. They "rebelled" and were "glad" to see him go.[56]

Unalaska city Aleuts now encamped at Burnett Inlet on Etolin Island had experienced the pre-evacuation military buildup and had come into more contact with non-Aleuts than had other islanders. They were familiar with change. This experience helped them face the challenges of evacuation.

The food at Burnett Inlet was no better than at the other camps. There was too much "macaroni," a starchy, unbalanced diet without green vegetables or meat. Staples were handed out to heads of households each week, but they included nothing fresh. Although evacuees could purchase better-quality groceries at Wrangell, wage earners had to pay for their camp food, a requirement they resented. All meals were dished out "camp style" at a mess hall.[59]

Like other Aleuts, Unalaska people repaired and built evacuation facilities. Their "duration village" was set close to Burnett Inlet's abandoned red cannery buildings and piles of rusty machinery. At first, they were optimistic about a good life there. The first baby girl born was named "Burnette."[57] Attitudes soon changed, however, and Burnett Inlet became synonymous with misery.

The buildings were "really unfit to live in," remembered an eleven-year-old Aleut. There were "small and crowded" cabins shared by too many people, the rest living in a two-story bunkhouse with "no running water, lights, or heat, only the cooking range in the kitchen." The camp had "one-toilet—'outhouse'—for the group," and no bath facilities. For those housed in the cabins, "only one water faucet was provided."[58]

Aleuts at Burnett Inlet attributed an outbreak of "boils" to the substandard diet and unsanitary conditions. One woman was permanently scarred by them. But there were worse health problems. Physicians seldom visited, dentists not at all. Midwives were present, but in case of emergency no transportation was readily available to hospitals at Wrangell or Ketchikan. One young woman and her husband felt that their son would have been spared permanent handicap if medical help had been available. Ironically, before the evacuees left this camp they were given physical examinations they felt were "unnecessarily gross and rough."[60]

In spite of such conditions, Burnett Inlet claimed comparatively few fatalities. Not as many data are available about Aleut mortality there, so reasons for the lower death rate remain speculative. No doubt the building of new cabins relieved overcrowding. Many Unalaskans worked elsewhere, freeing up additional space. The water supply drew no complaints, and sanitation facilities—while primitive—were not unhealthy. Although no baseline statistics are available, Unalaska city Aleuts might have been in better physical condition prior to evacuation, when they had the only Indian Service hospital in the Aleutians. Because they had had more contact with the outside, Unalaska being quite cosmopolitan, the shock of evacuation was less traumatic. Unlike that of the Atka people, moreover, Unalaska's age profile seems less prone to decimation. There were no members of the community over age sixty-eight, and only four infants one year old or less. Five Unalaska evacuees died, fewer in number and percentage than those of other camps.[61]

Because the Burnett Inlet camp was situated "on a rocky promontory of a bleak and lonely island," its Aleuts were especially homesick in its isolation. Their leader, William Zaharoff, expressed it best: "We want to go back. Oh, how we want to go back!" Boredom was the major problem at Burnett Inlet. Previously an active and competent people, the Unalaskans were relegated to inactivity and feelings of worthlessness. They felt cooped up and deprived of their normal life.[62]

Even though Burnett Inlet was reputed to be better than other camps, it too had its share of problems for evacuees. In the winter of 1942, an epidemic of influenza hit. Although none died from it, it was so widespread that school could not open until April 1943. Burnett Inlet was also the only community having three Aleut wives separated from their Caucasian husbands as a result of the blood quantum test for Unalaska city evacuation.[63]

Some consolation was provided these Aleuts by their makeshift church, which was graced with ecclesiastical articles carefully brought in evacuation by Anfesia Shapsnikoff, the renowned basket weaver. They named the church after their abandoned house of worship, the Church of the Ascension. It occupied the central "place of honor" at Burnett Inlet. In addition to the church, another touch of normal life was provided by pet cats and dogs, which brought reminiscences of home.[64]

As time wore on, Aleuts attempted to give meaning to their camp existence. Men hunted and fished to put meat on the table, worked elsewhere for wages, and were joined in cannery labor by the women. The wages were spent on supplemental food and needed extra clothing. Community members repaired and rigged devices for more creature comforts, including a steam bath like those at Unalaska city.[65]

Despite the Aleuts' attempts to be self-sufficient, not enough jobs were available. Their teacher, Edythe J. Long, reported to Superintendent Hirst early in 1943 that 110 of them were still "dependent on Evacuation funds for subsistence." Most hated it, wanting instead to earn their living. Long praised their efforts. "We cannot help but respect and admire this group" for their "willingness to work." Because the goal of the Interior Department was to make them completely independent, eliminating forever their need for government assistance, evacuation was treated as a first step in that process. Fred Geeslin wrote to Hirst advocating the establishment of a Native store at Burnett Inlet. Proceeds would go to the Indian Service's evacuation fund. And in fact, by February 1943, $727.39 had been collected from the commissary at Burnett Inlet. Hirst reported that "these collections" were "deposited to the credit of the Emergency A Fund," which reduced "the total cost to the Government accordingly."[66]

This parsimony irked Martha Newell, who had been separated from her Caucasian husband. Like William Zaharoff, who in 1942 had protested Burnett Inlet's facilities, Newell protested the requirement to pay for food, since "we didn't ask to come." She asked her husband in Seattle to write to Washington, D.C., for an explanation of "why we have to pay for our food and other things when we have no way to make a living."[67]

Alaska Delegate to Congress Anthony J. Dimond received Kenneth Newell's letter. Incarcerated Japanese were being treated better than these Aleuts, he charged. He demanded to know why Aleuts were not allowed to return to Unalaska city. The whole thing, he claimed, "really smells rotten." He felt Martha deserved better because she had helped others in the influenza epidemic at Unalaska years before. "Now, when it is really up to Uncle Sam to do his stuff, some knot-head says these Unalaska people must pay for their food, and live in any kind of a warehouse or shack that is available."[68] The letter was similar to the one sent to President Roosevelt in 1941 by John Yatchmeneff. In response to Newell's accusations and demands, Fred Geeslin attempted an explanation to Delegate Dimond. He admitted that "conditions were not so good at Burnett Inlet" before building materials arrived. But afterward, the Indian service had provided lumber for their church even though it might have been a violation of church-state separation. This infraction of the First Amendment was justified, argued Geeslin, "in order that they be happy in their new environment." The aim, of course, had been to make Aleuts "as self-sustaining as possible." Although they received no "compensation for the necessary labor" in refurbishing and building the camp, they were given food and supplies. They were also aided by

Elmer D. Long, the teacher's husband, who, like Magee at Killisnoo, was paid six hundred dollars extra for his labor.[69]

According to Geeslin, these special efforts were appreciated by the Aleuts, and they expressed relief to be "out of the reach of the Japs. All possible has been done to accommodate them," and there was "no reason for complaint." Geeslin mistakenly claimed that only one complaint about conditions was ever made. Yet Geeslin did confess that "these evacuees may be receiving less than Japs in concentration camps." He conceded that if Martha Newell were "estranged from her husband," we would "furnish supplies to her as long as she remains at Burnett Inlet and cannot obtain employment."[70]

The Burnett Inlet teacher, Edythe Long, however, had a different opinion about Martha Newell's complaints. She described Martha as a "trouble-maker" who raised a commotion in the community so she would be sent back to Unalaska. Newell's complaint, said Long, was a "gross misrepresentation." Newell was mistaken—she had not been required to pay for her supplies. The Burnett Inlet Aleuts were well taken care of and "complaint of hunger here is ridiculous," argued Long. "I doubt if very many people in the world today are faring as well." Interestingly, Edythe Long previously had fired Newell as her babysitter. She wanted Newell to leave the camp, and not charging her for supplies would make it easier for her to save money and leave.[71] Eventually, Martha Newell died at Burnett Inlet, the cause unknown. Kenneth Newell was not present at her death.

Teacher Long may have been negative about Martha Newell, but she treated Aleut leader William Zaharoff gingerly. He was "a problem" too, but "we felt he could be of great help to us." Unfortunately, noticed Long, he had developed a "childish attitude" about paying for supplies. It had made him "extremely disgruntled." Long did not mention that the Indian Service refused to pay hospital expenses for Zaharoff's wife, who died while hospitalized. His mood, she thought, would dissipate once he found employment. Because Zaharoff grieved over the death of his wife, the teacher commiserated and ignored "his attitude."[72]

The desire to return home was common at Burnett Inlet. Rumors in 1943 that the Pribilof people were soon to be sent home flew into camp, raising hope that Unalaskans would follow. But word had also come that Aleut property left behind at Unalaska had been damaged. Wanting to verify this, forty Aleuts, calling themselves "The Unalaska Community Members," signed a petition and sent it in October 1943 to Governor Gruening. If the rumor were true, they wanted Gruening to assist in repairing their homes before they returned. Gruening was gone from his office, leaving Secretary Bartlett to respond. His research indicated that the Alaska Indian Service was competently watching over Aleut interests on the Aleutians. Aleuts should, however, direct any future concern about the matter directly to Hirst and Geeslin.[73]

The Aleuts from Akutan, Biorka, Kashega, Makushin, and Nikolski at Ward Lake at first seemed blessed by a favorable location. Unlike other evacuees, they were near a city with health services. A few days after arriving, a young Akutan woman and one from Nikolski gave birth in the Ketchikan hospital to baby girls.[74] Although already cramped, the Ward Lake camp would have to be stretched farther to accommodate the newborns.

Ward Lake was unique because it held Aleuts from several villages. They had come from remote places and were not accustomed to the environment surrounding Ward Lake. Forest Service officials complained when camp children played with toy "cap pistols" near department buildings vulnerable to fire. The children were also suspected of breaking windows and automobile headlights. Pauline A. T. Whitfield, the Nikolski teacher, and her husband, a special assistant, were informed about this. As camp managers they pledged "full cooperation" to prevent "needless destruction of Forest Service property." Thereafter, children were not to play near Forest Service buildings. Other restrictions were implemented also: "No taking piled cord wood. . . . only windfalls and dead standing trees" could be cut for firewood.[75]

Alaska Indian Service policy for Ward Lake was identical to that for the other camps. Aleut labor would be used to repair facilities and build new dwellings. That being completed, Aleuts would find employment and pay their own way. Fred Geeslin recommended establishing a Native store for Ward Lake to meet this goal. The process at Ward Lake, however, moved slowly. In January 1943, teacher Whitfield reported that thirty families were "entirely dependent upon the Evacuation Fund for their subsistence." One problem was that fourteen wage earners at Excursion Inlet were remiss in sending money to their Ward Lake families. Whitfield suggested that ways be found to reverse this drain on the Indian Service budget. In response, Geeslin decided to "arrange with evacuees to have their checks deposited" directly to the Juneau office. This money would then pay "for supplies issued to their families." The Nikolski people, Superintendent Hirst reported, had already saved enough to pay the government the balance of four thousand dollars on a previous loan.[76]

Having never before had so much money, some of the fortunate Aleuts who earned good wages spent it freely and not always on necessities. Whitfield complained when Aleuts spent "their money for liquor instead of buying food for their children." She felt, nevertheless, that "the majority of the evacuees are doing a fairly good job of adjusting themselves to their new surroundings."[77]

In fact, Aleuts at Ward Lake had much difficulty adjusting. Because of overcrowding and unsanitary conditions, they became ill and depressed. According to Luke Shelikoff of Akutan, the camp was a "damp old thing"; the ground "was wet all the time." Tents used before cabins were built leaked, and "everything including blankets" was soaked. Ward Lake conjured the image of "swampy," a "place wet with constant rain," where the sun was blocked out by huge trees and Aleuts were placed "under the woods."[78]

They received little help from the Alaska Indian Service. "No government agency provided us with transportation into town" or "helped us with finding employment," charged Dorofey Chercasen from Nikolski. They were even denied use of the telephone in the school building. They walked the eight miles to Ketchikan or were taken by Eugene Wacker, a local taxi owner, for thirty-five cents. Wacker also helped "bail our people from the city jail." To improve his taxi service, Wacker purchased "a small bus so he could transport more people," allowing Aleuts to work away from camp during the day but remain with their families the rest of the time. Aleuts owed "a lot to the kindness of this dear man."[79] As soon as Aleuts found outside employment, the Indian Service no longer supplied their food.

The worst problem at Ward Lake was lack of medical care. Leonty Savoroff remembered that after "two or three weeks" a team of physicians arrived. They found many Aleuts ill, so a quarantine was instituted. Because the camp had no resident physician, teacher Whitfield served as a "camp health aide." When Savoroff contracted pneumonia, he was confined to camp, not placed in the Ketchikan hospital. He resumed work before cured, came down with "double pneumonia," and "was laid up for six months at camp trying to get well."[80]

Such factors made Ward Lake the second deadliest camp in Southeast, behind Killisnoo. Twenty Aleuts died there, most of them victims of tuberculosis and pneumonia. They were buried at Bayview Cemetery. Only one newborn lived; four died. The two smallest villages, Makushin and Kashega, lost one-fourth of their people.[81] Only the Attuans in Japan suffered a worse mortality rate.

Aleuts at Ward Lake did not receive the expected benefit of Ketchikan's hospital or city services. In fact, their camp experience was complicated further by proximity to the city. In 1943, for example, Aleuts were accused of causing health hazards for Ketchikan's citizens. The city quarantined the camp, claiming that Aleuts were spreading "virulent sex diseases." This move came at the request of former mayor Harry G. McCain, chairman of the city council's Committee on Police, Health and Sanitation. He wrote to Governor Gruening protesting Aleut presence at Ward Lake. McCain charged that they "infect the public places," causing an epidemic in the city. "Their latrines empty directly into Ward Cove Lake, a recreation area, one of the most beautiful . . . in this part of the country or in all of Alaska." This scourge caused wildlife to die off. Aleuts, he claimed, hurt local business because they were "unsanitary and diseased and thus obnoxious." He wanted to rid the city of this "dangerous menace." The governor, he suggested, should find a "way in which the welfare of the Aleuts can be properly cared for without menacing established communities of white people."[82]

The Ketchikan city council debated this issue and heard testimony on behalf of Aleuts from Coast Guard Captain Frederick Zeusler, teacher Pauline Whitfield, Leonard Allen of the Indian Service, Aleut friend Eugene Wacker, the Reverend George Beck, and Hugh McGlashen, an Aleut evacuee from Akutan. McGlashen argued that Aleuts should have been left in their island homes. The others claimed that most of the charges against Aleuts were untrue. To move them again would be unjust and expensive. By a vote of one nay and five ayes, the council agreed to petition Governor Gruening to move the Aleuts or provide "proper medical attention for them."[83]

In this flap, Aleuts were used by McCain and Mayor J. A. Talbot to seek funds from the Alaska Indian Service and Territorial government for a Native hospital they wanted built at Saxman, a nearby Tlingit community. Mayor Talbot mentioned the proposed hospital in the council debate and in the petition to Gruening. McCain as mayor had previously asked for funds from the Indian Service for venereal disease control even before the Aleuts arrived at Ward Lake. The evacuees were also caught in a battle between the city health officer and a part-time Indian Service physician, the one apparently stressing Ward Lake's unhealthy conditions and the other supporting the Indian Service's contention that the camp was not too bad after all.[84]

The governor's office would have nothing to do with these matters. It was an Indian Service affair. Consequently, Superintendent Hirst wrote to Mayor Talbot that, based on an investigation by Dr. J. P. Eberhardt, Territorial medical director, the Aleuts would not be moved from Ward Lake. But he pledged "further efforts . . . to improve their health conditions." Plans were being made to provide another nurse for Ketchikan's Natives and for Aleuts at Burnett Inlet and Ward Lake. Yet the public airing of these matters failed to improve conditions. Reports came from the camp that "there are quite a number of sick with the flu." When

Superintendent Hirst summarized the donnybrook over health conditions for the commissioner of Indian affairs, he admitted that "we have had and may expect a continuance of such situations during the emergency in the Territory." Although he allowed that Native health in Alaska was worse than in the states, he said, "We are doing all we can to meet the situation with our limited funds and personnel."[85]

Eventually, some Aleuts were moved out of the camp to relieve overcrowdedness. Although the council's complaints had precipitated this, the clinching factor was the camp's impact on Ward Lake's recreational value. Early in January 1944, the lake's water was found to be contaminated. Water samples "showed positive with coliform organisms present." Warning signs were posted. At the camp where 142 Aleuts lived, the "septic tank facilities . . . were designed" for only "sixty-five persons." Pollution from the camp had migrated into the lake and would prevent Ketchikan citizens from swimming in it. Dr. Ralph W. Carr, the Indian Service's part-time physician in Ketchikan, "suggested no action be taken until the Aleuts were moved . . . after which the polluted condition" would "be remedied." By May 1944, Aleuts from Biorka, Kashega, and Makushin, approximately forty-six people, were moved to Burnett Inlet in yet another evacuation, the only action of its kind in the whole episode.[86]

Given the odds, Aleut accomplishments at Ward Lake were impressive. They actually improved the facilities. Fred Geeslin remarked that "these people are the hardest workers I've ever seen." He called them "practical, frugal, . . . resourceful." Some women, like Sophie Pletnikoff of Kashega, found jobs in Ketchikan as housekeepers and cannery workers. Pletnikoff paid for her own living quarters in the city. Others who could also left the camp for "modern conveniences." Aleut construction workers provided most of the labor that built the city's Creek Street bridge. Cannery representatives actively recruited Aleut workers.[87]

Morale in the camp was sustained by one means or another. Church activities helped. Luke Shelikoff of Akutan was overjoyed that church articles from the island were used at Ward Lake. For internal governance, a ruling body of the various village leaders elected Mark Pettikoff of Akutan as spokesman, a kind of ombudsman. The Whitfields acted in an advisory capacity and took appeals. Aleuts agreed that money earned would be pooled and distributed by village leaders. To break the boredom, "some of the younger people organized dances and get togethers."[88]

Some Aleuts went into Ketchikan to provide musical entertainment, a kind of civic service. In 1945, thirty of them "sang Christmas carols in Russian and Aleut . . . at the Ketchikan General Hospital" and for military servicemen at the USO. Ketchikan citizens were invited to the traditional Aleut New Year ceremony and were introduced to a colorful display of church adornments. In February, eight Aleuts entertained the Ketchikan Rotary Club with songs in "Old Church Slavonic." These activities were encouraged by the new camp managers, Mr. and Mrs. Henry W. Benedict, who replaced the Whitfields.[89]

Such participation erased some of the bad feeling caused by Ketchikan Police Department arrests and court fines, which Aleuts considered unfair. In 1943, police recorded thirty-eight arrests, mostly for drunkenness. Some of these were repeat offenders. The figure for 1944 fell to fourteen. In a rugged city like Ketchikan, hard drinking was not uncharacteristic. But Aleuts were offended by Chief of Police Jake Zeldenrust's harsh arrest policy. One of them confronted the chief. "We don't want to do anything wrong. Please be good to my people," he implored. "They don't mean any harm."[90]

Mark Pettikoff, their leader, also spoke out for Aleuts in the fray over sanitary conditions. He protested their being called "undesirables." Venereal disease was not used as an excuse to disgrace other ethnic groups, he noted. Moreover, Aleuts served in the United States military and bought "their share of war bonds." No "special favors" for Aleuts were necessary, but they wanted to be treated like others. If the politicians who now wanted to remove Aleuts from Ward Lake, Pettikoff argued, "had shown the same zeal in keeping away the whiskey bootleggers and white exploiters . . . they might have accomplished some useful purpose." As for Pettikoff, he frankly resented "un-American efforts to kick" Aleuts "about from pillar to post."[91]

The Aleuts from Attu village held in distant Japan experienced the worst of the "dark valley" encounters.[92] The forty Attu Aleuts living in cramped quarters at the northern end of Otaru starved, some literally to death. They ate primarily rice, which to them became a synonym for no food at all. After their return, the mention of it made them tense, triggering memories of extreme hunger. One report attempted to downplay starvation but nevertheless acknowledged that lack of protein contributed to Aleut illness and death. Innokenty Golodoff was fortunate because his Japanese girlfriend gave him extra bread, fish, and "a little bit of pickled radishes." For the less fortunate, much of the food they got gave them "very bad stomach aches, and they were very painful." Children "were starving." One mother resorted to scavenging "orange peelings off the ground." When she fed them to her offspring, they would "stop crying for a while."[93]

Attuan children remembered Otaru as the worst time in their lives.

John Golodoff wanted to blot it completely out of his memory. "The less I remember the better." He claimed to have been beaten for not working at a pace demanded by guards. Angelina Hodikoff carried scars from beatings she received. One wound was "caused by a stone thrown at her by a Japanese guard because she had stopped working."[94]

Most Aleuts worked at digging and hauling a claylike substance used as a polishing agent and in ceramics. When it lodged in the right eye of Olean Prokopeuff, she feared loss of vision, although that failed to happen. The work was difficult and unpleasant. Mike Lokanin had to crawl into a hole to direct the powdery fan-blown material into storage. It plugged his nose, ears, mouth, and eyes until he could "hardly breathe." The residue deposited in his lungs was later noticeable on X rays. Even Aleut women worked "from seven in the morning to five at night and got one day of rest in two weeks."[95]

These evacuees had little or no medical care in Otaru. Innokenty Golodoff testified that they had none. Some of the seriously ill, however, were hospitalized; others who were sick remained at their guarded house. In the summer of 1943, a visitor there recorded that "only seven were healthy." Thirty-two seemed to be afflicted with tuberculosis. Some of these were sent to a nearby sanatorium. Some Aleuts felt they were given medical attention for a diabolical reason: experimentation. One writer charged that "Aleut prisoners were used as guinea pigs for experiments with vaccines," and the Aleuts suspected this was true. When they returned from hospital checkups, Olean Prokopeuff asked what happened to them. "They replied, 'We are being inoculated.' We did not know what was being done." Mike Lokanin said Japanese doctors took blood from one Aleut and injected it into another. He and Mike Hodikoff were subjected to this, and afterward, Lokanin complained of vision problems.[96]

In Otaru, whole families were threatened with extinction. Mike Lokanin's only two children died of starvation in 1944. Two of the three members of the Peter Artumonoff family died from tuberculosis. Of the fifteen people in the three Golodoff families, six died, five from beri-beri, caused by a vitamin B deficiency and resulting in pain, paralysis, emaciation, and swelling of the body. Of the ten Hodikoffs, five died. Mike, the Attu leader, and his son, George, died in 1945 of poisoning from eating rotten garbage.[97]

Sixteen of the forty Attu evacuees—40 percent—died at Otaru. One died during Japanese occupation, and one en route to Japan. Five babies were born; one who was born near the end of the imprisonment survived. The major causes of death were beri-beri, starvation, food poisoning, tuberculosis, and pneumonia.[98]

Other scenes at Otaru haunted Aleuts for years after their release. For twenty-three days, Mike Lokanin watched his daughter slowly fade toward death. His son died the next day. Three days later his wife, Perascovia, was hospitalized. "It was the hardest time we had," he concluded. Alex Prossoff's stepmother was admitted to the sanatorium for tuberculosis treatment, but because of "no heat and very little food . . . she died." No "Red Cross packages of food or clothing" and "no medicine ever came." Olean Prokopeuff lost three children to beriberi. When she visited them in the hospital, "they would say, 'Mother, come here and scratch me.' " They "could not move."[99]

The Japanese required cremation of the dead, a custom repugnant to Aleut religious faith. Some considered it a "sin." Mike Lokanin recalled that one of the deprivations at Otaru was not being able to bury their dead. Aleuts had to transfer by hand crematory remains of their loved ones into boxes sometimes too small to hold them.[100]

Like other Aleut evacuees, Attuans missed their island's snow-topped mountains, verdant slopes, marine life, and birds. They were strong people and did what they could to make life at Otaru meaningful. Desire to see Attu again and to worship in their church gave them hope. A significant coup in the Otaru episode was Alex Prossoff's shepherding of $388.22 in American money through three years of captivity. Prossoff, the church's treasurer, had buried the money next to his house in the Japanese occupation, hid it under a blanket on the evacuation ship, and buried it once more near the Otaru camp.[101]

What little they enjoyed was related to the church calendar. One of the guards who befriended them, civilian policeman Takeshiro Shikanai, procured turkey and goat meat for an Aleut Christmas party. On Christmas eve 1944, "the party lasted late into the night, the Aleuts playing the accordion, and dancing folk dances. Everyone forgot the passage of time on this night."[102]

Most of the time, however, was spent working. Instead of giving in to despair, Aleuts refused to submit to some aspects of their captivity. When Innokenty Golodoff and others were weakened by hunger, they refused to work. Others threatened to strike for more wages. They were paid one yen a day but through negotiation gained a tiny increase. Julia Golodoff excoriated the Japanese for the death of her daughter and was given no food or water because of her outburst. "They made her shovel snow" in bare feet, "but she did not die."[103]

Some Aleuts used more subtle forms of protest. Officials who came to inspect asked them about the quality of food. They were met by icy Aleut silence. "We refused to talk." Others used stealth. Mike Lokanin stayed alive by sneaking past guards to rummage for "fish heads and guts" and potato peelings from a garbage dump. It was "better than nothing," he claimed. Others once "killed two dogs and ate them." In the worst year of hunger, 1944, "we would dig in the hog boxes," said Alex Prossoff, "when the guards were not looking."[104]

Only Mike Lokanin and Alex Prossoff would talk to Japanese interrogators, although all Aleuts were forced to learn Japanese. Following instructions from one of the elders, they gave the Japanese false information about America and affirmed loyalty to their country. They criticized the Japanese government for ruining their Attu homes, imprisoning them, and taking their people to "a land" where they could not "talk his language." Alex Prossoff "had arguments with the guards over their gods. One of them wanted me to pray to their gods but I told him I would pray to my own God."[105]

"Optimism and happiness," their inner strengths, helped to bring them through. After the war, a teacher noticed these qualities in five of their children. They were "good-natured children with a wonderful sense of humor." The Attuans constantly thought about returning home, and this, too, sustained them. Conscientiously, they visited the crematorium to collect "the little boxes" containing "the bones of our loved ones. We kept all our boxes carefully," Alex Prossoff remembered, "because we wanted to take them home to be buried some day." Once, while at this task, he humorously engaged a guard: "I noticed that when a Jap body was burned the bones did not fill the box. . . . I told a Jap guard that his people have small frames, much smaller than Attu people. Must be because his people eat too much rice."[106]

9

Pribilof and Aleutian Homecomings

In 1942, my wife and our four children were whipped away from our
homes—like dogs. . . . All our possessions were left . . . for mother
nature to destroy. . . . I tried to pretend it really was a dream and this
could not happen to me and my dear family. The dream . . . was not a
dream it was the very vision we experienced on our return to
Akutan. . . . I knew I had to salvage my house for my family [and] I
worked till my hands bleeding with pain made the wood red.
—Bill Tcheripanoff, Sr., Akutan Aleut Evacuee
Commission on Wartime Relocation Hearings

Aleuts dreamed that one day the wind of evacuation would be a river no
more. Then the joy of homecoming would replace the horrors of the
camps. Their communal wholeness would be restored to them on familiar islands in beloved homes and churches. They dreamed the lights of
their Aleutian and Pribilof islands would disperse the darkness of the
camps, to which they had not succumbed. They did not give up hope.

But when and how the dream would materialize remained unknown.
In one traditional Aleut story, the Chuginadak Woman searching for a
husband used dried sea lion gut that turned into a horsetail-grass
bridge. It took her from island to island—Chuginadak, Samalga,
Unalaska, and Unalga. Stymied when the wonderful gut would not
stretch far enough, she was carried to a cave shelter on Akutan by two
friendly North Pacific murres, birds that provided their wings for a
mattress and blanket. After much tribulation, she found a mate, and
equilibrium in village life was restored.[1] Although Aleut evacuees could
not appropriate its magic, the ancient story contained elements of their
present plight: struggle, homecoming, and triumph.

Except for Attu, the war that had prompted the Aleuts' hasty evacuation never actually reached their Aleutian and Pribilof islands. Still,
it stood in the way of their return. The area was considered a combat
zone and was restricted. Even if the signal to return the Aleuts had
been given earlier, the Department of the Interior would have been
reluctant to rush into a resettlement that might repeat the errors of

the poorly organized evacuation. The probability of return for the Attuans could hardly be imagined, for their fate had been unknown since June 1942. Perhaps they would one day be part of a prisoner of war exchange.

Eventually, resettlement did begin in starts and stops, just as evacuation had. It was deemed a civilian responsibility—after permission was granted by military authorities. In a routine by now unnervingly familiar, the return of the Aleuts varied in kind, in place, and in time. Some of the deserted villages required more rehabilitation than others. Some were not rehabilitated at all. Government officials refused to fund restoration of four communities, virtually ringing the death knell for Attu, Biorka, Kashega, and Makushin. This loss affected seventy-one Aleuts, and Aleutian settlements were thereby reduced in number by half, to Akutan, Atka, Nikolski and Unalaska. Some Aleuts, also, chose not to go back. But of those who did return, the Pribilof people, second to be evacuated, were the first to return, the only ones granted the privilege in 1944. They were followed the next year by the remaining Aleuts, about one-half of all those evacuated. Attu's people, the last evacuated, were also the last to return.

As the Aleutian campaign wound down, an end to the camps was anticipated. The war's focus in the central Pacific made them superfluous. Aleut expectation of resuming village life rose as the war dragged slowly to an end. Anxious about their prospects, Aleuts could not have imagined, however, the shambles in which they would find their homes and villages. Only those who chose not to return or were not allowed to were spared this further degradation and sorrow. Bill Tcheripanoff, who had earlier felt some uncomfortable premonitions, was nevertheless shocked when he saw the devastation.

Nearly everything the Aleuts owned had been left behind when they were evacuated with only what they could carry on board the evacuation ship. Even before the elements had time to destroy their property, United States soldiers and sailors did. Some were souvenir seekers who simply took Aleut possessions. Others mindlessly vandalized Aleut homes, furnishings, and equipment. Servicemen raided unprotected community buildings and churches. Personal, community, and ecclesiastical articles disappeared or were destroyed. And making matters worse for the Aleuts upon their return was the discovery that their valuable subsistence equipment for fishing, hunting and trapping either was no longer usable or was gone altogether.

The homes, churches, indeed the villages they left had been altered by misuse, neglect, and the elements. Anticipating happiness at last, the Aleuts were shocked and saddened by the sights they encountered upon returning. Traumatized by evacuation, repulsed by camp life, they experienced now more frustration and disappointment. But they characteristically turned immediately to tasks of reconstruction and resettlement. In this, they were winners, not losers. They were creative, innovative builders and responsible organizers. They set about to refashion new communities and a new order for themselves. Like the Chuginadak Woman, they were successful in the end.

The first evacuees to go back to the Aleutians were sent on a temporary mission. Soon after Nikolski people arrived at Wrangell in July 1942 they were visited by two army officers. The military wanted "two Aleuts from Nikolski Village, who had trapped blue foxes on Adak," to show them the island's terrain. This knowledge would be used for building a military airfield. For this scouting trip, the two Aleuts were each given five hundred dollars and a rifle. Mission accomplished, they were back in the Wrangell camp in two weeks. Also several Aleuts from the Ward Lake camp were employed at the Nikolski sheep ranch for two summers.[2]

But the largest group to return was a crew for harvesting Pribilof fur seals in the summer of 1943. Evacuation had deprived the U.S. Treasury of over a million dollars of seal harvest income. While Aleuts were in relocation camps, they were costing the government, not producing revenue. In November 1942, Secretary of the Interior Harold Ickes complained to Secretary of War Henry Stimson, "Without consulting me or any official of this Department, our armed forces evacuated" the Pribilof Islands, taking Aleuts to Funter Bay, "where presumably they would be less subject to enemy attack." The loss of government revenue, however, remained a problem for him. Ickes urged the return of all Pribilof Aleuts for sealing operations in the spring of 1943. To Ickes, the move only made good sense. It would "remove the natives from their present unsatisfactory status as refugees, improve their health, and at the same time will produce revenue for the Government."[3]

Rational as this seemed, Secretary of War Stimson was not impressed. St. Paul Island was garrisoned with 875 servicemen busily building an airfield. There was no room for Aleuts, Fish and Wildlife Service personnel, or sealing operations. When Stimson responded to Ickes on December 4, he defended Pribilof evacuation as a "military necessity." Aleuts could not be returned now because "conditions in the Aleutians still are not sufficiently stabilized." Moreover, "occupation of the Pribilof Islands was made possible by using the housing of the former occupants." The Pribilof Islands, Stimson argued, were strategically important; also, transportation to supply civilians there would be difficult if not impossible to find.[4]

Early in 1943, however, Stimson relented somewhat. On January 2, he told Ickes that a party of approximately 150 Aleuts and government employees would be allowed back in the spring, but "only in order to direct the pruning of the seal herd by military personnel." Furthermore, Stimson added, beginning in June 1943, the St. George people could be resettled.[5] That meant nearly 180 Aleuts at the gold mine site would leave Funter Bay and return to their St. George homes.

What had changed Stimson's mind? Apparently the prospect of military attack on the Pribilofs had abated. St. George Island was a small post. Only one officer and forty enlisted men were stationed there. In fact, both Pribilof Island bases were disappointing from a military standpoint. Efforts to supply them in stormy weather were fraught with accidents. One officer was killed. Only a few aircraft landings actually were made. Construction projects remained uncompleted because of equipment shortages, and foul weather, high seas, and ice floes that prevented off-loading of supplies. The water supply was inadequate, morale was low, and the men were bored. Stimson finally agreed it would be better to give the Pribilof Islands back to Aleuts who belonged there. By June, the decision to leave both islands was final, and all troops except a small caretaker contingent of ten on St. Paul were removed by September 1943.[6]

In spite of Stimson's no-return position in January 1942, Fish and Wildlife Service personnel had anticipated the move and had begun preliminary planning for the return as early as November 1942. Superintendent Johnston inquired whether military occupancy had resulted in any damage to Aleut homes and villages. If so, supplies should be ordered accordingly. He and his superior in Chicago, Ward Bower, believed the Pribilovians would be eager to move back. When reports from the Pribilofs reached Director Ira Gabrielson that military personnel in "small boats have been known to make use of fur-seal herds . . . for target practice," matters became urgent. Seal depredation was so alarming that Gabrielson asked the commander of the Thirteenth Naval District for help in "preserving and protecting this valuable natural resource."[7]

After Secretary Stimson relented, the Fish and Wildlife Service geared up for summer sealing and resettlement of St. George Island. Governor Gruening and General Buckner were notified. Contacts were made with the Fouke Fur Company of St. Louis, Missouri, to receive the pelts. A survey of the islands, to be led by Johnston, was planned. Personnel needs were discussed. A small increase in wages for Aleuts was contemplated.

Supplies and transportation were, in a preliminary way, arranged. The army approved a May 15 arrival date for St. George people.[8] The return was moving along in fine shape.

Anxious to put the Funter Bay fiasco behind him, Governor Gruening was pleased. He wrote to General Buckner urging cooperation. The governor took this opportunity to lecture the general. "It is the Department of Interior's view," he pointed out, "that the interruption of the sealing industry, a government monopoly, last year was most unfortunate and unnecessary." Perhaps this mistake would be corrected and only "conditions arising from absolute military necessity" would get in the way.[9] Without actually accusing the military outright, Gruening was the first government official to express doubt about the justification for evacuating the Pribilofs in the first place.

Governor Gruening's analysis—on hindsight quite valid—was nonetheless irrelevant. The push to resume sealing operations and restore the St. George community was fully underway in spite of a planned military offensive in May aimed at retaking Attu and Kiska from the Japanese. The military apparently was so confident of victory they paid no heed to the Pribilofs. At the time of the evacuation, the military had expected the enemy would attack the area. Back then, their takeover of the islands and garrisoning of troops had been crucial to Alaska defense. Now, apparently, the North Pacific situation had changed radically.

If Fish and Wildlife officials were optimistic about the return to the Pribilof Islands, their enthusiasm was dampened in March 1943 when they were made aware of difficulties surrounding the move. The bad news came from an unexpected, nonmilitary source, Agent Lee McMillin. When rumors circulated that all Aleuts at Funter Bay were to be resettled on the Pribilofs, McMillin reported that not all Aleuts wanted to go. Some Aleut men "do not want to return until the war is over and stated emphatically they will not go," McMillin said. Several factors were at work, he explained. At Juneau, where a number of Aleuts had gone for employment, the governor's office was busy recruiting Territorial Guards from among the Pribilof people. Men from the St. Paul group signed on willingly for the Guards; men from the St. George group refused, hoping that they would be resettled soon. Aleut sentiment was mixed. Some felt the Pribilofs might still be attacked. They wondered about the fate of Attu people. If Attuans had been killed by the enemy, might not the same fate befall them if they prematurely returned to the Pribilofs? Furthermore, many Aleuts now understood clearly that sealing would pay less than work at Juneau or Excursion Inlet. If they returned for summer sealing, would they be given a bonus to compensate for the higher wages they now earned? McMillin thought that when departure came, it would be difficult to persuade many workers to go.[10]

Superintendent Johnston of the Fish and Wildlife Service was willing to take some blame for Aleut hesitancy and confusion. Previously, in attempts to mollify them about conditions in the camps, he had warned Aleuts that military action in the Aleutians would most likely take place, indicating they were actually safer where they were. Now, however, he wanted sealing workers available. It was no longer necessary to make them fear the danger posted by military action on the islands. Consequently, he withheld approval of Guard recruitment. He promised Aleuts who stayed for camp duties a share in the sealing proceeds. He also threatened that those who refused to go sealing would "forfeit any share of the sealing division." Worse yet, Johnston warned that anyone refusing to work in the seal harvest would be denied a permit to return to St. Paul when it eventually would be resettled. And if a St. George person refused to return in the summer when sealing operations were to resume, he "will not share in the sealing division and will not be allowed to return at any later date if I can help it." Disobedient Aleuts would lose for all time "all privileges as an island resident."[11] Such threats, Johnston thought, would convince all needed Pribilof Aleuts to return for the seal harvest.

After making these declarations, Superintendent Johnston had second thoughts. He decided to seek validation of his position from Chief Bower. He wanted an endorsement of this policy and clarification of Pribilof Aleut legal status. Johnston posed the essential question, "What is the extent to which government is legally obligated to the natives and the natives to the Government?" Not surprisingly, lawyers for the Department of the Interior came up with no definitive answer. Bower then reported that the issue of rights of occupancy had not been determined, and when it is, "it may hamper instead of aid our desired operations." Governmental maintenance of "natives is not defined in an existing law," but is established practice and "takes into account also the moral obligation of the Government." Johnston's concerns, arising "out of the present abnormal war conditions," ought to be for the present laid to rest. Yet, declared Bower, "in view of war conditions, the forced evacuation of the islands, and the designation of the area as a war zone, it is scarcely possible or equitable to require complete forfeiture of all rights of return to the Pribilofs."[12]

There were others who had a vested interest in allowing Aleuts to stay in better paying jobs. The War Department's Juneau engineering office complained of a potential drain on the labor force. "Many of those native Aleuts," wrote the resident engineer, "are employed here in laboring and in skilled capacities." They were essential. "A protest must be filed against the withdrawal of these workers who are engaged in . . . national defense construction." An urgent request was made to allow them to work in Southeast Alaska "in line with the best interests of the National Defense Program."[13]

Plans for an easy return to the Pribilofs and the smooth resumption of sealing had collapsed. As it turned out, there was no full Aleut sealing crew in the summer of 1943. The Fish and Wildlife Service was also forced to abandon St. George resettlement until 1944. Aleut activism had been an important factor in these developments. A clash with government policy no longer intimidated Aleuts. They were now more interested in and capable of bettering their own lives and determining their own fates. Because of their experience in the camps, automatic concert of interest between Aleuts and the government no longer existed. In early April 1943, the Alaska Indian Service was able to recruit four Burnett Inlet evacuees and eight from Ward Lake for the sealing party. However, Fred Geeslin informed Johnston that the president of the Alaska Native Brotherhood, Roy Peratrovich, had been visited by a "delegation of the Funter Bay group." They were interested in knowing their rights should they refuse to join the sealing expedition. Ruth Gruber, a frequent Harold Ickes emissary in Alaska, told Aleuts there is strength in unity. "If all the natives as a group refuse to go, nothing can be done against" you, she advised.[14]

Aleuts were further supported by a protest of citizens from Juneau. A public outcry by Mary Jane Gaither and telephone calls to the Juneau Fish and Wildlife Service office by her mother, Mabel Hoopes, and by local attorney Grover Winn, accused the government of mistreating Aleuts. In "An Open Letter to the Public" sent to Delegate Anthony Dimond, on April 7, Gaither claimed that Pribilof people were victims of "shameful . . . 'slavery.' " Aleuts for many years had been deprived of nourishment, and "medical and hospital care." The upcoming sealing venture was designed, charged Gaither, only to make money; and Aleuts were threatened by banishment if they refused to go. She urged: "LET'S all HOLLER and HOLLER LOUD and LONG until our own back yards are clean!"[15]

The evacuations themselves had not raised such a furor because few people, especially on the outside, had knowledge about them. But this most recent and public commotion from Alaska during wartime was embarrassing to the Department of the Interior. Fish and Wildlife Service Director Ira Gabrielson was especially sensitive to the criticism. His office explained away the Gaither letter to Dimond by praising the administration of Pribilovian caretakers and describing Funter Bay conditions as "make-shift." Aleuts "have suffered no real hardships, although some inconveniences have been unavoidable." Chief of Alaska Fisheries Ward Bower was told that the Gaither and Hoopes protests were launched because they might lose their Aleut housemaid. Attorney Winn was considered an interested party because he "has been renting some shacks to the evacuees in Juneau." Winn's fangs, however, were doubly lethal because he threatened to " 'blow the lid off' the whole sealing plan through the medium of two nationally known writers" (one of whom was believed to be Corey Ford and the other Joseph Driscoll of the New York *Herald-Tribune*).[16]

When Johnston visited Funter Bay on April 26, 1943, determined St. George and St. Paul men met with him. Rumors of impending military action in the western Aleutians still had them worried about safety should they resume sealing at that time. Johnston assured them that they would be as safe there as if they were on coastal Alaska or in cities like Seattle, San Francisco, or Los Angeles. Before evacuation, he reminded them, the Pribilofs had been vulnerable to attack. Now, because an attack on the islands was very unlikely, their presence there was safer than it had been when they were removed. That issue covered, the Aleuts pressed Johnston for more pay per skin taken. Johnston hedged that request by saying he would have to have it in writing and would then wire it to his superiors. Having begun negotiations, however, Aleuts pressed further. They wanted payment for camp wages until sealing could be resumed. It is possible these Aleut negotiators were aware that wages for non-Aleut Pribilof employees had been raised 25 percent in January, " a pleasant surprise" announced to Johnston by Bower.[17]

Not so pleasant to Johnston was a signed statement by three St. George leaders stating their unwillingness to join the sealing crew without a raise in pay. They also were not in favor of taking women and children to the Pribilofs until the war was over. Although St. George women were anxious to leave Funter Bay, they were more concerned about safety. Better that some die in Southeast than all be killed at St. George. A skeptical Johnston attributed this new activism to "outside influences." He charged that "99 out of every 100 people . . . say how foolish it is to send them back at this time." Talk like this "has the result of stirring up the natives."[18]

After Johnston received the written request for more pay for Aleuts, Chief Bower in Chicago extricated him from the question of the return of St. George people by canceling the St. George resettlement. He said

PRIBILOF AND ALEUTIAN HOMECOMINGS 143

a sealing party could be dispatched for the spring season but would have to return to Funter Bay. Johnston was relieved. "From the standpoint of safety," he sighed, "I am glad the change was made." It was a dangerous situation, Johnston concluded. "If we had rehabilitated St. George and afterward a single bomb had been dropped there our whole course of action would have been open to criticism." Johnston said the cancellation also improved Aleut morale. "The men are going . . . in a much better state of mind now that they do not have to worry about their families. Johnston had also been attempting to form a work force to take fox skins, and he intended for this group to stay on at St. George after the seal hunt was finished.[19]

Although the sealing operation appeared diversionary, it directly affected resettlement a year later and life at Funter Bay in the interval. Sealing in an active combat zone was indication to some that government policy was primarily driven by economics. But for Pribilovians, it was the first return home, albeit for only an interlude, and an intensely emotional experience. When the sealing crew was ready to depart on May 6, 1943, they boarded the *Delarof.* This ghostlike ship had carried them in evacuation. "As we drew away from the dock," a non-Aleut remembered, "a choir of native voices began a farewell chant in Russian which was answered by those remaining on shore. Many of the women were crying their farewells, never before having experienced a parting with their loved ones."[20]

When they approached St. Paul Island on May 15, Aleuts stood in awe. "They doffed their hats" and sang praises of thanks to the Lord.[21] For the St. Paul sealers, this island was home.

As the sealing progressed, the government's fur-seal industry began churning out Treasury revenue for the first time since the war began. Treasury revenue, however, was not given as justification for taking Aleuts back for the seal harvest. Fish and Wildlife Service personnel instead stressed defense needs. "In all discussions of the Pribilof operations with our critics," offered one of them, "we have placed particular stress upon the production of oil, meal and glycerin bearing fats by the by-products plants there." Asian sources of these commodities had been cut off, so we "must utilize to the utmost every source of these vital war necessities." The crew tackled its assignment with gusto. For the first time, moreover, the United States military participated in sealing. Among the sealers were 180 enlisted men, twelve of whom were Aleuts. The other 116 sealers were experienced Aleuts from Southeast camps. The Aleuts were paid more than ever for each skin processed, as a result of earlier demands by St. George and St. Paul leaders. The sealers produced a record harvest, "the largest number of skins taken under controlled conditions in the history of the islands."[22]

This was done, however, at great cost to those remaining at Funter Bay. Deprived of labor and leadership for nearly six months, they endured worsening conditions. It had been assumed all along that the St. George people would be sent back to their island. When Bower reversed that, "the sudden change of plans," wrote the storekeeper, "threw us a bit out of kilter." Supplies had been laid up only for the St. Paul people at the cannery. Since the St. George group had not gone, there now was a critical need for food. So depressed was Ira Gabrielson by his visit to Funter Bay in the late summer of 1943, he initiated moves to evacuate. "Checked Funter Bay situation," he announced in a telegram, "and under conditions it is desirable" to "make arrangements return natives to Pribilofs this fall."[23]

Goaded into action by Gabrielson's recommendation, Fish and Wildlife Service officials in Chicago and Seattle set out to make Gabrielson's desire a reality. Hoping the military would not stand in the way, officials consulted with General Buckner. "It seems likely that favorable action will result," predicted Charles Jackson, Gabrielson's assistant director. General Whittaker of Buckner's Alaska Defense Command received a number of inquiries about resettling the Pribilof Islands. He contacted Governor Gruening for answers. The Governor responded that arrangements would be "handled directly from Chicago." If, as it appeared, the military had given the green light, Whittaker wanted to know which person on St. Paul would sign for supplies.[24] Resettlement again appeared definite.

Johnston's assistant, Frederich Morton, wrote to Chief Bower on September 14 "that action has already been started to return the St. Paul group on the island, as well as the St. George personnel." Plans, he said, "are working out nicely." Supplies were ordered and the *Penguin* was already underway toward Funter Bay. Only one puzzle remained. "It is difficult to complete rehabilitation plans," Morton judged, "without knowing conditions on the Pribilofs." Johnston, who was there with the sealing crew, "would be of valuable help in bringing these plans to a successful conclusion."[25]

Unbeknownst to Assistant Morton, however, Superintendent Johnston had left St. Paul Island, feeling that resettlement was impossible for the fall of 1943. After Johnston left, Aleuts in the sealing crew became "very dissatisfied." Sealing was over. They missed their families. They refused additional work and demanded to know whether they were

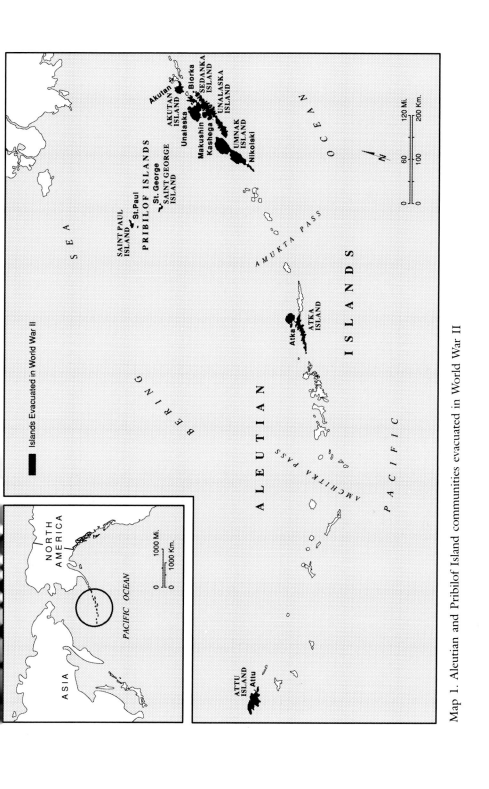

Map 1. Aleutian and Pribilof Island communities evacuated in World War II

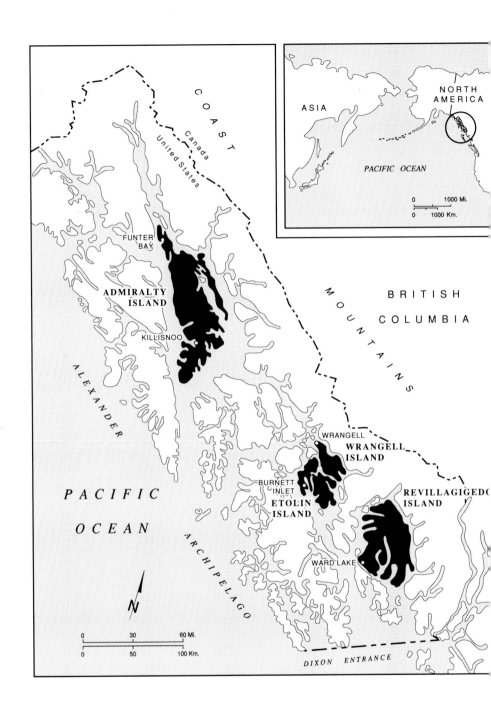

Map 2. Aleut evacuation sites in Southeast Alaska

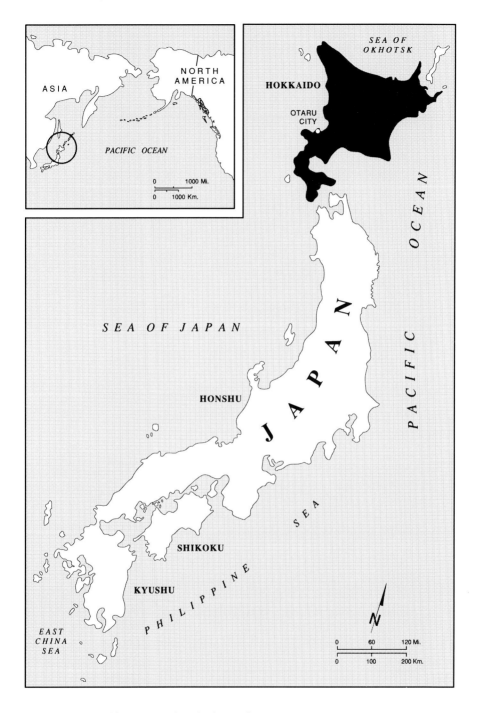

Map 3. Attu Aleut evacuation site in northern Japan

Abandoned Nikolski village in the winter of 1945. Ten Aleut communities were evacuated, and all of them looked similar to this. The church was the most prominent structure and stands out dramatically against houses and the landscape. (*National Archives, Still Picture Branch*)

Next 3 pages:
Shortly after Atka evacuees arrived at Killisnoo, they were visited by an artist, W. Langdon Kihn, whose hand-sketches of five Aleut faces appeared in *Natural History* (February 1943). These sketches are the only such pieces of art depicting Aleuts known to exist. They reveal a strong, proud people.

Larry and Periscovia Nevzoroff, husband and wife. Periscovia, sixty-five, moved from her birthplace on Unalaska to Atka, her husband's home island. Larry, seventy-two, was skilled in boat construction, trapping, and making fish nets and hooks.

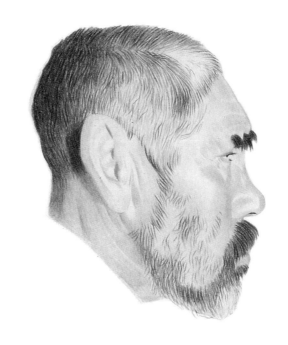

(Above) Mary Snigaroff, forty-two, was known for her weaving of extremely fine Atka grasses into beautiful small baskets famous for their minute detail. Born on Attu, Mary was the aunt of Alice Snigaroff Petrivelli, another Atka evacuee, now president of the Aleut Corporation.

(Top left) Mike Mercheenen, seventy-two, was a bachelor whose prowess as a hunter was tested before evacuation when he was stranded and survived for three months by living off hand-caught seals.

(Bottom left) Nick Prokopeuff was a lay Orthodox priest from Atka serving his people and those on Attu Island. He was fluent in Russian and was sixty-nine years old at this sketching.

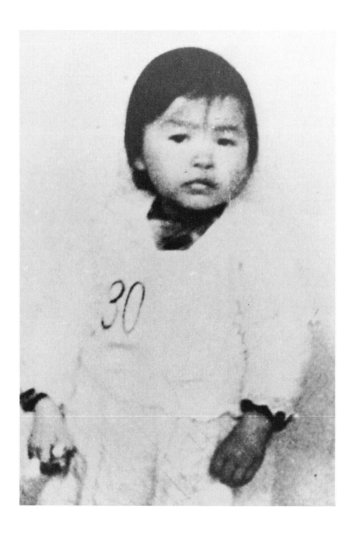

Elizabeth Golodoff of Attu was about eighteen months old when this photograph was taken by a Japanese captor at Otaru city. An identification number is visible on her blouse. She was one of seven Golodoff children evacuated to Japan. Her father, Laurenti, died of tuberculosis there and three of the Golodoff children died of beri-beri. (*Alaska State Historical Library, Goforth Collection, courtesy J. Penelope Goforth*)

The Civilian Conservation Corps camp near Ward Lake, about eight miles from Ketchikan, was physically the most attractive of the Southeast evacuation sites. Yet Aleuts were crowded there in unhealthy conditions and found the thick surrounding forest oppressive. (*U.S. Forest Service, Ketchikan*)

These dwellings at Funter Bay were photographed after Aleuts had been returned to the Pribilof Islands and the buildings cleaned up. The board walkways still appear hazardous and were doubly so when iced over in winter. Nearly five hundred Privilovians were crowded into buildings like these. Other campsites in Southeast Alaska were similar. (*National Archives*)

The front of Wrangell Institute with army tents pitched on the grounds as temporary shelters for Aleuts from Akutan, Biorka, Kashega, Makushin, Nikolski, and Unalaska. Some of the evacuees lived in these crowded makeshift accommodations for more than five weeks. (*National Archives, Still Picture Branch*)

Eva Borenin stands next to her mother, also named Eva, in the doorway of an army tent on the grounds of Wrangell Institute. The daughter was fifteen, the mother fifty-five. They were evacuated from the smallest Aleut village, Makushin, with only eight Aleuts in residence. (*National Archives, Still Picture Branch*)

Mark Pettikoff, fifty-one-year-old leader of Akutan's Aleuts, with his wife Sophie, forty-four, and daughter Irene, two, in the entrance of their tent at Wrangell Institute. (*National Archives, Still Picture Branch*)

Lukenia Prokopeuff and her daughter Annie aboard the army transport ship
David S. Branch on their return to Atka in 1945. Annie was born during the
stay at Killisnoo. The soldier who took this photograph wrote that Lukenia
"appears sad at seeing the village almost entirely destroyed by fire." (*National
Archives, Still Picture Branch*)

Luke Shelikoff, in his army uniform, poses with a relative, Mike Shelikoff, in 1946. They are standing in front of Polly McGlashen's house at Akutan. Luke was an evacuee who left the Ward Lake camp for military service. Aleut loyalty and patriotism were never questioned. Twenty-five served in the military during World War II. The largest group of these were from St. George. Three Aleuts saw action in the battle of Attu and were awarded bronze stars. (*Alaska State Historical Library, Goforth Collection, courtesy J. Penelope Goforth*)

George Borenin (left), fifty, and Cornelius Kudrin, forty-nine, in August 1948. Both were from Kashega, where Borenin had been the community's leader. Although their village was not resettled, they appear happy to be back in the Aleutians. They represent Aleut optimism and an indomitable spirit. (*Alaska State Historical Library, Catron Collection*)

going back to Funter Bay or whether their families were coming home. Agent McMillin, left in charge at St. Paul, called them "mutineers." He wired Morton with disconcerting news. St. Paul household goods had been seriously depleted by military personnel. There was "no furniture or cook stoves here for native families, and natives say they refuse to remain under these conditions." McMillin wired that "St. Paul rehabilitation impossible this Fall. Supplies now on hand will last only to end of October." Frightened by the prospect of being abandoned himself, McMillin requested that "unless assurance is forthcoming for sufficient winter supplies and proper help, including doctor, please furnish me transportation to Seattle and endeavor to get my wife to Seattle."[26]

Agent McMillin, however, had no real control over the resettlement question. He could only advise. But he feared being left in the isolated, unsupplied islands along with Aleuts. His superior, Johnston, had overseen harvest operations and then disappeared. McMillin thought returning any more Aleuts would be entirely foolhardy. Calling the proposed return of more Aleuts a kind of fantasy, he warned against hazardous "Bering Sea landings" of supplies, women, children, and the sick. So incensed was he over the prospect, he asked permission to contact Delegate Dimond. Without proper arrangements, he said, a return would bring "criminal charges."[27]

McMillin's warnings were taken seriously. Although headquarters still wanted the St. George people to go back, all plans for resettlement were abandoned. McMillin and the sealers were eventually returned to Funter Bay. Supplies slated for the islands were also diverted back to the camps. It was urged, again, that every effort be made to improve conditions there. Ira Gabrielson, explaining to Governor Gruening why the Pribilofs had not been resettled, blamed the lack of transportation and supplies. However, he said, the Service would now have more supplies for the upcoming winter at Funter Bay. Improvements would make "conditions far less crowded than they have been in the past." Based on his visit there, however, Gabrielson was skeptical: "What we will be able to do this winter is all too little, but it seems to be the best that is possible."[28]

Members of the sealing crew from St. Paul were the first to rejoin their families at Funter Bay. They arrived on October 11, 1943, and were followed on November 21 by the St. George sealers on the *Penguin*. The St. George group had been held up by measles and by dangerous winter seas. "Mr. Johnston's request for men to remain . . . for foxing operations" on St. George "was turned down—all of them wishing to return to their families."[29]

Sealers and government officials were informed that St. Paul village would need extensive repairs because of neglect and harsh military use. Any plan for return would have to include definite appropriations for repairs and supplies. Still, the likely prospect of return the next year reinforced in the minds of Fish and Wildlife personnel the notion that Funter Bay really was a temporary location. And rumors and talk of returning continued to stir Aleuts who were longing for home.

But they would have to spend nearly another year at Funter Bay. On his return, McMillin noticed that conditions had not improved. His wife was assisting Funter Bay nurse Beatrice Porter in the measles epidemic of 1943. There were three deaths in two weeks in October, and others were expected. McMillin realized the Service was "being very severely criticized" for lack of medical care and administrative incompetence. A month later an overworked nurse Porter suffered "a nervous breakdown." Chief Bower had "thought all along that the natives would go back to the Pribilofs this fall." Consequently, not much had been done to improve conditions in the camps.

In November 1943, Superintendent Johnston wrote General Buckner to line up another seal pruning enterprise for the summer of 1944.[30] Johnston, apparently, was playing the odds. Should a return in 1944 be impossible, at least there would be another sealing expedition that year. But a resettlement would accomplish the same end. In December, therefore, Johnston opened negotiations with the Alaska Defense Command for the return. He asked General Buckner to form "a company of Alaska natives to be detailed to the Pribilof Islands for the sealing operations in 1944." He added that for the return of the St. Paul Aleuts "all native dwellings on St. Paul would have to be completely refurnished with stoves, bedding and other furniture." Johnston asked the army for repair funds, ordered supplies, and earmarked nearly $100,000 from the government budget to pay for resettlement.[31]

Unfortunately, Funter Bay still desperately needed attention. A consulting physician was sent, and emergency medical aid was arranged in response to four deaths in early December. Army Quonset huts had arrived, and six dwellings for Aleut families at the cannery site had been completed. The food distribution system was improved, and "the elevated walks . . . have been repaired and where frosty or icy walks were dangerous they have been covered with wire mesh."[32] When an earlier departure was anticipated, these improvements had been forestalled. Now they were being completed, in spite of the belief that in only three months the camps at Funter Bay would be abandoned.

In a parting shot, Ruth Gruber, Department of the Interior field representative, reported to Secretary Ickes early in 1944 about Funter

Bay's "vitiated and unwholesome atmosphere." It had made the physician, Dr. Smith, "a disillusioned, broken man" and caused him to resign after less than a year's service at the camps. Dr. Smith "had been refused even the most common medical facilities; he had never had less cooperation from other Government employees; he had never felt so hopeless about the careless treatment of our Alaskan natives." Then the nurse resigned, and "the school teachers of St. Paul Village, feeling utterly frustrated, resigned." Funter Bay's conditions the past winter, Gruber charged, "were scandalous."[33] It definitely was time to leave.

No Aleuts were happier to leave than the children at Wrangell Institute. Separated from their families, they waited and waited in April to rejoin them at Funter Bay and then return home. Would that a dried seal gut or friendly murre could magically carry them back! The school reverberated with anticipation. Rumor circulated that the *Penguin* would pick them up. They believed departure was just ahead. "When is the *Penguin* coming? Is the *Penguin* coming today?"[34] This refrain became a wish, as if the repetition would hasten its arrival.

Before the *Penguin* did come, the children were treated to a picnic at The Point, a rustic site four miles from Wrangell on Zimovia Strait. It was a beautiful sunny day. "Everyone sang gaily—the Aleuts have a musical ear and sweet voices," wrote a participant. The next day, April 26, "eager eyes" spotted a small dot on the water's horizon. A joyful cry went up: "The *Penguin* is coming! The *Penguin* is coming!" Immediately, the pier was filled with Aleut children "carrying the suitcases that had been packed for days." They left in the middle of the night for Funter Bay, the first step in a long journey home.[35]

They arrived to greet their parents on April 28, a homecoming of sorts before the real one. Everything was in readiness. Government officials had arranged for health examinations upon arrival on the Pribilofs by "two prominent medical specialists and an equally competent dental surgeon."[36]

Their Pribilof priest, Father Makary Baranoff, noted that evacuation had scattered his people into many different places. But, he predicted, "we are all going back" to the Pribilofs "some day." This diaspora would eventually end. Though not all Pribilovians returned in 1944, those who did boarded the army transport ship *William L. Thompson* on April 30. Forty-four Aleut sealers from Burnett Inlet, Killisnoo, and Ward Lake were also taken aboard. The Pribilof-bound transport left Funter Bay on May 4, a day of Aleut deliverance.[37]

The ship stopped at Dutch Harbor and then anchored on May 13 at Village Cove, St. Paul Island. Advance crews were landed on both islands to prepare the dwellings after military occupancy and, except for the sealing crew, nearly two years of Aleut absence.[38]

What they found in their communities was not entirely unexpected because sealers had spread the word. But its impact could hardly have been felt until it stood before their eyes. St. Paul needed considerable refurbishing. St. George needed somewhat less. The same tasks of cleanup and repair they had encountered at Funter Bay faced them at home. More than eight hundred soldiers had been quartered at St. Paul. It was "found in very poor shape—all dwellings . . . left dirty and altered; furnaces, radiators and pipes broken . . . no water system . . . lights off . . . broken lines." St. George, however, "was found to be in good order. . . . Apparently nobody had visited the island all winter."[39]

As stewards of the government's seal industry, Fish and Wildlife Service personnel, with the help of Aleuts, set about to ready the plants for the summer seal harvest. First, though, "every cottage for white employees and bunkhouses required repairs." They completed that by May 28, and readied the sealing facilities damaged by winter weather. All summer, water from a nearby lake was hauled by truck.[40] The extra effort on both islands was worth the cost. Aleuts were home, reconstruction was underway, and sealing revenue would soon embellish the federal Treasury.

Less attention by officials, however, was devoted to Aleut losses. Most mattresses, furniture, and utensils were missing, especially at St. Paul. Although these could be replaced, personal possessions that had fallen into the hands of soldiers could not. Some of it was stolen, some simply used up. One military radio operator, apparently on St. Paul for thirteen months, remarked that "there was no life on the island when we landed." Soon, however, he discovered signs of former life in one Aleut "shack": a "half-fried egg . . . and a half cup of coffee." He spied a phonograph and records. Bedding down in the Aleut house with his musical find, the soldier became extremely popular. Other soldiers visited regularly. Record playing became "the favorite source of recreation. Playing cards and gambling were next." He admitted, "we played the records over so much, we practically wore them out." Most often played was Ella Fitzgerald's "It Ain't What You Do—It's the Way You Do It."[41]

The condition of their homes and the loss of their property grieved the startled Pribilovians. Decades afterward they remembered vividly. Mary Bourdukofsky from St. Paul reported that "all our furniture and personal belongings were gone." Her family's house had been converted "into a gambling club. . . . The walls were full of dart point holes," and hundreds of cigarette burns were etched into the rug and linoleum. The house of Heratina Krukoff's grandparents also stood empty, their family possessions lost. The military "had used the house for a mess hall." One Aleut attempted some humor to lighten her testimony. "When I got home," she recalled, "my house was just bare, everything was gone. All I found in my cupboard was a man's shorts big enough to fit a giant." Natalie Misikian remembered: "My mom cried, oh, where's my furniture and everything. . . . I was worried about my Shirley Temple doll. . . . I started crying. . . . We didn't have anything."[42]

Anne McGlashen of St. George said, "What hurt most" was that "our artifacts were broken" and "our gold and silver Icons" were stolen. Anatoly Lekanof, Jr., recounted having to throw away mildewed clothing and use "scratched up" furniture. His house had been converted into a military "day-room" because it held a piano. The Lekanofs lost musical instruments, "Holy Icons . . . all the radios, fishing gear and hunting guns." Also, his father's chickens and two pigs were gone. Another reported that "all wooden dories and outboard engines . . . were either missing or no longer seaworthy." It was a serious setback. William Shane declared that Aleuts had to "start all over again," and this was difficult because they had scant resources—only what they had managed to save in evacuation packed in one suitcase per person and "little money."[43]

Much that was lost could not be assigned a monetary value. In addition, Michael Lestenkof of St. George smarted over the methods used by the military to clean up before pulling out. They burned many Aleut possessions, some in the garbage dump. On the side of his porch, Lestenkof found half-buried in dirt and ashes articles that had belonged to his wife. He discovered the remnants of an item that had been especially treasured by her: a pincushion dresser doll he had given her for Christmas. He was never able to fathom why the military had insulted him this way, why they could not have thrown the pincushion doll away instead of burning it next to his porch.[44]

Such disappointments aside, Pribilof Aleuts were home to put together a new life. Just being there energized them for the tasks ahead. Paul Merculief symbolized the restored vitality they felt on return to St. George. "It was toward evening," he remembered, "and I was like a young antelope prancing around the village because of the grass, the green and wide open spaces that we did not have at Funter Bay." Although Anatoly Lekanof, having to make another adjustment, thought the island seemed "bald" with "no branches, no trees," it was still wonderful. He said "it was a happy time, coming back home again."[45]

The same feeling lay ahead for other Aleuts left behind in Southeast camps. Their chances of return to the chain improved with the retaking of Attu and Kiska in the summer of 1943. This ending of the Aleutian campaign, the only military engagement on American soil in the war, cost some three thousand Japanese, American, and Canadian lives. But it erased all danger and heralded resumption of normal life in the area. For Aleuts still remaining in Southeast, return in 1944 seemed assured. Alaska Indian Service personnel, burdened by costs, wanted to abandon the camps, and evacuees were enlivened by this prospect. They looked forward to a 1944 return. Why should they not follow on the heels of the Pribilovians?

Unfortunately for the evacuees from Akutan, Atka, Biorka, Kashega, Makushin, Nikolski, and Unalaska city, they had no profitable industry that could bring revenue to the government. The urgency that had driven the Pribilof resettlement, a seal harvest, was missing when return of Aleuts in Southeast was considered. There were different forces at work. As a result, their homecoming did not take place until almost a year after that of the Pribilovians.

Adverse publicity about the camps in Southeast had in fact turned officials to consider seriously their abandonment as soon as possible. Furthermore, evacuees were a financial burden on the Alaska Indian Service. The policy of self-sufficiency had been a failure and costs were mounting. As early as April 1943, the Department of the Interior was eager to put an end to financial outlays for evacuation. In its fiscal 1944 planning, the estimated cost for camp food was approximately ten thousand dollars per month.[46] When Aleuts could return to subsistence living, this outlay would be greatly reduced.

The question of resettlement, then, was predicated on financial considerations. In October 1943, Benjamin W. Thoron, director of the Division of Territories and Island Possessions, told Superintendent Claude Hirst that evacuation funds would be used up by July 1, 1944. Hirst thought the Aleuts were not likely to be returned by that time. A budgetary crisis, Hirst felt, could not be avoided, with expenses at the camps, even with Funter Bay people returned, now estimated at $4,500 per month. He recommended that planning be started for the return of Aleuts in Southeast camps, except perhaps for Aleuts from Unalaska and Atka. War Department officials, he suggested, should be contacted immediately for permission to go forward.[47]

Assistant Commissioner of Indian Affairs William Zimmerman in Chicago was supposed to coordinate the move. He agreed with Hirst that running out of funds would result in serious difficulties. He admitted, however, "I am not sure how to proceed about the Aleutian Evacuees." The Division of Territories, the War Department, and the Alaska Defense Command would have to be involved. Zimmerman asked

Hirst if he had broached the subject with the army. In the meantime, Director Benjamin W. Thoron of the Division of Territories pushed the issue by informing Assistant Secretary of the Interior Oscar L. Chapman that $200,000 for evacuation had been spent and "$60,000 additional will be required . . . between now and July 1, 1944." Thoron said the secretary's office should request additional funds to resettle all evacuated Aleuts. Chapman, however, had another idea in mind. He suggested to Commissioner John Collier that the navy be asked "to assume responsibility of transporting these people back to their homes."[48] That seemed logical to him because the navy had been responsible for their evacuation.

Thus, the Department of the Interior was caught in another squeeze. Whether officials kept the camps going or attempted to return the Aleuts, they needed additional funds. In Director Thoron's letter to Chapman, he pointed out that emergency funding had been designated as "Civilian Food Reserve Funds." These monies and the cost of navy evacuations were not expenses charged, he claimed, to the Department of the Interior. Contacted about this, Assistant Commissioner Zimmerman mistakenly thought that the food reserve revenues that had been used in evacuation were still available to be used for the return. Zimmerman pointed out to Thoron, however, that the navy had refused to pay $23,241.91 for Alaska Steamship Company transportation of Aleuts to Wrangell.[49] They might also refuse to pay for their return.

Responding to this dilemma, Department of the Interior officials initiated discussions with the military. In November 1943, Secretary Ickes wrote to Secretary of War Stimson. He desired the return of all Aleuts and asked whether funding would be available from the War Department. Stimson stated that when "the military situation permits," Aleuts would be returned. His War Department would fund the return and restoration of Aleut homes except for Atka, which was "a Navy responsibility."[50] On the eve of a new year, 1944, a glimmer dawned. All Aleuts might soon be back home.

Stimson's response indicated that the decision to return the Aleuts had been made by the military. Planning for the move began. Details would have to be worked out between military and government officials, so Zimmerman sent to the Juneau headquarters copies of the Stimson letter. The army would arrange transportation and repairs when the Alaska Indian Service informed them of the number of Aleuts and the costs involved. Superintendent Hirst wired the deputy commander of the Alaska Defense Command in January 1944, informing him of the approximate number to be resettled, including "six teachers and school equipment." He also volunteered to assist in the reorganization of the villages. He could not, however, send any estimate of repair costs since department personnel were not aware of local conditions. Hirst coolly reminded the deputy commander that Aleut property had been a military responsibility.[51]

So far, no serious difficulties had emerged. Everybody at this stage wanted the return to happen—and soon. The camps had too many disabilities. Assistant Superintendent Fred Geeslin reported to Zimmerman in February that needed repairs to the Ward Lake Camp had not been made "and the new septic tank toilet had not been constructed." The culprit had been "shortage of labor." Moving would be the right solution. To Geeslin, all that had to be done was to make arrangements with General Buckner's command. Only one dark spot appeared on the horizon. In a conversation with Harry Wilson of Unalaska city, Geeslin learned that Caucasian citizens there were opposed to the return of Aleuts. The houses in which the Aleuts had lived "had been broken into several times and the contents pilfered." Residents knew about this and wondered where exactly the returning Aleuts would be housed and how their lost property would be restored. Geeslin said he thought Indian Service personnel had compiled inventories of Aleut personal belongings at the time of evacuation, which would "aid in establishing claims for their rehabilitation."[52] There should be no problems when Aleuts returned, Geeslin believed.

At this crucial time, Commissioner John Collier removed Claude Hirst as general superintendent. Beginning in 1944, Geeslin became acting superintendent until Hirst's replacement, Don C. Foster, arrived. Hirst was cashiered at least in part for "fishing activities" and not attending to duties in his office. Secretary Ickes felt Hirst left Alaska "in very bad shape." Collier wanted more effective leadership and a better staff in the Alaska office. "I believe," he wrote to Ickes, "that Mr. Hirst's immediate staff have acquired some of Mr. Hirst's indolent attitudes."[53]

Acting Superintendent Geeslin immediately picked up on plans for the return. He wrote to General Buckner at the end of February for details and asked for Buckner's opinion on sending Aleuts back to Unalaska city. "There is a question in our minds regarding the advisability" of moving Aleuts there at this time, he admitted, no doubt referring to the protests put up by Caucasian residents. But "these people will be more anxious to return when they learn of others being returned," he contended. There was no question about the desirability of evacuating Aleuts from Ward Lake. Planning should be undertaken immediately, although there were reports of damage to Aleut houses and Indian

Service buildings at Akutan, too. The Ward Lake group, Geeslin recommended, should be "returned in May or early June to permit them to get settled during the summer months."[54]

Cooperation and aid were forthcoming from the navy. Acting Navy Secretary James Forrestal wrote to Ickes on April 7 that the navy took responsibility for rehabilitation of both Atka and Akutan and would pay for it. Akutan, he said, "is now ready for occupancy, while about five more houses will be required at Atka for which the necessary construction material is available." The people returning to these communities would need "cooking utensils, bedding, and trapping equipment. Fox farming conditions remain unchanged, and reindeer on the western portion of the island have been unmolested." Forrestal stated that the area commander would arrange and pay for transportation if Interior Department efforts to obtain it failed.[55]

But soon after this navy offer, planning was temporarily frozen solid by the Alaska Indian Service. The glacial chill came from newly appointed General Superintendent Don Foster, who wired to Zimmerman, "Please delay further action." He wanted time to assess the Aleutian situation and send Zimmerman a realistic recommendation. Foster had doubts about a return in 1944 because military servicemen still on the islands would cause "social problems." He also claimed "inability to obtain teachers who should accompany" Aleuts. Furthermore, a survey of village conditions and needs had not yet been completed. Another factor, Foster claimed, was opposition from the commander of the Seventeenth Naval District, in spite of Acting Naval Secretary Forrestal's support.[56]

Secretary of the Navy Frank Knox earlier had ordered the commander of the North Pacific Force to proceed with Aleut return. Now Knox informed Secretary Ickes that Juneau Indian Service officials were unwilling to move ahead, claiming a schoolteacher shortage. Indian Service officials also wanted to avoid "intermingling," a code word for sexual encounters between Aleut women and military personnel. Knox mentioned another drawback that concerned the newly-appointed Foster: "the difficulty in supplying the villages." According to Secretary Knox, the Indian Service, rather than returning all Aleuts, would instead move those at Ward Lake to Funter Bay when the Pribilovians were gone.[57]

This was shocking news to Zimmerman, who wired his reaction to Foster. "Our view here," he notified Foster, is that "evacuees should be returned" at the "earliest practicable date." The move from Ward Lake to Funter Bay he called "wholly unnecessary." Foster's inability to obtain schoolteachers should not be a factor. "Many villages will be without teachers." Such stalling by his Alaska staff, given Ickes's desire and the concurrence of the military, Zimmerman felt was "embarassing."[58]

Zimmerman could be very direct when he wanted to be. He insisted the return be completed in 1944. Foster knew that Aleutian villages had been badly damaged. He told Zimmerman that a recently completed report of village conditions "beggars imagination." Foster realized, however, that camp conditions were equally bad. He appeared to back down, saying "that it is a wise thing to return them." Natives from Ward Lake who were exposed to the social conditions at Ketchikan—he ironically called them "something terrific"—would be helped immensely if returned. Conditions at Unalaska, with servicemen abounding, could not be worse than at Ketchikan, with "hordes of outside fishermen swarming all over the place." But Foster expressed doubt that General Buckner would actually be helpful. So far, "he has shown no disposition to assume responsibility for securing funds." Foster was not eager to move without promise of funding, and he saw many difficulties ahead: "If we are to get these people returned . . . by August and not later than September, it is certainly going to take some rapid action by all of us."[59]

It seemed that the plans for returning the Aleuts would move ahead. Governor Gruening gave his blessing. Geeslin, however, who in a turnabout now shared Foster's doubts, blamed delay in planning for return on the military's misconstruing of the Indian Service's position. Foster continued to have serious misgivings. He insisted military presence on the islands along with the Aleuts would bring "nothing but human misery and social results that will be a headache to the service for sometime to come." He needed more personnel, including teachers, to protect Aleut interests when they arrived back home. "This is particularly true at Unalaska," Foster argued. In spite of Foster's protests, however, the higher-ups in the Interior Department and in the army and navy arranged the resettlement for May. Foster reluctantly, prepared a draft agreement between the parties, spelling out responsibilities. In July, Stimson, Forrestal, and Ickes signed the agreement. Steps were taken for a special U.S. Treasury appropriation. On August 7, 1944, President Roosevelt allocated for resettlement $200,000 from the "Emergency Fund for the President, National Defense, 1942–1945."[60]

Throughout the summer, funding had been one, though not the only, concern of Foster and Geeslin. Geeslin had opposed making any move without seeing army and navy money flowing into the Juneau office.

He advised against "any commitments against our current appropriations for the rehabilitation of these people." If they were to be moved, Geeslin's schedule demanded that "funds . . . be made available *not later than June 30* to insure the return of these people by the latter part of August or the first part of September." Foster and Geeslin asked for a commitment by the military "in writing" that the Indian Service would be reimbursed for resettlement expenses. Foster and Geeslin felt trapped between having no assurance of military funding and being pressured by the Interior Department to complete the job. In a memorandum to Ickes in July, John Collier insisted that "we need to act promptly in order to effect resettlement of the natives this summer." By July 20, the Department of Interior had in hand a military agreement for funding. The "last hurdle" had been cleared.[61] Would this and President Roosevelt's allocation be timely enough?

No, they would not. On September 2, Foster telegraphed Zimmerman recommending that the return be cancelled. He now claimed that Aleutian weather in the fall hampered transportation. Also, the cost of construction "during winter months will be increased not less than 50%." Furthermore, Foster had been unable to obtain supplies and arrange shipping. Military lists of supplies had not been available until August 31. Foster urgently recommended that the return be postponed until March, 1945. He argued that this would "permit ample time for purchase and assembling supplies and equipment." Four days later, Paul Fickinger, temporarily acting as commissioner of Indian affairs, wrote to Zimmerman that Foster reported "considerable feeling and some protests from the Aleutian groups that they should not be returned . . . before next Spring," because "in the winter . . . it would probably not be possible to complete the necessary shelters." Fickinger felt this Aleut "protest" had "considerable merit." Even though the money was now available, Foster should be heeded. On this office memorandum, Zimmerman finally caved in and wrote the death warrant to Aleutian Chain resettlement in 1944: "It is now agreed that Aleuts will not be moved until Spring."[62]

In letters by Geeslin to military officers announcing the cancellation, he blamed the tardy receipt of funds and Aleut unwillingness to return late in the season.[63] But the Alaska Indian Service was responsible for allowing time to run out. Foster, as a new general superintendent, was reluctant to take on this difficult task of resettlement. Assistant Geeslin, perhaps influenced by Foster's arguments, also resisted the move. They harbored considerable skepticism about the military paying for resettlement. They argued that Aleuts and servicemen would cause problems if living in close proximity. They claimed lack of teachers and difficulty of supply. When headquarters refused to accept this rationale, they then demanded specific proof of military and governmental funding. Finally, they claimed that Aleuts did not want to return in the fall.

To the contrary, the sentiment of Martha Newell at Burnett Inlet in 1943 reflected typical Aleut feelings about return: "If I am able to go back I'll walk the ocean." Ward Lake Aleuts were especially disappointed when they did not follow the Pribilovians in 1944. Their teacher, Pauline Whitfield, had been quoted in Ketchikan's newspaper predicting that the return to the Pribilofs would be "the first move toward breaking up the Ward Lake" camp. They could expect to be home in May 1944. The newspaper also had printed an announcement by Foster that a construction foreman had been placed "in charge of rebuilding homes damaged by Jap attacks and Jap occupation, and general repair to structures."[64] Such rebuilding had not come to pass, but hopes were raised to new levels as 1945 approached.

"I surely will be glad to get back," Mark Pettikoff, the Akutan leader, said in an understatement. Most Aleuts at Ward Lake shared his sentiments, but those who were told they would not be resettled at their home villages felt a keen loss. An article in the Ketchikan newspaper in January 1945 mentioned that only Akutan and Nikolski would be reoccupied, leaving Biorka, Kashega, and Makushin abandoned.[65]

In 1945 the return actually got under way. Fred Geeslin assigned Virgil Farrell, Alaska Indian Service director of education, to be liaison to the Alaska Defense Command. The Army would send transportation between April 1 and April 10, 1945, to start from Ketchikan. Having delayed departure for nearly a year, Geeslin now apologetically explained that Indian Service planning had "been seriously handicapped" by the accidental death of its resettlement officer on August 13, 1944. "To date we have not been able to locate a person to fill this position due to the shortage of manpower." He said the military seemed cooperative. Supplies had been ordered, but not all of them could be obtained. Aleuts would have to "pack their belongings and household equipment including Indian Service supplies" and assemble for the journey. Lighterage to a ship at Burnett Inlet and Killisnoo would have to be arranged. Those at Ward Lake needed transportation to the Ketchikan dock. The whole operation was a demanding assignment, Geeslin complained.[66]

By the end of February, however, planning supposedly was complete. An Indian Service resettlement officer, Harley W. Covalt, would join a construction superintendent whose biggest task would be to rebuild the burned-out village of Atka. Schoolteachers were lined up to teach and to represent the Indian Service at the four communities of Akutan,

Atka, Nikolski, and Unalaska. The move would involve approximately 360 Aleuts, for "from casual surveys few of the Aleuts want to stay in Southeastern Alaska."[67]

The movement of Aleuts into the Aleutian zone, which was still restricted, required photographing, fingerprinting, and issuing travel permits complying with military regulations. Two Army servicemen completed this task in March, proceeding from Ward Lake to Burnett Inlet and Killisnoo. Aleuts thought these procedures strange. What complexities were involved in simply returning to their ancestral homes! At least, however, the Aleuts at Ward Lake were packed and ready to go. The camp was dismantled and the used lumber was given to Tlingit Natives at Saxman village near Ketchikan.[68]

The day of their departure, April 15, 1945, was—as if providence had planned it—Easter, the holiest day in their religious calendar. Aleuts held a worship service the night before, consoled by the knowledge that the next Easter celebration would be held at home and the Ward Lake camp would be only be a sad memory.[69]

Taken to the dock by the Coast Guard, 138 Aleuts left Ketchikan on the army transport ship *David S. Branch,* bound for Burnett Inlet, where on the next day 135 Unalaska city people boarded. Their last Southeast Alaska stop was at Killisnoo to pick up 77 Atka people. The ship did not tarry. The last were loaded aboard on April 17, and the ship headed for the Aleutians. Geeslin admitted that the "old people and the middle-aged people were very anxious to return."[70]

Akutan was the first stop. On April 21, thirty-five former villagers disembarked there to begin life anew. Twenty-one Aleuts from Biorka and eighteen from Kashega were settled with them. As the *Branch* approached the island, Aleuts smiled with excitement. Their church was the first building they saw, and everyone aboard was "animated." All "were glad to be back! There just wasn't any doubt about it," wrote their teacher. Yet homecoming was bittersweet. Although they were happy to be home, they were saddened by what they found there. Luke Shelikoff observed that his house looked untouched on the outside; seeing the inside, however, he "almost cried." It looked like "a chicken house, dirty . . . leaking all over, wall paper . . . down on the floor . . . my door busted." Guns left to him by his father and godfather had been stolen. Outboard motors were missing; his dory and skiff were gone.[71]

Others observed similar destruction and experienced similar losses. Matrona Stepetin's house was "bare," doors and windows broken. There were "no beds, nothing, no pots, pans or anything like that." George McGlashen was overcome. "We were lost," he admitted.

"Things that we lost we will never get back." It was "terrible." For him, going home was something like going to Ward Lake, maybe "worse." As for Bill Tcheripanoff, his earlier premonition was now realized. It was a "sad experience" which "makes my heart want to cry," he said. "All our possessions were gone or destroyed."[72]

Apart from the ruinous forces of nature, navy personnel had lent their hands to the destruction. The process began as early as July 1942, when crews broke into buildings, stole, and "turned upside down the whole village." Four separate navy ships were named in reports that surfaced later. A navy report of June 11, 1943, documented that sailors at the naval fueling station used Aleut possessions. The report listed seventeen categories of items, ranging from radios to paint. The church was broken into and the altar cloth stolen, but it was later returned. Another navy report in May 1944 admitted to "vandalism" at the village but asserted it had "been repaired." Damage after the spring of 1944 was not.[73] It is impossible to reconcile Aleut testimony with resettlement officer Harley W. Covalt's report that Aleut dwellings were found in "very good condition," a judgment even navy reports contradicted.

Covalt arranged the landing at the Coast Guard dock about one and a half miles from the village. The Aleuts were then reloaded on a lighter Army scow that proceeded to the village. There, the navy provided Aleuts three hot meals a day at cost until they could unpack. Indian Service employees Mr. and Mrs. Henry W. Benedict, who had been their Ward Lake teachers, were in charge. The Benedicts hoped to open a Native store for supplies soon after resettling.[74]

By the time Fred Geeslin arrived for an inspection, Aleuts had used all of the available building materials. Geeslin, who previously had complained that difficulty in getting supplies was a huge obstacle in resettlement plans, now acquired more materials from Dutch Harbor in one short week. Also, contrary to navy reports, Geeslin claimed there had been "little looting." Yet he admitted that "much renovation was needed." The efforts of Aleuts in rebuilding their village, he thought, was commendable, especially since they labored "under very adverse circumstances."[75]

Years later, those circumstances were vividly remembered by Aleuts. They had been left virtually alone and unaided. Matrona Stepetin's husband repaired their house and chopped wood for the upcoming winter. Luke Shelikoff repaired his house and built a boathouse that had blown down in a storm while he was away serving in the army. Bill Tcheripanoff "gathered beachwood and scraps . . . to patch the roof" over his family of four. He worked until his hands bled. "We were desperate yet could not find help, which we badly needed after the return to Akutan."[76]

Having discharged the Akutans, the *Branch* next stopped at Unalaska city on Unalaska Island. On April 22, Unalaska's 135 people disembarked at Captain's Bay along with five from Makushin. They were then loaded on trucks some distance from the city, which was hidden by hills. They wanted the church to be their first view of home. As the trucks bore them away, they impatiently awaited the sight of the church and their houses. Instead of being taken to them, however, they were unloaded and herded into a fenced-off area to stay in army Quonset huts, with no explanation of why or for how long. "Nobody was satisfied," Phil Tutiakoff remembered, because "everybody wanted to go home." The problem, of course, was that their homes were not habitable. "They had been broken into and the weather got at them." Tutiakoff's family never did get their house back. It eventually fell to a bulldozer and was replaced by "a couple of cabanas."[77]

The Aleut section of Unalaska city was a shocking sight. Reports received at Burnett Inlet before departure had been true. "Windows were torn out," along with the doors at most of the houses. So much damage had been done that none of them was "fit to live in," having been "vandalized, ransacked." Lost were personal items like guns, boats, and motors.[78]

Before leaving camp, Unalaska Aleuts had mailed to authorities their concerns about the condition of their homes and property. Copies had gone to the governor's office and to General Buckner. Acting Governor Bob Bartlett had urged on their behalf that General Buckner authorize a survey of their property and, if the reports of uninhabitable conditions were accurate, explore what could be done about restoration. Prior to this, Geeslin had been assured by the commanding general of Fort Mears, Edgar B. Colladay, that all Aleut homes were being "guarded by a military police patrol." Deputy U.S. Marshall Verne Robinson also had indicated "that all reasonable protections are being furnished by Army authorities."[79]

Army authorities, however, failed to provide such security. At least part of the problem was the evacuation itself. Servicemen on military patrol duty who witnessed the evacuation on July 19, 1942, stated that only on the day before had Army Captain Hobart W. Copeland ordered Aleuts to board the evacuation ship, giving them less than twenty-four hours notice. They were "allowed to take with them only such belongings as they could carry, mainly clothing." Many valuables had to be left behind. "A detail from the Post went around later and nailed the doors shut and put slats over the windows. None of us recall having ever seen signs posted against trespassing."

Later, servicemen reported looting by all branches of the military stationed there or passing through. Unalaska city, with its stores, taverns, theater, and Native village was a "natural congregating place," alluring to off-duty military personnel. "Large numbers of men were in the area during the salmon run in Unalaska Creek in the autumn of 1942 and when Naval task forces visited . . . in the summer of 1943." When the army "conducted its cleanup of the village in June of 1943" to "remove rubbish and outbuildings . . . many houses were entered unofficially and souvenirs and other articles were taken." Probably "some of the furniture found in Army and Navy quarters," they thought, came from Aleut houses.[80]

Official damage reports verify the story told by these eyewitnesses. One, signed by General O. H. Longino and sent to General Buckner, documented the loss of more than keepsakes. "Typewriters, guns, radios" have been taken and "clothing, bedding, books and personal papers have been scattered about. Most of the icons are gone." It was "housebreaking, thievery and vandalism." Another survey party, accompanied by Verne Robinson, inspected "34 of the 38 native homes. All buildings were damaged due to lack of normal care and upkeep." Aleuts "were so hurriedly evacuated . . . they had no time to properly secure their homes, cover stove pipes and chimney to prevent rain from blowing in, to turn off water supply, or otherwise protect their homes." There was considerable "weather damage and damage by rats." Both "armed forces personnel and civilians alike have been responsible for . . . vandalism." Blackouts "increased the difficulties of adequately policing the area in which native homes are located."[81]

To Aleuts, this mess at home was as bad as, if not worse than, the one they had encountered on arrival at Burnett Inlet. Probably unbeknownst to them, however, the Alaska Indian Service now had President Roosevelt's "Emergency Fund" appropriation to ease the financial burden of correcting the problem. Whether in fact the funds were ever made available to the Aleuts is questionable. Resettlement officer Harley Covalt had visited Unalaska before the Aleuts returned. He had been assured by Foster that the non-Aleut residents there "will co-operate in every way possible in their rehabilitation." The army had already set aside Quonset huts and promised to furnish meals at cost to the Aleuts upon their arrival. The Alaska Indian Service school needed "cleaning, painting, and some minor repair." So did the hospital building. Superintendent Foster calculated that "most of the needed supplies, equipment, building materials . . . to do a reasonably good job" had been ordered on "eleven hundred separate purchase requistions." Although both Foster and Covalt felt the navy gave "assistance . . . grudgingly," Covalt should move ahead with rehabilitation. He would be in charge at Unalaska until teachers could be hired. Foster planned to pay fifty cents per hour to Aleuts working on reconstruction, with three-quarters of it "impounded to purchase their needed supplies for the next year."[82]

Fred Geeslin, the experienced Indian Service agent, soon appeared on his inspection tour. From army engineers at Unalaska, he obtained a panel truck for use in the repair and reconstruction. He had Aleuts dismantle ammunition storage buildings for lumber, siding, and roof sheathing. Geeslin remembered later that Unalaska Aleuts had been most concerned about their church and had asked if he could get cedar shingles for its reroofing and a large oil heater. Geeslin negotiated with the navy and got the requested materials. In appreciation, the Aleuts later presented him with "a framed, glass covered ALASKA COTTON picture."[83] Any question that this material for their church might be a violation of state-church separation was ignored. The long process of Unalaska reconstruction was now underway.

After Unalaska's people were dispatched, the *Branch* sailed to Chernofski Harbor on the eastern end of Unalaska Island. There the Nikolski people were transferred to a power-driven scow for the eighty-mile journey to their home on Umnak Island. The fifty-nine who returned were greeted by three Nikolski Aleuts already there working on the Aleutian Livestock Company ranch. During the war, two sheep-shearing expeditions had returned to Nikolski for summer labor. Three Aleuts in 1943 and 1944 resided there for stints of two and one-half months.[84] These were similar to the advance Pribilof sealing venture of 1943, except that sheep-shearing was a private enterprise.

Like the others, the Nikolski Aleuts were happy to be back but dismayed at the sight of their homes. "Doors were torn, windows broken." Many of their personal belongings were "scattered, lost, damaged." The insides of dwellings were starkly uninviting, dank, and messed with debris. Valuable items like Sergie Savoroff's stove and dory were gone. The Nikolski church windows were broken, and the interior was "deteriorated." Leonty Savoroff remembered that "what was left in the house was wet and the clothing unusable." Some tools and hunting equipment were missing or damaged, and his house needed many repairs. "The inside walls, ceiling and floor," he said, "were bad." One of the residents estimated that "it took at least a couple of years to get back to normal."[85]

Although Nikolski was more isolated than Unalska city, this isolation had not prevented military vandalism, which began soon after Aleuts were evacuated. It was reported by the military on October 5, 1942. Locked buildings were broken into and raided, action that naval weather station personnel living in the Indian Service school building either participated in or could not prevent. "Practically every house in the village had been broken into and contents of cupboards, closets, dresser drawers had been removed and thrown carelessly around the rooms," an investigation revealed. Aleut houses were left in "an upturned condition." The Native store was "torn up and the merchandise was spread around on the counters and floors." Sailors claimed that soldiers were responsible for the pillage. Whoever the vandals were, "it was apparent," the report concluded, "that members of the Armed Services were guilty of a deplorable offense."[86]

From time to time, several military units had used the village. A 1944 report claimed that "in most cases troops have been quartered in native houses." This led to "extensive pilfering and looting of private property . . . in the homes of the Nikolski natives." In April, three Aleut workmen and the foremen of the Aleutian Livestock Company verified that "pilfering and looting was extreme" and "very little usable personal property" remained. The army did nothing to replace damaged or stolen property.[87]

Resettlement officer Covalt had earlier discovered that Nikolski had many problems. "A majority of the houses," he judged, "are not in condition to be occupied." The school and store would have to be used for "temporary quarters." Yet the school building, now occupied by soldiers, "is in a run-down condition and needs a thorough cleaning and minor repairs." Superintendent Foster placed in charge of the resettlement Mr. and Mrs. Chaney O. Beebe, two Indian Service employees who had been at Killisnoo with Atka people and therefore were strangers to Nikolski's Aleuts. By Foster's admission, this was risky—"we have our fingers crossed," he said—because "they are Seventh-Day Adventists and take their religion quite seriously." This was bound to create tension, given Aleut devotion to a different religious tradition. Geeslin visited Nikolski but spent only three days there. During that time he witnessed a "Navy plane" fly an Aleut to Dutch Harbor "for medical attention."[88]

In spite of adversities, Nikolski people eventually pieced together a meaningful life. As in the other villages Geeslin visited, everyone, he said, was "pleased to be back home where they could fish and hunt reindeer." They would have to rebuild their homes and reestablish their successful cooperative store. They would be aided in this by government payment of twenty-five cents per hour for their labor. As they settled in, they wondered if they would be able to resume fox trapping on the islands assigned to them by the Fish and Wildlife Service. Before the war, it had been the base of their economy.[89] Now their equipment had been destroyed or pilfered. Having lost much in evacuation, they asked for and got very little in return.

The people of Atka village were the first to be evacuated and the last Southeast evacuees to be returned. Their experience was incomparable because they had seen their village burning on the dark night they had been taken away. They did not know how much of it might have escaped U.S. Navy torches or Japanese bombing. Perhaps their church had been spared. They left at night and returned at night. All of the seventy-seven Atkans would have cheered the sight of their church if it had greeted them the next day as the dawn rose over Nazan Bay.

They did not see it or much of anything else. It was as if their village had disappeared, although some buildings remained partially standing. The villagers had been happy to be back in Atka, but their Atka was no more. Quonset huts and a mess hall in a special military area one-quarter mile from the village were their lot until the village was rebuilt. Vera Snigaroff Nevzoroff was especially saddened because their church was destroyed. Her "house was an empty shell," and "there was nothing left of the community that was once there." The church and the monies to maintain it had been consumed by fire, and gone were "all of our personal belongings that were packed and ready to go before the evacuation." Alice Snigaroff Petrivelli testified to irreplaceable losses: "All the pictures of my mother and three brothers, who were deceased . . . our beautiful church, our icons, everything."[90]

When the U.S. Army transport ship *St. Mihiel* had unloaded troops at Atka village on September 16, 1942, Aleut dwellings not torched were occupied by the military. Navy personnel aboard the seaplane tender *Teal* landed at the end of the month and established a weather station. Both military branches used Aleut dwellings. William Dirks remembered returning to find his house stripped, except for "my bathtub and toilet," still marked with an "Officers Quarters" sign. An official report indicated that some Aleut houses were used for "medical detachment . . . offices, mess, kitchen, store rooms and quarters. Certain dwellings were dismantled for building material." Household furniture, untensils, tools, and other items "were used by the troops."[91] Contrary to the assertion that flames had destroyed Atka village, the military had taken much of it, along with Aleut possessions. The church was likely burned because it was the most prominent building, a beacon for Japanese attack.

Atka did not rise from this nothingness like a phoenix. Aleut labor, not magic, restored it. Before the Aleuts returned, Interior Department officials had decided that "rebuilding homes would have to be performed by the Atka men." Some Atkans had to live in partitioned Quonset huts, each family with only one room measuring sixteen by eighteen feet. "Such rooms would accommodate a family on an emergency basis," concluded a report. "Pit toilets would have to be built." Army labor and food would be available for only a few days to assist in unloading. Indian Service Construction Superintendent Glenn Green oversaw the restoration. He and his wife, a teacher, were in charge of the resettlement project. Supposedly, Aleuts were to be paid fifty cents per hour for labor, but they claim to have received only twenty-five cents an hour for an eight-hour day. It took about a year to finish Atka reconstruction.[92]

Following visits to the other reinhabited Aleut villages, Assistant Superintendent Fred Geeslin spent one week in Atka. Its reconstruction was undertaken, he said, "under . . . adverse circumstances." Although he never discussed it with Aleut leaders, he noticed caged red foxes on nearby Adak Island, which he assumed were to be released by the military to eradicate rats brought by transport ships. He reported this to the Fish and Wildlife Service, fearing that red fox would decimate blue fox, an important source of Aleut income. This was a real threat to the economy of the Atka community.[93]

Aleuts hastened reconstruction by working in the evenings and on weekends without pay. Homes completed were filled immediately by families living in Quonset huts. Renewal was slowed when construction materials already unloaded were sent to the Indian Service school at Mt. Edgecumbe, Alaska. Atka Aleuts built a church that resembled the one burned down, replete with an "onion dome and double cross."[94] This signaled that revival had begun and the community would eventually be restored to Aleut life.

Only one group now awaited a homecoming. Attu people were still incarcerated in Otaru. And even when they were freed, in the fall of 1945, their return to the Aleutians did not include seeing Attu again.

Prospects for their return remained dim until August 1945, when Tokyo agreed to Allied terms of surrender and United States military forces landed in Japan. Thereafter, developments for their release moved rapidly. The roof of their house was marked "P.W.," for prisoners of war, making it a target for American airlift supplies. Aleuts were visited by American and Japanese officials planning their release. When asked if they wanted to go home, they all said, "Yes, yes." Having been incarcerated and mistreated for so long, Mike Lokanin released some outrage by defiantly engaging in a fistfight with a zealous Japanese guard who attempted to restrict Aleut movements.[95]

American occupation troops entering Otaru on September 3 were a welcomed sight. Attu's people were told they would leave Japan in several weeks. Free at last to move about, they discovered in walks around Otaru "a church that looked like our own church at Attu" superintended by an elderly couple, immigrants from Russia, who could speak English. Other than a "little holy picture" smuggled in by Mike Lokanin, Aleuts had had no visual reminders of their Attu church until now. As if engaging in a preview of return to Attu, the Aleuts asked the couple if they could worship "again in a church like ours." They worshipped there twice before leaving Otaru.[96] On the evening before departure, they celebrated with one of their favorite Japanese guards, Officer Takeshiro Shikanai. A civilian had donated a generous volume of sake.[97] This party was an Aleut goodbye to three years of imprisonment.

In the early morning of September 17, twenty-five Attuans left their quarters through the windows, an act symbolizing their newly gained freedom. Dressed in clothes provided by Shikanai, they were loaded on a bus, accompanied by United States officials and a representative from the International Red Cross. Thus began the most difficult and round-about return in the evacuation story.

The first destination was Chitose, an air base approximately twenty miles south of Sapporo. They arrived there the first afternoon, but bad weather held up their scheduled airlift until September 20, when they departed at 2:05 P.M. for Atsugi air base between Tokyo and Yokohama. This was the first airplane flight for any of them. Authorities at Atsugi—the Aleuts remember this as Osaka—required them to change into new clothing. Their other garments were burned behind the air-plane hangar. Attu people were about to leave the country, with no fond memories. They flew from Japan at 8:00 A.M., September 21, 1945, their destination Okinawa Island in the East China Sea.[98]

They flew over the atomic-bombed ruins of Nagasaki, perhaps the first civilian group of Americans to see this devastation. It reminded Olean Prokopeuff of the American bombing of Otaru and their having to be evacuated for protection because of it. Nagasaki, she recalled, "looked like a bundle of kindling wood. The place appeared demolished when viewed from the airplane." Their stay at Okinawa was extended by a vicious typhoon that lashed the area in late September, something like an Aleutian storm. The Attuans also came down with measles and were kept there for about three weeks until the middle of October, when they departed for Manila in the Philippine Islands.[99]

They stayed at Manila for five days before boarding the USS *General Brewster,* an army transport ship. Two Aleuts were left behind in a Manila hosptial, too sick to continue the journey home. On October 20, the others sailed for San Francisco, passing close to the Aleutian Chain on their way. They reached the Golden Gate and touched American soil on November 3 for the first time in over three years. Their exodus came to an end near Bodega Bay and Fort Ross, where Russians had brought Aleut relatives for sea otter hunting in the nineteenth century. In transit, Attuans were told of being in Alaska waters only 220 miles from the Aleutians. So badly did they want to go home, one said, "we were hoping that they could let us off at Unalaska," rather than continuing on.[100]

San Francisco, however, was a delight to them. It was "a new world . . . like heaven to me," an exultant Mike Lokanin remembered. In this "very beautiful city," Alex Prossoff's favorite one, they were met by Red Cross, welfare, and medical personnel. They were given spending money, clothing, and rooms in a hotel. Then they went sightseeing. "We were so busy walking and looking," Prossoff confessed, "we did not have time to go to church." After a week in San Francisco, Attu's people were put on a train, their first railroad trip, and sent to Seattle.[101] Slowly they were wending a way toward the Aleutians.

Fulfilling its historic role of entrepôt for Alaska, Seattle became the processing point for the Attuans' return. They were put up in a hotel, then at "a house with kitchen and everything." Staying in Seattle for a month, they found it extremely pleasant. Innokenty Golodoff was able to stay with his brother's family, and Aleuts attended the Greek Orthodox Church of the Assumption.[102]

Delays in their return to the Aleutians were primarily caused by Department of the Interior officials not knowing where to send them. Housing at Atka, a likely relocation site, was not completed. Also, numerous government agencies took time to process these former prisoners of war. Expenses for the layover of this small group of people were minimal, and officials were eager to give the Attuans a pleasant experience after their ordeal.

But there would be no return to Attu. They were finally told that they would be resettled with the Atkans, an Aleut people with a different dialect and with whom there had been ancient tensions and rivalries. At first only eleven out of twenty-five were settled at Atka village, although eventually fifteen ended up there. By November, two were still in a Manila hospital. Three, sick with tuberculosis, were in the Tacoma, Washington, Indian hospital. Four Attuans wanted to live in Unalaska city, and five youngsters were sent to the Indian Service school at Eklutna, Alaska.[103]

Officials had been notified for the first time on September 22 that some Attuans were still alive in Japan. No news of their whereabouts had been uncovered since the Japanese occupation of Attu in June 1942. Subsequently, even before the Attuans set foot on California soil, Alaska Indian Service officials began efforts to resist the restoration of Attu village. Assistant Superintendent Geeslin learned on September 11, while engaged in Atka reconstruction, that Attu had been demolished. Having already experienced troubles with an "incompetent" resettlement officer, Harley Covalt, Geeslin anticipated further problems when he learned that some Attuans had survived and were coming home. Thinking ahead, he broached this topic with Atka's leaders. They "agreed to having the Attu people . . . resettled in their village providing they would . . . be permitted to trap the islands assigned to the Attu people." On October 4, Superintendent Foster telegraphed Collier's office, recommending that Attuans be resettled at Atka.[104] The decision was not made until early December.

Upon learning of the surviving Attuans, the military immediately gave clearance for Attu's resettlement. Secretary of the Interior William A. Brophy, who had succeeded Harold Ickes, was notified in November that the Alaska Defense Command had "no objections," and the commandant of the Seventeenth Naval District "suggests habitation be located on site of former village." Foster, however, was set against it. He visited Seattle on December 1, and "the facts" were "presented" to the Attuans. "Each of them agreed that it was best for them," he claimed, "to be resettled at Atka village." The day before his departure, Foster wrote to Zimmerman, "Since the Atka Natives are more than glad to accept the Attu people and they are perfectly willing to return to Atka it is our plan to send them there." He wrote a disclaimer. "No coercion, force or any other undesirable tactics were used."[105]

Contrary to Foster's claim, Attuans later maintained they were given no choice. Many of them, in fact, wanted to return to their home island. Innokenty Golodoff declared, "We tried to go to Attu," but "the Government wouldn't let us go." They said Interior officials told them there were insufficient numbers of Attu people to justify a hospital which would have to be built. "The Government told us to live with the Atka people." Alex Prossoff was also clear on this matter. "We wanted to go to Attu," he insisted, but were told "we must come to Atka" because Attu was occupied by soldiers and the village destroyed.[106]

Indian Service refusal to restore Attu village was based on economic concerns more than on the wishes of Aleuts. When Foster reported to Interior Secretary Brophy about it, he claimed that "settling the Attu people at Atka has saved the government an enormous amount." Some construction at Atka was completed by salvaging army materials for the six Attu dwellings "at no cost to our Department."[107]

Their long journey about to end, Attu's people boarded the same ship that had returned other Aleuts, the *David S. Branch,* an apt finale to this episode. They sailed on December 12 toward Unalaska Island, arriving a week later at Captain's Harbor. From there the ship went to Adak Island, where it unloaded military personnel and the Aleuts. A small tug took them to Atka on December 21, 1945, in time to celebrate Christmas once again in the Aleutians.[108]

Attuans traveled by truck from the tug to the Atka village school building, where they were assigned living spaces in Atka homes or Quonset huts. Although their coming did place a strain on the Atkans as well as on themselves, they all overcame the inconveniences. Eventually, as in the Chuginadak Woman story, the people of these two rival villages reached accommodation. Olean Prokopeuff, however, said she was never happy in Atka. It was not like her home in Attu. "A year passed, then the houses were built for us . . . so we moved in. Since then they have been our houses for a long time. Today, whenever there is a storm, I don't trust my poor house."[109]

10

Victory and Redress

> Some called the ordeal suffered by . . . Aleut-Americans the
> "craziness of war," and dismissed that ugly portion of our history
> with that excuse. Not many of our people until recently . . .
> realized the ultimate insult of the entire story. The evacu-
> ations were not necessary; the Aleuts suffered for nothing.
> —Agafon Krukoff, Jr., St. Paul Aleut
> Commission on Wartime Relocation Hearings

The war was over, victory was gained, and Aleuts were home at last.
The storms of evacuation had finally blown out. The wind was a river
no more.

Evacuation had been a harsh experience for Aleuts and had threatened their survival as individuals and as an ethnic group. Finding their
way through those devastating times had been extremely difficult. Their
religious faith had sustained them when there was little hope and no
reassurance that their communities would be resettled after the war, or
ever. As evacuees, they had struggled in the camps to hold their lives
together in meaningful ways. They had learned that concerted protest
could change matters over which they previously felt they had little
control. As a people, they had not been defeated. Survival against overwhelming odds is their personal victory.

Life in the camps, however, had transformed Aleuts forever. Exposure to the influences brought to bear on them while in exile from their
Aleutian island homes demonstrated to them their previous isolation
from the forces of society at large. They understood that they had been
a people set apart. From their non-Aleut neighbors, they had learned of
the importance of participation in the democracy by which their lives
were governed. They soon wanted to participate in it fully as citizens of
the state, not wards. Evacuation had created in them a heightened sense
of self-awareness and self-worth.

This exposure became a catalyst for a new Aleut era. Aleuts began
choosing different directions for themselves as they entered the world
of capitalism and politics after the war. Early leaders in adjusting to
these developments—Flore Lekanof and Philemon Tutiakoff—had
been evacuees. They became models for a cadre of younger leaders

who would end Aleut quiescence and signal a new political expression and ethnic pride.

For many years, however, the horrors of evacuation hovered over them like a dark cloud. Not unlike survivors of the Japanese American camps in the States, some refused to speak about it at all. Many felt too ill just thinking of the years of hardship and deprivation. They only wanted the memories to fade away, believing that reviving them served no practical purpose. They would consider evacuation to have been their contribution and sacrifice to the war. That should suffice. Then, forget it! Aleuts breaking camp at Ward Lake burned the temporary church altar they had made and buried the ashes in villages at home. They and the Atka people brought back trees to plant in the Aleutians.[1] Were not these symbolic acts enough?

They were not enough for some who remembered all that had been lost. As time passed and the stories came out bit by bit, some began to wonder about righting this terrible wrong. Younger Aleuts like Patrick Pletnikoff, Agafon Krukoff, and Dimitri Philemonof, who heard the tales told by their elders, came to believe the entire evacuation experience had been an unnecessary insult to all Aleut people. Eventually, they joined with willing evacuee survivors to pursue redress through political action. This was the American way. Evacuation had generated a new Aleut consciousness moving toward restitution. Aleut remembering, a tradition tied to love of home and church, was stimulated. Those who counseled forgetting about the camps, not wanting to relive the experience, were not heeded. The evacuation experience was an indelible part of Aleut history that could not be ignored.

The end of the Aleut evacuation story came on August 10, 1988, with the passage of Public Law 100-383. That victory culminated a long and hard-fought battle for restitution. The story of the Aleuts' Southeast Alaska friends, the Tlingit people of Angoon near Killisnoo, stands in contrast. In 1882, their village had been pillaged, burned, and bombarded by order of U.S. Navy Commander E. C. Merriman. Six children had been killed. Ninety-one years later, in 1973, the case was settled under threat of a lawsuit. Tlingits won a monetary settlement but not the apology they wanted from the government and the navy. Forty-three years after evacuation, Aleuts had in hand a public law for financial restitution and an apology from Congress and the president on behalf of the people of the United States.[2]

Nevertheless, restitution was slow in coming. The effects of the evacuation were felt for years, and postwar conditions were difficult to mitigate. Aleuts could not simply resume community life as it had been before. One Aleut historian, Lillie McGarvey, judged that "next to the coming of the Russians . . . World War II was the greatest upheaval experienced by the Aleut people."[3]

Like patterns on their grass baskets, the deprivations of their evacuation experience continued to be woven into the postwar years. Aleuts still needed medical care. The mayor of Unalaska, R. B. Patterson, informed Governor Gruening of this urgent need. He and military authorities wanted a physician and nurse to relieve the pressure on army medical personnel who were caring for the Aleuts. When asked for this help, General Superintendent Don Foster of the Alaska Indian Service complained to Congressional Delegate Bob Bartlett that the demand was "out of line and unreasonable at this time." But the truth was that Aleut health problems, which had worsened in the camps, had followed them home. Indian Service Medical Director E. W. Norris explained that the health of the evacuees was poor because their "high wages" in Southeast had been spent "for liquor and other luxuries, to which they were unaccustomed." Although this had been "detrimental to their health," it would end, he predicted, as they settled in at home.[4]

General Superintendent Don Foster believed this, too, even though army medical officers in Atka asked him for desperately needed help to improve Aleut health. He responded, "It has not been possible to recruit and maintain an adequate staff to satisfy all the demands for medical care." Foster said the villains were profligate Aleuts and "the Bureau of the Budget and the Congress," who had cut appropriations for medical services. Evacuation had caused health problems, Foster admitted, but "our staff was considerably below normal strength due to circumstances beyond our control." Only two field nurses were available for Unalaska. One of them "is to be sent, in the near future, to Atka and the other Aleutian communities."[5]

The Unalaska Native hospital had served as a center for Aleutian health care before the war. Damaged in the Japanese attack on Dutch Harbor, it needed restoration and staffing. Only a public nurse served there. A year after Aleuts returned, the Indian Service still had not acted. Moreover, it planned to reduce the size of the Unalaska dispensary. Army Post Commander Elbert F. Foster protested the move. It would curtail the service of the nurse and the one army physician who helped Aleuts on an advisory and emergency basis. Superintendent Don Foster's justification for scaling down the medical quarters was "excessive costs." His plan was to station "a field physician at Unalaska," and when Aleutian mail runs would resume in October 1946, "this would facilitate the transportation of patients to Unalaska and would enable the nurse and physician to make field trips . . . along the chain." After that, he felt, the Alaska Indian Service would be "justified in requesting the reopening of the Unalaska Hospital."[6]

In spite of the need and Superintendent Foster's intentions, nothing was done. A year later, Unalaska's mayor, Arthur J. Harris, wired Governor Gruening about the "extremely serious" lack of medical resources. He informed the governor in October 1947 that the army and navy were removing their physicians. There would be no doctor in a radius of five hundred miles of Unalaska. The governor's office admitted the Unalaska Indian hospital should be "reopened and restaffed," but whether funds would be "forth-coming . . . before next year" was "very questionable." Washington, D.C., might help, but unfortunately, according to the governor, neither the Indian Service nor the Territory had sufficient money to fund health care.[7]

In contrast, this failure to provide medical help did not prevail on the Pribilof Islands. There, the Fish and Wildlife Service wanted to care for its sealing labor force. It organized a medical mission for St. George and St. Paul in July 1944. The Service said this was necessary "due to the long enforced absence of the natives from the islands." The announcement inspired Dr. Samuel R. Berenberg, the St. Paul physician before evacuation. He wrote a note of gratitude to Secretary of the Interior Harold Ickes. Berenberg mentioned, however, "the enormous mortality rate" at the Funter Bay camps and suggested "some investigation be made." To Director Ira Gabrielson, this was like a dreaded fire bell in the night. His office wrote to Ickes concerning a reply to Berenberg, "We have found it necessary to revise your draft letter." As a result, the revised letter, under the secretary's signature, informed the physician that "our records indicate . . . the mortality rate at the evacuation camps . . . was no higher than normal despite the rigorous handicaps that were necessarily imposed on these people due to the war."[8]

Contrary to Gabrielson's denial, mortality rates had escalated at Funter Bay camps. Also, Aleuts were returned to the Pribilofs in very poor physical condition. When the Pribilovians finally reached home, a medical team of two physicians and one dentist performed sixty-three tonsillectomies and fifty-one adenoidectomies on the children of St. Paul and thirty-six similar operations at St. George. They could have done more, but the seal harvest was underway, making it impossible "to spare the men from sealing operations." The dentist also "did a large amount of good work."[9]

Although both St. Paul and St. George Islands had been assigned a physician each and a dentist to share, the Department of the Interior did not follow recommendations by the medical team to provide additional medical personnel. Superintendent Edward Johnston opposed the appointment of a medical inspector. It "would mean," he wrote Bower, "a considerable additional expense to the Service."[10]

Gradually, the physical health of most Pribilovians was restored. A visiting study group in 1949 found that hospitals and medical facilities were "adequate." But the emotional wounds inflicted by evacuation were another matter. The visitors noticed that "there is still evident some resentment and bitterness" over Funter Bay. "The sufferings, deprivation, and uncertainties that resulted from this war-time tragedy have not been forgotten."[11] This resentment and bitterness was harbored by Aleuts because of the many deaths of their relatives and friends at Funter Bay. Yet Secretary Ickes had depicted these death rates in the camps as "normal."

Restoration in the other Aleutian communities took longer than it did on the Pribilof Islands. The Alaska Indian Service was more penurious than the Fish and Wildlife Service, which could use revenues from its sealing operations. Assistant Superintendent Geeslin of the Indian Service protested when resettlement officer Covalt mistakenly paid one dollar per hour to laboring Akutans. Only fifty dollars per month should have been paid, and that only to the people of Atka. Aleuts at Akutan, Nikolski, and Unalaska were supposed to donate their labor for rebuilding their homes. Anything else would be "an unnecessary obligation." Geeslin argued that "if we were outright 'Santa Claus' and had all the money in the world, we probably could pay these bills." Instead, "we have very limited funds to rehabilitate these people and must do so at the least possible legitimate expense."[12]

After six months, according to Superintendent Foster, the Aleutian resettlement program was "moving along quite well." Yet his November 1945 report to Zimmerman cited numerous problems. Resettlement officer Covalt was "entirely incapable" and apparently ineffective. Assistant Superintendent Geeslin took his place on the islands in August. Foster went on to report that Atka people depending on "tents and Quonset huts," which had not "proven too satisfactory," would soon "have a roof over their heads." But these houses probably would not be finished inside by the time they were occupied. The military, furthermore, was not "in a position to furnish" sufficient "materials" for Akutan and Nikolski, Foster stated, explaining "delays and inconvenience." Then the Akutan teacher resigned, so the Benedicts had to split their duties between Akutan and Nikolski. Biorka Aleuts had been transferred yet another time from Akutan to Nikolski. They wanted, however, to return to their home at Biorka. Superintendent Foster claimed that although it normally "would be the policy of the Office to help these people rehabilitate at Biorka," this "would mean an added cost and some inconvenience."[13] It was never done.

Again, Unalaska was a special problem. Foster, who had resisted resettlement of Aleuts there, was still worried about servicemen "mingling" with Aleuts. He consequently supported making the city, with its Aleut residents, out of bounds to army and navy personnel. "When the sailors and soldiers came into Unalaska," he charged, "Aleuts went out of circulation as far as work was concerned and everything came to a standstill." The out-of-bounds policy was opposed by non-Aleut businessmen, especially the liquor dealers, but many Aleuts were concerned that unbridled liquor sales hurt their community. On October 18, 1945, thirty-three of them petitioned the city government and Judge Anthony Dimond of the Territorial Third Judicial Division to halt all liquor sales beginning with the new year.[14]

This petition expressed other Aleut complaints about their lot. "Our whole economic livelihood was upset due to our evacuation," they wrote. Aleut houses and their church desperately needed electric lighting. Streets lights were needed for safe passage after dark. Their "light plants which were lost" during the war had not been replaced. Furthermore, they complained, the sailors roaming around lacked effective disciplinary control. All in all, they wanted better and safer living conditions.[15]

Changing economic circumstances were at work here, too. Unalaska's herring fisheries and commercial salmon and cod industries were nearly gone. In the judgment of long-time resident Henry Swanson, this was "the worst time for Unalaska" because there were no jobs. Along the Aleutian Chain, transportation for passenger and mail service had been provided by the U.S. Coast Guard. But this was discontinued in July 1946, and Superintendent Foster lamented the loss of this service and its accompanying dental and medical help from Coast Guard vessels. In a very real sense, Aleuts were stranded. Because the government was bent on cost-cutting, the Indian Service experienced "difficulty and delay," Foster complained to Delegate Bartlett, in transporting "medical patients to and from the villages." Vocational students also were without transportation. Trappers had no way of reaching distant islands to trap fur-bearing animals. The situation, he believed, was "entirely unsatisfactory" and one the Aleuts should not have to endure. Stymied and empty-handed, Foster admitted, "We do not have any appropriation for transportation and neither do we think it advisable for this office to propose such a venture."[16]

In addition to shriveled-up services, Aleuts had trouble with their fur harvests. "Nikolski Aleuts experienced a very poor trapping season last winter as they had to confine" their hunting "to their home island of

Umnak," which had "only red foxes," rued Foster. Unalaska Aleuts also complained of taking only a few foxes because "Army personnel brought in numbers of dogs" that "killed the fox on Unalaska Island." Moreover, the Atka people, who owned the fur stock on Adak Island, found non-Aleut blue-fox trappers there. Another threat came from the navy's desire to take Attu, Agattu, and Tanaga islands for strictly military use. "Should these islands be withdrawn as military reserves and the Aleuts not permitted to trap them," Foster warned, it would "be necessary to put these villages on relief or some sort of a dole system."[17]

The military also prevented Attuans from trapping on Attu, Agattu, and the Semichi Islands. Moreover, Atka's Aleuts were required to obtain a special permit to trap blue fox on Amchitka Island, and Unalaska's Aleuts were required to get permits to trap on Carlisle Island. These islands had been set aside as bird refuges by the Fish and Wildlife Service. But non-Aleuts received permits "to stock and trap blue fox on Kagamil, Seguam, Kanaga, Samalga, Rat and Little Sitkin Islands." In order "to have adequate islands assigned to the Aleut groups as near as possible to their villages" to alleviate transportation problems, Foster's office attempted negotiations with Fish and Wildlife officials. But they were interested in creating additional "bird and sea otter sanctuaries." The Aleuts, he wrote, depended "almost entirely for their livelihood" on trapping.[18]

Aleuts were not the only ones who regarded the Aleutians to be in rough shape after the war. An Unalaska resident, James A. Harris, described the area's plight to a Juneau radio commentator in November 1947. A decline in fishing had been caused by "Japs bombing the oil dump." Our ships had emptied "oily bilge water into the bays." The army and navy had dumped gas and ammunition into the ocean nearby. Sunken ships with "cargoes of oil and gasoline" still lay off the beaches. Servicemen had barricaded and exploded inland spawning grounds "with rifles and hand grenades." Harris said that "trapping was ruined during the war by the wholesale slaughter of foxes by servicemen."[19] His letter was given to Governor Gruening.

This "upheaval of their economy," the governor wrote to the Interior Department, ought to be remedied. He endorsed Harris's suggestion that surplus war equipment be made available to Unalaska residents and suggested two additional possibilities. Maybe through the Reconstruction Finance Corporation, payment could be made for "war caused loss or damage to property." Other claims might be processed through the War Damage Corporation. If that were unsuccessful, Gruening suggested "introduction of a general relief bill." But Washington, D.C., offered no relief. "The War Damage Corporation is now in the process of liquidation," Gruening was informed. Any claim would have had to be filed by June 30, 1946. As for legislation, the director of the Division of Territories and Island Possessions believed "that there is not sufficient certainty as to the extent of damage done." Also the uncertainty of identifying "persons who suffered losses" would make legislation questionable. Unalaskans would have to work through the Reconstruction Finance Corporation for "alleviating in some measure the economic dislocation caused by the war." The number of Alaska property damage claims, including those from Unalaska city, eventually totaled 207. The War Damage Corporation later settled these claims for just over eighty thousand dollars.[20] Aleuts, however, always claimed they received no part of this compensation.

The damaged environment and the weak economy were consequences of the Aleutian campaign that weighed heavily on Aleuts. But, their evacuation and return had also been costly for the government. Several emergency funds were established in the Department of the Interior by special appropriations, the original one for $500,000. President Roosevelt subsequently allotted an additional $200,000 for the resettlement. But this $700,000 was insufficient. In 1944 and 1946, a combined additional $79,500 was earmarked for the camps and resettlement. These funds, of course, do not account for Japanese costs to take the Attuans to Otaru or for U.S. military expenditures for transportation, damage repair, and replacement. It seems safe to say that the total cost above normal budgets of the entire evacuation process, not counting the lost sealing revenue of 1942, amounted to well over a million dollars. Many Aleuts were self-sufficient in the camps, and Superintendent Foster claimed to be "satisfied the resettlement of the Aleuts has been handled on the most economic basis possible under the circumstances." When returned, each Aleutian Aleut, he figured, cost the government only $593.51, including "food supplies for approximately one year."[21]

Damage claims against the government were filed by non-Aleuts almost immediately after evacuation began and continued for several years. Settlement of these accounts was handled with more dispatch than the final restitution for Aleut losses, which did not come until 1988. It took the government more than forty years to pay Aleuts for evacuation-related losses. Several Caucasian sheep ranchers on different islands were the first to claim war damages. A representative of the ranch on Kanaga Island complained to the commander of the Thirteenth Naval District in December 1942 that navy personnel had taken over its property in the winter of 1941. But the commander was busy fighting a war and did not reply "by reason of military operations" until the middle of January 1943, and then with no definite recommendation. A resident of Unalaska, James I. Parsons, asked Governor Gruening for help in recovering damages for property he claimed the army commandeered when they forced him to evacuate in July 1942. Acting Governor Bob Bartlett referred the matter to General Buckner to determine whether this was a "just claim against the United States Government." After investigation, Buckner's office decided "there is no basis for any claims against the government for Mr. Parsons."[22]

The most persistent claimant was Carlyle C. Eubank, president of the Aleutian Livestock Company, whose Nikolski sheep ranch suffered losses from evacuation of its personnel, including Aleut workers, and from military vandalism. Immediately after evacuation, he pursued the case like a hound, engaging Governor Gruening, Delegate Dimond, General Buckner, and Senator Mongrad C. Wallgren of Washington State. Eubank persisted for over four years. Finally, on July 3, 1945, Delegate Bartlett introduced legislation in the U.S. House of Representatives on Eubank's behalf, a private claims bill "arising out of the evacuation of the civilian population" from Umnak Island. It was referred to the Committee on Claims. In March 1946, a compromise was reached on equipment losses, and Eubank was awarded a $1,500 settlement.[23]

Not so fortunate was John P. Olson from Makushin on Unalaska Island, who had an Aleut wife and son. The Olson family left behind a ranch and nearly seven hundred sheep when evacuated to Wrangell. Olson claimed a $36,000 loss. He believed a just settlement should be made and tried to interest Governor Gruening in his cause. Yet as late as October 1947, Acting Governor Lew Williams wrote to the chief of claims and litigation in the office of the judge advocate general that "Mr. Olson's case has been before your Department . . . and no definite action" has been taken.[24]

Speculation about further claims crossed the minds of government officials, especially when the camps were abandoned. Ward Lake belonged to the government, and U.S. Forest Service officials were satisfied when its buildings were razed. Damages to Southeast camps, however, might result in claims, for some were privately held property. Owners of the Funter Bay and Killisnoo canneries had been paid monthly rent, which, it was hoped, diminished the possibility that depreciation compensation would be sought. The Funter Bay gold mine and Burnett Inlet sites had been used free of charges. Owner Sam Peckovich expected to be unhappy with the condition of the Funter Bay camp after the St. George people left. Fish and Wildlife Service personnel, however, visited the camp and said it was better than acceptable.

They estimated that improvements worth $3,000 had been made to the property. After inspecting the place himself, Peckovich was convinced that the improvements and cleanup were adequate. A. R. Brueger, owner of the Burnett Island cannery, which received an estimated $3,495 worth of improvements, was also satisfied. This would be "in full settlement of any claim he might have against the Government."[25]

Although the major claimants were Aleuts whose property was destroyed or stolen in evacuation, the first compensation was paid to the Fish and Wildlife Service for a cottage on St. Paul Island that the Army Weather Bureau took permanently. The Service was reimbursed three thousand dollars, but no such payment went to Aleuts for loss of personal property. When Aleuts did file claims "for damage occurring to their real and personal property" on the Pribilofs, the War Department found only one legal provision that might be pertinent, and the Army Claims Division discouraged the use of this 1943 statute because it did not provide payment for damages "resulting from combat activities, pilferage, depredation or vandalism." It would be "extremely difficult, if not impossible," to determine "the cause and extent of the damage sustained by each claimant."[26]

This did not stop the Fish and Wildlife Service from submitting to General Buckner's headquarters claims of $16,131 for "government-owned property lost or damaged by the armed forces." Interior Department Under Secretary Abe Fortas requested that the Bureau of Budget provide payment for all claims arising from damage to the Pribilof Islands from the president's $200,000 allocation for Aleut resettlement. Originally that fund inlcuded $10,000 for personal property damages. President Roosevelt amended this appropriation, directing the secretary of the treasury on September 28, 1944, to extend this coverage to other Aleut evacuees and increase the total amount available for claims to $25,000.[27]

Pribilovian Aleuts remembered receiving totally inadequate payment for their personal losses—some as little as twelve dollars. Many difficulties got in the way of processing the claims. Michael Lestenkof of St. George blamed the army for not listing valuable items on inventories of Aleut belongings. Hence, total losses to Aleuts were understated from the beginning. Chicago-approved claims and vouchers had to be sent to the Juneau office of the Alaska Indian Service because the president's allocation was designated only for disbursement from Superintendent Foster's office. Chief Bower refused to approve three claims from the two Pribilof Russian Orthodox clergymen, Fathers Makary Baranoff and Feodosy Kulchizsky. Other church claims were also rejected.

Bower, however, did submit claims of "the St. Paul Baseball Club . . . and the St. George Native Canteen."[28]

As the claims process moved forward, Pribilovians and other Aleuts recovered little for losses of their personal belongings. Store supplies on Atka and Nikolski were replenished and houses in the four communities repaired or substitutes found, but personal belongings were not replaced in spite of a plan to do so. Geeslin blamed some of this on the incompetence of resettlement officer Covalt. Lists of personal articles to be replaced had been ordered in 1945 but had not been received by early 1946. Geeslin was so upset about this that he traveled to Seattle to investigate. Furthermore, ordering had gone so awry that excess supplies received were "sold to the Aleuts and the money deposited to the credit of the President's Fund." When Geeslin left the Aleutians, he designated Deputy U.S. Marshal Verne Robinson as his officer in charge. Robinson later testified that shipments to replace Aleut personal belongings never arrived and he never received an answer to his inquiry about them from the Bureau of Indian Affairs in Seattle.[29]

By the middle of March 1946, Geeslin had updated an inventory of Aleut losses of personal belongings. He learned that even more money than originally estimated would be needed to replace destroyed or stolen items. Yet not replacing them would be costly, too, because guns and traps were needed for Aleut subsistence harvesting. Faced with an almost no-win situation, Geeslin admitted to a "guilty conscience," when he asked Aleuts "to waive numerous items" that had been lost and to substitute less costly ones. "There were several thousand dollars worth of items," he confessed, "which would not have been acceptable to any white person." He felt Aleuts were justified when they complained in Southeast camps of "not getting as much as the Japs were in their concentration camps." Back then, he said, "our only answer to them was that they were citizens and that they should not even compare themselves to the questionable Jap population in America, and that we were doing the best we could for them with funds available."[30] Now, he reflected, the situation had not changed much.

The Department of the Interior was notified on June 18, 1946, that the President's Fund would expire on June 30, and any balances on "that date will be rescinded." To extend the allocation would be "extremely difficult if not impossible," so all "legitimate items" should be encumbered before the expiration date.[31] Apparently Geeslin did not pursue the matter; and Aleuts were, by his own admission, left shortchanged.

The business of redress took on a different twist for Attu's people. Before leaving Okinawa Island in October 1945, Mike Lokanin, who became leader after Mike Hodikoff's death at Otaru, broached the topic of restitution with American Red Cross official Monroe Sweetland. "The Japs took our church," Lokanin claimed, and all its icons. The church was valued at $1,400, and its three golden crosses were worth $450. Payment on the loss would help when the rebuilding began. Sweetland was sympathetic and wrote to Assistant Secretary of the Interior Oscar Chapman endorsing this claim. It should be included in "Japanese Reparation" and compensation from the government "comparable to that being given to other American civilians who were prisoners of the Japanese." Chapman felt the Attuans should also be provided "new guns" and "a school for the children, most of whom now speak only Japanese!"[32]

In October 1945, Interior Department officials decided to file Attu claims "against the Japanese Government" through the State Department. Procedures would have to be worked out, however, and the State Department needed data from the Alaska Indian Service substantiating the claims. This would entail "a great deal of field work by . . . Don Foster's staff." So far as "the claim for the church and fixtures" was concerned, steps had been taken "to have this claim settled from money provided from the President's Emergency Fund." Attuans felt they also deserved $74,425 for loss of income during imprisonment and destruction of their "fox breeding stock" as a result of combat on Attu. Monetary damages for loss of human life amounted to $220,000, for a combined total claim of $294,425.[33]

While moving toward a March 1, 1951, deadline, the Attu claims were lost temporarily by the Department of the Interior. They were eventually filed with the War Claims Commission on January 9, 1951. This commission was established by act of Congress on July 3, 1948, to handle World War II claims, including those of noncombatants. Claimants were regarded as victims "who suffered personal and economic injuries" as a result of "violations of well-established principles of international law." Any compensation received would not be "forms of gratuities or bonuses." Attuans qualified. They had been imprisoned and had paid a heavy toll. While only "3.5 percent of the internees detained by the German Government" had died, the death rate among all prisoners in Japan had been more than double that, "7.1 percent." Only twenty-five Attu people had come out alive, carrying the remains of twenty loved ones, a 44 percent mortality rate.[34]

The War Claims Commission awarded "detention benefits at the rate of $25 per month during internment for those under eighteen years of age, and $60 a month for those older." No benefits were paid for those who had died in Otaru. "In the event of death of the eligible internee" after the return but before restitution, benefits would go to "eligible survivors, including the widow, the dependent husband, and children." Accordingly, twenty-three claims were paid to Attuans in 1951, ranging in amounts from $19.99 for Alfred Prokopioff, Jr., the only survivor born in Japan, to a maximum of $2,358 for those older than eighteen. Although Attuans had asked for over $290,000 in damages, they received just over $32,000. These funds did not come from the Japanese or American government but from "proceeds of enemy property vested and retained by the Office of Alien Property, Department of Justice."[35]

The War Claims Commission had provided Attuans a way to get "money back from Japs."[36] But how could other Aleuts recover their losses? Prospects were not promising. By the middle of 1946, claims money had been depleted and the processes terminated, signaling an end to restitution. Aleuts had no politically powerful advocates and no organization through which to further their cause.

Having recognized the need for both even before evacuation, they now began a more organized, thorough approach and took steps that eventually led to final restitution. As far back as the 1920s, Pribilof people had attempted to gain more control of community affairs from Fish and Wildlife Service agents and caretakers. In evacuation, they had defied authorities by leaving the camps for more rewarding employment elsewhere. In efforts to gain some control over their lives, the women at Funter Bay and other Aleuts at Burnett Inlet had mounted protests. By the beginning of 1950, Aleuts were ready to establish a corporate charter at St. Paul and institute a "new wage plan." These developments strengthened their determination to establish themselves as viable citizens and to take a more active role in political and economic decisions.[37]

In 1951, Pribilovians brought a lawsuit against the federal government for alleged long-standing violations of agreements over goods and services. They sent a St. Paul evacuee, Iliador Merculieff, to Washington, D.C., as their emissary for this legal action under the Indian Claims Commission Act. Although it took until 1978, Aleuts finally won this lawsuit.[38] More importantly, though, Merculieff's journey to the nation's captial became an important lesson for evacuation redress strategy. It was a forerunner to the final victory gained some thirty-five years later.

That victory was preceded by significant developments in Aleut organization. The Aleut League was formed in 1967 to coordinate Aleut community associations and to seek funds for Aleut projects in education, health, and housing. Flore Lekanof, a St. George evacuee, was its first chairman. He and other Aleut leaders were active in an Alaska-wide movement that led to passage of the Alaska Native Claims Settlement Act of 1971. This act gave Natives title to land and set up regional corporations. It created the Aleut Corporation, a profit-seeking entity. In 1976, the Aleut League and the Aleutian Planning Commission, whose executive director was Dimitri Philemonof, were merged to form the Aleutian/Pribilof Islands Association (APIA). Its board chairman was Anthony Philemonof, and the executive director was Patrick Pletnikoff.[39] The APIA, a not-for-profit organization, was joined in promoting Aleut concerns by the Aleut Corporation. These two agencies were guided by young Aleut descendants of evacuees, who demonstrated assertive leadership.

In 1977, Patrick Pletnikoff launched the movement for evacuation redress that was later carried on by APIA leader Philemon Tutiakoff, an Unalaska city evacuee, and executive director Dimitri Philemonof of St. George. Pletnikoff explored legal action as the best possibility for recovery of losses. Early that year, Lael Morgan, an Alaska author, offered Pletnikoff help in "checking out material for the lawsuit." Then, during a visit in Anchorage with Attorney Gary R. Frink from Washington, D.C., Pletnikoff "hit the topic of damages done to the Aleutian Islands and her Native peoples during World War II" and requested that Frink's firm "represent us in this regard." Because there was no money to pay legal fees, Pletnikoff approached the Department of the Interior. The Department responded to Pletnikoff's request by claiming it had "no funds for support of a law suit." Further pursuing this matter, on January 23, 1978, Pletnikoff retained the Washington, D.C., law firm of Cook and Henderson. A young lawyer for the firm, John C. Kirtland, began to research "the historical context and setting" and to compile data on "human suffering" and "property loss."[40]

Pletnikoff's intent was to sue the Japanese and American governments. He wrote to the Japanese consul's office in Anchorage and received an icy reply. The "Treaty of Peace" between the two countries contained an "Allied Power waiver of all reparations claims" arising from the war. Undaunted, in June 1979, on the eve of his replacement as APIA executive director by Gregg Brelsford, Pletnikoff wrote to Verne Robinson doggedly maintaining that "we intend to sue the U.S. and Japanese Governments." He had already taken an important first step when he retained John Kirkland's law firm.[41] That turned out to be a stroke of good fortune. A graduate of the U.S. Naval Academy and a military veteran himself, Kirtland proved an effective advocate and practitioner of jurisprudence. He led the attempt for congressional legislation to correct the injustices that had been inflicted upon Aleuts.

By the time Pletnikoff relinquished APIA leadership, he had established a liaison with Alaska Senator Mike Gravel. Pletnikoff was interested in federal funding for an Aleutian health care facility and for a cleanup of World War II debris. He had been working with the senator's staff on these projects when Gravel, in a March 1, 1978, letter to Pletnikoff, mentioned a house bill "to give Japanese-Americans civil service retirement credit" if they had spent time "in internment camps." Perhaps, the senator suggested, "similar compensation should be made" to Aleuts, although their situation "was not completely comparable."[42]

Japanese Americans with grievances over wartime relocation were on the move for "repairing America," in the words of one of them, William M. Hohri. Aleuts were welcome to join them. It was felt the objectives of each group could be pursued as one. The Japanese Americans and the Aleuts forged a campaign together. The alliance helped both groups by increasing their political influence in Congress. Hohri thought he noticed another benefit of this cooperative movement: it allowed "self-conscious Japanese-Americans to say, 'See! We're not just for ourselves.' "

John Kirtland and the Alaska congressional delegation—Senators Ted Stevens and Frank Murkowski and Representative Don Young— were responsible for guiding the appropriate legislation through Congress. They were able to amend the congressional bill that had created a special Commission on Wartime Relocation and Internment of Civilians (CWRIC) for investigating Japanese American internment to include the investigation of Aleut evacuation.[43] This bill, the Commission on Wartime Relocation and Internment of Civilians Act (Public Law 96-317), was signed on July 31, 1980, by President Jimmy Carter.

This linkage assured a political agenda for the cause in Washington, but funds still were not available for expenses involved in gathering and documenting the claims of Aleuts scattered among the far-flung islands. Kirtland therefore made an emphatic point: *"There is absolutely no way that the Commission, with its limited staff, will be able to document the full range of hardships and deaths suffered by the Aleut people."* On that note, the APIA galvanized its forces and convinced Alaska State legislators to fund the effort. Gregg Brelsford engaged Alaska's congressional delegation to lobby Governor Jay Hammond to support a $165,000 appropriation for the project. It seemed to Brelsford that Hammond might veto the bill, but Governor Hammond finally signed it and the gathering of Aleut testimony commenced in 1981.[44]

Using this grant from the state of Alaska, Kirtland published a memorandum in equity law with voluminous documentation, the first of its kind in Aleut history. It formed the basis for the Aleut section of the CWRIC report, *Personal Justice Denied*. The publication of this volume led to legislative action to implement the commission's findings. Subsequently, the APIA appointed a "World War II Task Force," chaired by Philemon Tutiakoff and composed of three APIA members and three from the Aleut Corporation. The task force in turn created the "World War II Project," a blueprint coordinated and implemented by Alfred Stepetin to obtain data and depositions from people on the islands.[45]

Testimony for the hearings of the CWRIC were held on September 14, 17, and 19, 1981, at Anchorage, Unalaska city, and St. Paul. Brelsford and Kirtland had earlier lobbied successfully with Senator Stevens to expand the commission membership to include Father Ishmael Gromoff, an Aleut from St. Paul. Many pitched in to prepare for the hearings: Anna Lekanof of St. Paul, Father Paul Merculief and Susie Merculief of St. George, and Alice Petrivelli of Atka, among others. Fifty-three Aleuts testified in person, and over 135 depositions and written testimonies were collected. It was an impressive accomplishment given the underlying resistance to probing painful old wounds. Philemon Tutiakoff said evacuation "was such a bad experience there was a tendency to let it go—forget about it." Most Aleuts had remained silent until their children had begun asking about the camps.[46]

The testimonies given were video-recorded, and a written transcript was microfilmed for the archival record. Aleuts said they knew they could never recover family keepsakes, icons, and ecclesiastical heirlooms, but they were emphatic about redress for other losses. They wanted repayment for rebuilding their houses, churches, and community buildings. When Kirtland spoke on their behalf, he suggested that the principle of "military convenience" explained why they had been evacuated. "It was convenient to have the Aleuts removed and taken away. It cut down," he contended, "on the problems of administering the area." But why, he asked, at Unalaska was blood quantum made a factor and only Aleuts forced to leave? His evidence, Kirtland thought, said it all: "There was a racial element, there was a question of racial distinction which was made as to the need for the evacuation."[47]

Evidence suggests there indeed had been a racial thread that wove itself among the many strands that make up the fabric of this tragic story. The record is so tangled, however, it is difficult to measure precisely the intent of racial bias to the exclusion of other factors more easily identified. Military advantage was certainly at work, but Aleut safety also was a genuine concern of some government and military officials. Such war exigencies as difficulty of supply, shortage of medical personnel and teachers, and budget strains help to explain, but certainly not to justify, camp conditions. Bureaucratic bungling by both civilian and military personnel resulted in well-intentioned officials making all-too-human mistakes. When Aleut protests had fallen on deaf ears, it was at least in part because Aleuts had no political strength or advocates. The reparation attempt signaled an Aleut resolve to reverse this.

After the hearings, the struggle for reparations began with a strategy developed by the APIA. An advisory committee of Aleut leaders was formed to represent the various island constituencies. Gregg Brelsford in Anchorage and John Kirtland in Washington, D.C., coordinated efforts, and all were connected through frequent telephone conferences. They felt there was "no guarantee of success," but Kirtland pragmatically insisted there be unanimity among the Aleut people. Positions taken had to be acceptable to the Alaska congressional delegation. Funded by Atlantic Richfield, Exxon, the Aleut Corporation, and Aleut village corporations, Kirtland worked out draft legislation with Senators Stevens and Murkowski that was completed at the end of October 1983. They decided that Representative Don Young should introduce the bill to be the "vehicle" for implementing their reparation goal.[48]

Aleut leaders, the Alaska politicians, and Kirtland had to be adroit in shaping this legislation to avoid pitfalls. Other congressmen also introduced a variety of redress measures. Seven were introduced, but no action was taken on them between 1983 and 1985. Because Japanese American leadership was split, a situation that threatened defeat or more stalling, separate Aleut bills with identical texts were prepared for the House and Senate. In 1986, budgetary constraints under the Gramm-Rudman-Hollings rubric posed more problems. Then, Assistant Attorney General John R. Bolton announced Department of Justice opposition to Speaker of the House Jim Wright's bill, H.R. 442, which had been submitted in 1985. First Bolton complained on philosophical grounds. "Wartime hardships" caused by "untimely or poorly planned" governmental action, he argued, should not "form the basis for special compensation." Next, he expressed constitutional objections. The bill did not provide for administration by an Executive Branch appointee. Bolton also felt that funds for church restoration would violate First Amendment church and state separation.[49]

As the reparations issue neared resolution in 1987, Kirtland compromised by revising the bill's language, tailoring it to Justice Department objections. Agafon Krukoff, Jr., and Dimitri Philemonof submitted supporting statements and appeared at congressional hearings on the revised provisions. One year later, the end was at hand. On July 27, 1988, the Senate approved the conference report. The House agreed on August 4 by a margin of 257 to 156, and President Reagan signed Public Law 100-383 on August 10, 1988.[50] Redress was won.

The act, "to implement recommendations of the Commission on Wartime Relocation and Internment of Civilians," was predicated on a "human rights" assumption. Title II of the act was named "Aleutian and Pribilof Islands Restitution." It created a U.S. Treasury "Restitution Fund" and appointed the APIA as administrator. A trust was established for $5,000,000 to benefit Aleut evacuees and their descendants. Because the Attuans were evacuated by the Japanese, they were not included in the bill's provisions. It would also benefit eligible Aleuts not included in other sections of the act. "Compensation for damaged or destroyed church property" in the amount of $1,400,000 was provided. Eligible individual Aleuts were awarded $12,000 each "as damages for human suffering." Many, however, like Philemon Tutiakoff, died before receiving payment. Then, "to make restitution for the loss of traditional Aleut lands and village properties on Attu Island," which were placed into the National Wilderness Preservation System, the Aleut Corporation would be paid a valuation not to "exceed $15,000,000."[51]

Redress had drawn Aleuts to Washington, D.C., in unprecedented numbers to support their claims. They asked for fairness and equity. One of them, Dimitri Philemonof, who was born six months after his parents returned to St. George from Funter Bay and was not eligible for an award, nevertheless felt the redress issue "very close to my heart." In the shadow of evacuation, he and other Aleut leaders nevertheless looked ahead to a brighter future. "Compensation," he predicted, "will assist in the rebuilding process." The trust account would benefit the "elderly, disabled or seriously ill" and "students in need of scholarships." It could lead to "the preservation of the Aleut cultural heritage and historical records, the improvement of community centers." It would help the remembering. Aleuts always held dear their island homes. Dimitri Philemonof put the evacuation story in that perspective.

These villages were deprived of their elders in many cases through death and through ravage of disease in the camps. The people returned after the war to find their village centers looted and destroyed, their property taken and vandalized. This trust would help . . . remind all Aleuts, young and old, of the suffering of the generations that found themselves caught up in the severe dislocation of the war years. Its earnings could be used to train new leaders, to carry out the traditions of the Aleut culture that were tested so severely by the relocation experience.[52]

UNITED STATES OFFICIALS INVOLVED IN ALEUT EVACUATION

DEPARTMENT OF THE INTERIOR

Harold L. Ickes, Secretary
Oscar L. Chapman, Assistant Secretary

FISH AND WILDLIFE SERVICE

Ira N. Gabrielson, Director
Charles E. Jackson, Ass't. Director

DIVISION OF ALASKA FISHERIES

Ward T. Bower, Chief

SEAL DIVISION

Edward C. Johnston, Superintendent
Frederick G. Morton Asst. Superintendent

Daniel C.R. Benson, Agent & Caretaker, St. George
Lee C. McMillin, Agent & Caretaker, St. Paul

BUREAU OF INDIAN AFFAIRS

John C. Collier, Commissioner
William Zimmerman, Jr., Ass't. Commissioner

ALASKA INDIAN SERVICES

Claude M. Hirst, General Superintendent
Frederick R. Geeslin, Ass't. Superintendent

Donald W. Haggerty, Field Agent
Virgil R. Farrell, Director of Education
George T. Barrett, Principal, Wrangell Institute
Langdon R. White, Medical Director

DIVISION OF TERRITORIES AND ISLAND POSSESSIONS

Benjamin W. Thoron, Director
Ruth Hampton, Ass't. Director

ALASKA DIVISION

Paul W. Gordon, Director

ALASKA TERRITORY

Ernest Gruening, Governor
Edward "Bob" Bartlett, Secretary

MILITARY

ARMY

Henry L. Stimson, Secretary of War
John M. McCloy, Ass't. Secretary of War

John L. DeWitt, Commander, Western Defense Command

Simon B. Buckner, Commander, Alaska Defense Command

Edgar B. Colladay, Commander Ft. Mears
Hobart W. Copeland, Captain, Ft. Mears

NAVY

Frank Knox, Secretary of the Navy
James V. Forrestal, Under Secretary of the Navy

Charles S. Freeman, Commandant, 13th Naval District

Ralph C. Parker, Commander, Alaska Sector
William N. Updegraff, Commander, Dutch Harbor Naval Station

A Note on the Sources

This is intended to explain and supplement the research that is fully cited in endnotes. Because no one involved in the evacuation kept a diary or written record, the book rests on various archival materials plus Aleut memory. Manuscript collections are scattered in a wide arc from Alaska to Seattle to Washington, D.C. Aleut recollections are recorded on microfilm and videotapes.

I started piecing together the story in Rasmuson Library at the University of Alaska Fairbanks. Its archives and its Alaska and Polar Regions Department contain a rich document cache. Governor Ernest Gruening's personal papers and the official papers of Delegate Anthony Dimond are there. They reveal some of the Territory's responses to evacuation. The archives also have videotapes and printed transcriptions of hearings held in 1981 at Anchorage, Unalaska, and St. Paul by the Commission on Wartime Relocation and Internment of Civilians. Many Aleuts testified at these hearings, making this a major record.

Research at other Alaska repositories also turned up valuable data. Correspondence files at the Anchorage headquarters of the Aleutian/ Pribilof Islands Association were especially helpful for my understanding of the redress movement. The Alaska State Archives at Juneau houses Record Group 101, "Papers of the Territorial Governors," with Gruening's official papers. At the nearby State Historical Library, I read on microfilm the Pribilof logbooks kept by Fish and Wildlife Service officials at Funter Bay. Ketchikan's Public Library and Museum has police records that I used to track Ward Lake evacuee relations with civil authorities.

But not all of my Alaska research was in archives. For awareness and verisimilitude, I visited the abandoned Wrangell Institute and camped where evacuation tents had covered the grounds. To comprehend Aleut distaste for Southeast Alaska trees, some of my favorite flora, I went to Ward Lake where, as Aleuts had said, it was dense, dark, and foreboding. One afternoon I spent at Bayview Cemetery outside Ketchikan. Several Aleut grave markers are there, watched over by beautiful ravens, my favorite birds. In these ways, the evacuation story became connected to my own consciousness.

I traveled to Alaska six times to pursue the evacuation narrative. Yet I am not completely satisfied with this rendition, and I hope a better account will emerge at some future time. To that end, I wish one day to visit Atka, Nikolski, Unalaska, Akutan, St. George, and St. Paul to view the communities and talk to the people. I also want to visit Funter Bay, Killisnoo, and Burnett Inlet to look at what remains of the camps, although I have heard that a fire completely destroyed buildings at Burnett Inlet.

I used the National Archives system at several branches. Its Pacific Northwest Region branch in Seattle provided two essential sources. Record Group 22, "Records of the Fish and Wildlife Service," includes the Alaska Sealing Division's Funter Bay correspondence. Record Group 181, "Records of the Thirteenth Naval District," contains some scanty material on Admiral Freeman and evacuation. Relevant parts of both sources, however, have now been transferred to the new National Archives Alaska branch in Anchorage.

The nation's capital holds a wealth of material that occupied me for parts of two summers. At the uptown National Archives building, Record Group 75, "Records of the Bureau of Indian Affairs," and Record Group 126, "Records of the Division of Territories and Island Possessions," are indispensable. The Modern Military branch at Suitland, Maryland, has Record Group 338, "Records of the Alaska Defense Command." Army and navy records there were disappointing because they revealed little about Aleut evacuation and had not been worked into shape.

Before I started the research for this manuscript, several other attempts to reconstruct the evacuation story had been published. I benefited from them. Unlike this volume, however, they were aimed at litigation and legislation for reparations. Pioneer work was done by John C. Kirtland and David F. Coffin, Jr. Their nine volumes, *The Relocation and Internment of the Aleuts during World War II* (Anchorage: Aleutian/Pribilof Islands Association, 1981), consist of a master index, Aleut depositions, and other data. Kirtland also wrote an additional piece, *A Case in Law and Equity for Compensation* (Anchorage: Aleutian/Pribilof Islands Association, 1981). These publications were a major resource for the Commission on Wartime Relocation and Internment of Civilians, but the Commission's focus was on Japanese American claims. This allowed the staff little time to research Aleut cases. The commission's report, *Personal Justice Denied* (Washington, D.C.: U.S. Government Printing Office, 1982), consequently has an Aleut section based largely on Kirtland and Coffin's volumes. A brief companion volume, *Personal Justice Denied,* part 2: *Recommendations* (Washington, D.C.: U.S. Government Printing Office, 1982), contains a compendium of Aleut claims that were addressed in Public Law 100-383 (1988).

Some material I used concerning Attu people came directly from Japan. The Aleutian/Pribilof Islands Association commissioned Henry Stewart of Waseda University, Tokyo, to study the Aleut prisoners of war. His "Preliminary Report Concerning the 1942 Japanese Invasion and Occupation of Attu and the Subsequent Removal of Attuans to Japan 1942–1945" is based on secondary accounts and is found in the association's files. For future consideration, two books bearing somewhat on the topic have been published in Japan but are not translated: Kira Sugiyama, *Aleutian War Story* (1984) and Masami Sugiyama, *On the Trail of the Picture: A Trip to the Aleutians* (1987).

Film and video portrayals of Aleut evacuation have been quite helpful. The Alaska Historical Commission sponsored a fifty-five-minute presentation produced and directed by Lawrence Goldin in 1987 and entitled *Alaska at War*. In it, several Aleuts speak of their experiences. The film itself created a contextual setting for the event. But the most thorough documentary is found in a videocassette of fifty-nine minutes released in 1992 as *Aleut Evacuation: The Untold War Story*. It was produced by Michael and Mary Jo Thill of Gaff Rigged Productions, Girdwood, Alaska, for the Aleutian/Pribilof Islands Association. Dimitri Philemonof, the association's executive director, designed the cassette's jacket. The Thills and I worked independently of each other until about six months from the Alaska airing on June 12, 1992, the fiftieth anniversary of the first evacuation at Atka. Then they read my rough draft manuscript for its historical framework and followed some of my leads for photographs in the National Archives. In their documentary, the Thills graciously credited me as "academic consultant." This film is the only one of its kind and is reminiscent of the work of Kenneth Burns. Its perspective is similar to mine but different in tone and does not include the Attuan story. Anyone interested in this subject would do well to view this excellent documentary.

Secondary literature provided many valuable insights into the Aleut background. The work of Ivan Veniaminov is a necessary starting point. Two modern scholars, Lydia T. Black and William S. Laughlin, continue the Veniaminov tradition. Their research is basic material for an Aleut history that as yet remains unwritten.

Notes

1. OF ALEUTS AND ALASKA

1. For this interpretation, I am indebted to Jerah Chadwick, who graciously gave me his paper "The Cosmology of Community: Some Observations of Two Aleut Ungiikaax Narratives," prepared at the University of Alaska Fairbanks, 1987. The Chuginadak story is found in "The Chuginadak Woman," in Waldemar Jochelson, comp., Knut Bergsland, ed., *Unangam Ungiikangin: Aleut Traditions*, vol. 1 comp. (Fairbanks: University of Alaska Native Language Center, 1977), 17–50. These stories were told by the Umnak chief, Ivan Suvorov, written by the Unalaska chief, Alexei M. Yatchmeneff, and retranscribed by Knut Bergsland.

2. Ivan Veniaminov, quoted in Richard Henry Geoghegan, *The Aleut Language* (Washington, D.C.: United States Department of the Interior, 1944), 19; Lydia T. Black, "Early History," *Alaska Geographic* 7, no. 3 (1980): 89; Knut Bergsland, "Aleut Dialects of Atka and Attu," *Transactions of the American Philosophical Society*, n.s. 49, pt. 3 (1959): 18, 38.

3. Henry W. Elliott, *Our Arctic Province: Alaska and the Seal Islands* (New York: Charles Scribner's Sons, 1887), 179, 240. There is considerable debate over the derivation of *Aleut* and its meaning. Some recent Russian scholars argue that it was a term used by Aleuts to designate themselves and their community. See B. P. Polevoi, "The Discovery of Russian American," in Frederick Starr, ed., *Russia's American Colony* (Durham: Duke University Press, 1987), 23–24. Early ethnographic sources support the contention that *Aleut* is an Attu Island name for Attuans. See Lydia T. Black, *Atka: An Ethnohistory of the Western Aleutians*, ed. R. A. Pierce (Kingston, Ontario: Limestone Press, 1984), 8, 47.

4. William S. Laughlin, *Aleuts: Survivors of the Bering Land Bridge* (New York: Holt, Rinehart and Winston, 1980), 141.

5. Ibid., 10–15, 27–45, 96–104; Ivan Veniaminov, *Notes on the Islands of the Unalaska District*, ed. Richard A. Pierce, trans. Lydia T. Black and R. H. Geoghegan (Fairbanks: University of Alaska Press, and Kingston, Ontario: The Limestone Press, 1984), 217–39, 270–90, 297–313; Lydia T. Black, *Aleut Art, Unangam Aguqaadangin* (Anchorage: Aleutian/Pribilof Islands Association, 1982), and *Glory Remembered: Wooden Headgear of Alaska Sea Hunters* (Seattle: University of Washington Press, 1992); Lydia T. Black and R. G.

Liapunova, "Aleut: Islanders of the North Pacific," in William W. Fitzhugh and Aaron Crowell, eds., *Crossroads of Continents: Cultures of Siberia and Alaska* (Washington, D.C.: Smithsonian Institution Press, 1988), 52–82; Albert B. Harper, "Life Expectancy and Population Adaptation: The Aleut Centenarian Approach," in William S. Laughlin and Albert B. Harper, eds., *The First Americans: Origins, Affinities, and Adaptations* (New York and Stuttgart: Gustav Fischer, 1979), 314–21.

6. Veniaminov, *Notes,* 2–8, 11–14, 47–55, 257; Ethel Ross Oliver, *Journal of an Aleutian Year* (Seattle: University of Washington Press, 1988), 157, 169.

7. Margaret Lantis, "Aleut," in David Damas, ed., *Arctic,* vol. 5 of *Handbook of North American Indians* (Washington, D.C.: Smithsonian Institution Press, 1984), 163, and "The Aleut Social System, 1750 to 1810, from Early Historical Sources," in Margaret Lantis, ed., *Ethno-history in Southwestern Alaska and the Southern Yukon: Method and Content* (Lexington: University Press of Kentucky, 1970), 293.

8. Lantis, "Aleut," 163, and "Social System," 179; Laughlin, *Aleuts,* 15, 133, 145.

9. This phenomenon also developed in other groups. See Robert R. Rathburn, "The Russian Orthodox Church as a Native Institution Among the Koniag Eskimo of Kodiak Island, Alaska," *Arctic Anthropology* 18, no. 1 (1981): 12–22; and Nancy Yaw Davis, "Contemporary Pacific Eskimo," in *Arctic,* 201–02.

10. Richard Dauenhauer, *The Spiritual Epiphany of Aleut* (Anchorage: Center for Equality of Opportunity in Schooling and Alaska Native Foundation, 1978).

11. The figures are for the "Aleutian Islands District" locales of Akutan, Atka, Attu, Biorka, Kashega, Makushin, Nikolski, St. George, St. Paul, and Unalaska. U.S. Census, 1941, vol. 1, *Population,* "Number of Inhabitants: Alaska," 1193. Population statistics for the Aleuts are often conflicting. I have relied on the Census of 1940, various reports, and Office of Indian Affairs evacuation lists.

12. This was applied to Aleuts at Unalaska by one of their teachers. See Mary E. Winchell, *Home by the Bering Sea* (Caldwell, Idaho: Caxton Printers, 1951), 32.

13. Will F. Thompson, "Resources of the Western Aleutians" (M.A. thesis, University of Washington, 1950), 4. General Superintendent Claude M. Hirst to Commissioner of Indian Affairs John C. Collier, Sept. 10, 1940, National Archives, Washington, D.C., Record Group 75, Bureau of Indian Affairs, Central Classified Files, Alaska (hereinafter cited as RG 75 Alaska), folder 36881-1940-125, box 31; Olaus Murie, *Fauna of the Aleutian Islands and Alaska Peninsula* (Washington, D.C.: U.S. Fish and Wildlife Service, 1959), 3; Ray Hudson, ed., *People of the Aleutian Islands* (Unalaska, Alaska: Unalaska School District, 1986), 285–87.

14. "Report on Survey of Atka," RG 75 Alaska, file 7469-1944-123, pt. 1A, box 31; Phebe West, "An Educational Program for an Aleut Village" (M.A. Thesis, University of Washington, 1938), 27–29; Hudson, *People*, 263–69; "Activity Report for Week Ending March 29, 1941" from Donald W. Hagerty in Papers of John Collier, Sterling Memorial Library, Yale University, microfilm edition, reel 13:138, April 15, 1941.

15. "Report on Nikolski Village," RG 75 Alaska, ibid.; Collier Papers, ibid.

16. "Report on Kashega Village," RD 75 Alaska, ibid.; "Native Evacuees, Passenger List," *Kashega Natives,* RG 75 Alaska, file 27167-1943-220, box 29.

17. "Report on Makushin Village," RG 75 Alaska, file 7469-1944-123, pt. 1A, box 31; "Native Evacuees, Passenger List," *Makushin Natives,* RG 75 Alaska, file 27167-1943-220, box 29.

18. "Report on Unalaska Community," RG 75 Alaska, file 7469-1944-123, pt. 1A, box 31; Hudson, *People*, 293.

19. "Report on Biorka Village," RG 75 Alaska, ibid.; "Native Evacuees, Passenger List," *Biorka Natives,* RG 75 Alaska, file 27167-1943-220, box 29.

20. "Report on Akutan Village," RG 75 Alaska, file 7469-1944-123, pt. 1A, box 31.

21. "Native Evacuees, Passenger List," *St. George, St. Paul,* RG 75 Alaska, file 27167-1943-220, box 29; Merle Colby, *A Guide to Alaska: Last American Frontier* (New York: Macmillan, 1939), 347; Edward C. Johnston, "The Home of Milady's Seal Coat," in B. W. Denison, ed., *Alaska Today* (Caldwell, Idaho: Caxton Printers, 1949), 214–25; Dorothy Knee Jones, *A Century of Servitude: Pribilof Aleuts Under U.S. Rule* (Washington, D.C.: University Press of America, 1980).

22. Johnston, "Seal Coat," 257; Lawrence Carson, "Maybe Tomorrow," *Alaska Sportsman,* Oct. 1943, 24.

23. Hubert Howe Bancroft, *The Works of Hubert Howe Bancroft,* vol. 27, *History of the Northwest Coast* (San Francisco: A. L. Bancroft, 1886), 32–69; Raisa V. Makarova, *Russians on the Pacific, 1743–1799,* trans. and ed. Richard A. Pierce and Alton S. Donnelly (Kingston, Ontario: Limestone Press, 1975), 37.

24. Gilbert T. Rude, "Reminiscences of a Chechako," *United States Naval Institute Proceedings* 66 (April 1940): 555.

25. The clearest expression of this duality came in Alaska's split and segregated educational system. Territorial government provided schools only for Caucasians.

26. Governor Ernest Gruening to Secretary of the Interior Harold L. Ickes, June 17, 1943; and "Alaska Native Villages Without Voting Precinct Which Have 30 or More Votes," Alaska State Archives and Records Center, Juneau, Record Group 101, Papers of the Territorial Governors, series 130 (hereinafter cited as RG 101 Juneau), box 462.

27. Harold L. Ickes, *The Secret Diary of Harold L. Ickes,* vol. 3, *The Lowering*

Clouds, 1939–1941 (New York: Simon and Schuster, 1955), 71; Renee M. Jaussand, comp., *Preliminary Inventory of the Records of the U.S. Fish and Wildlife Service, Record Group 22* (Washington, D.C.: National Archives and Records Service, 1977), 1–2, 8.

28. This organization's procedures I have determined from research into correspondence on Aleut evacuation.

29. U.S. Census, 1940, vol. 1, *Population,* "Characteristics of the Population: Alaska," 5.

30. "The Alaska Native Service, History," National Archives–Pacific Northwest Branch, Seattle, Record Group 75, Bureau of Indian Affairs, Juneau Area Office (hereinafter cited as RG 75 Seattle), Correspondence 1934–56, file "Survey and Report of A.N.S. 1949" (540.6–540.64); Edward E. Hill, comp., *Preliminary Inventories of the Records of the Bureau of Indian Affairs,* vol. 1 (Washington, D.C.: National Archives and Records Service, 1965), 229–30.

31. These statistics are derived from "Office of Indian Affairs–Alaska Service Directory of Personnel, 1941–42," RG 101 Juneau, box 460.

32. Ibid.

33. Ibid.; Collier to Delegate Anthony J. Dimond, July 7, 1938, Anthony J. Dimond Papers, Alaska and Polar Regions Archives, University of Alaska Fairbanks (hereinafter cited as UAF Archives), Political Correspondence Files, box 23.

34. Wilfred H. Osgood, Edward A. Preble, and George H. Parker, "The Fur Seals and Other Life of the Pribilof Islands, Alaska, in 1914," *Bulletin of the Bureau of Fisheries* 34 (1914): 142–43. Edward C. Johnston described the new dwellings as "modern concrete houses"; see Johnston, "Seal Coat," 223.

35. "Alaska Conferences," February 5, 1937, RG 75 Alaska, Office File of Commissioner John Collier, 1933–45, entry 178, file Alaska 1935–40, box A–B.

36. "Agreement Determining the Mutual Responsibilities of the Office of Indian Affairs and the Department of Public Welfare for Care of Certain Natives," Feb. 10 and Mar. 4, 1939, RG 101 Juneau, box 428.

37. H. Dewey Anderson and Walter Crosby Eells, *Alaska Natives: A Survey of Their Sociological and Educational Status* (Palo Alto: Stanford University Press, 1935), 212, 218–19.

38. Barbara Elizabeth Callarman and Jay Ellis Ransom, "To the Westward Islands" (unfinished manuscript, circa 1940 [?]) Papers of Jay Ellis Ransom, University of Washington Archives, Seattle, file "Research Materials," box 1.

39. "Community Activity Reports," May 31, 1939, RG 75 Alaska, series entry 819.

40. Bernard R. Hubbard, *Cradle of the Storms* (New York: Dodd, Mead, 1935), 26–28.

41. Helen Wheaton, *Prekaska's Wife: A Year in the Aleutians* (New York: Dodd, Mead, 1945), 42, 65, 67.

42. Colby, *Guide to Alaska*, 16. This guide "took the record" for most printings, 13 by 1959. See also Monty Noam Penkower, *The Federal Writers' Project: A Study in Government Patronage of the Arts* (Urbana: University of Illinois Press, 1977), 246.

43. Joseph Driscoll, *War Discovers Alaska* (Philadelphia: Lippincott, 1943), 33. The term *Japs* is retained throughout for historical context.

44. Ibid., 51.

45. Ralph A. Ferrandini, "They Sing, Dance and Play," *Alaska Sportsman*, Nov. 1941, 9, 30.

46. Ibid., 30.

2. RUMORS OF WAR

Epigraph: Corey Ford, *Short Cut to Tokyo: The Battle for the Aleutians* (New York: Charles Scribner's Sons, 1943), 122.

1. This view resulted in a refusal by Congress to fund defense installations in Alaska. See Forest C. Pogue, *George C. Marshall: Organizer of Victory, 1943–1945* (New York: Viking Press, 1973), 147–48; Mark S. Watson, *Chief of Staff: Prewar Plans and Preparations* in *United States Army in World War II* series, *The War Department* section, Kent Roberts, ed. (Washington, D.C.: Department of the Army, 1950), 454–58.

2. Emile Gauvreau and Lester Cohn, *Billy Mitchell: Founder of Our Air Force and Prophet without Honor* (New York: E. P. Dutton, 1942), 83–85.

3. Maurice Matloff and Edwin M. Snell, *Strategic Planning for Coalition Warfare 1941–1942* in *United States Army in World War II* series, *The War Department* section, Kent Roberts, ed. (Washington, D.C.: Department of the Army, 1953), 2–3; Louis Morton, *Strategy and Command: The First Two Years* in *United States Army in World War II* series, *The War in the Pacific* section, Stetson Conn, ed. (Washington, D.C.: Department of the Army, 1962), 27, 39–42.

4. Samuel Eliot Morison, *Coral Sea, Midway and Submarine Actions*, vol. 4 of *History of United States Naval Operations in World War II* (Boston: Little, Brown, 1961), 74–75, 161–62; Armin Rappaport, *Henry L. Stimson and Japan, 1931–33* (Chicago: University of Chicago Press, 1963), 176.

5. Mary Childers Mangusso, "Anthony J. Dimond: A Political Biography" (Ph.D. diss., Texas Tech University, 1978), 315–59.

6. Ibid.; Jonathan M. Nielson, *Armed Forces on a Northern Frontier: The Military in Alaska's History, 1867–1987* (Westport, Conn.: Greenwood Press, 1988) 97–102; Stetson Conn, Rose C. Engelman, and Byron Fairchild, *Guard-*

ing the United States and Its Outposts in *United States Army in World War II* series, *The Western Hemisphere* section, Stetson Conn, ed. (Washington, D.C.: Department of the Army, 1964), 223–52; United States Army, Alaska, "Building Alaska with the U.S. Army, 1867–1962" (Pamphlet), Aug. 10, 1962, p. 87.

7. Melody Webb, *The Last Frontier* (Albuquerque: University of New Mexico Press, 1985), 143–70; Claus-M. Naske and Herman Slotnik, *Alaska: A History of the 49th State,* 2d ed. (Norman: University of Oklahoma Press, 1987), 118–23.

8. Jonathon M. Nielson, "Should Soldiers Be Governors?: The Military on the Alaska Frontier, 1867–1884" in *Governing Alaska: Pre-Territorial Days* (Anchorage: Alaska Historical Society, 1983), 95.

9. Gruening to Dimond, July 1 and 12, Aug. 9, and Oct. 22, 1940, Anthony J. Dimond Papers, UAF Archives, Political Correspondence Files, box 29.

10. Ibid., July 18, 1940; For Gruening's wartime complaints see his *Many Battles: The Autobiography of Ernest Gruening* (New York: Liveright, 1973), 308–27.

11. John Haile Cloe, *Build-up to Dutch Harbor, June 1940–June 1942,* pt. 2 of Sherry Faller, ed., *The Air Force in Alaska* (Anchorage: Office of History, Alaska Air Command, Elmendorf Air Force Base, 1986).

12. Captain Ralph C. Parker to Commanding General, Alaska Defense Command, Feb. 20, 1942, National Archives Modern Military Branch, Suitland, Maryland, Record Group 338, Alaska Defense Command, Alaskan Department (hereinafter cited as RG 338 Suitland), Official Correspondence of Maj. Gen. Simon B. Buckner, 1941–44.

13. Hirst to Commissioner Collier, Sept. 10, 1940, RG 75 Alaska, folder 36881-1940-125, box 31.

14. United States Army, Alaska, "Building Alaska," 88, 90.

15. "The Chronological History of the Development of Ft. Glenn, Alaska, from 7 September 1941 to 1 June 1944," 2, RG 338 Suitland, Alaska, Department Historical Reports 1941–47, box E-G.

16. Ibid., 4.

17. Ibid.; United States Army, *Official History of the Alaskan Department* (Washington, D.C.: Office of the Chief of Military History, n.d.), n.p.

18. D. Colt Denfeld, *The Defense of Dutch Harbor, Alaska, from Military Construction to Base Cleanup* (Anchorage: Alaska District U.S. Army Corps of Engineers, 1987), 30–59.

19. Ibid., 34, 42.

20. Telegram, Harold R. Terpening to Governor Gruening, Feb. 14, 1941; RG 101 Juneau, box 462; and R. H. Kitts and C. R. Rose, "Statement Concerning Labor Conditions at Dutch Harbor," Feb. 24, 1941, RG 101 Juneau, box 489.

21. Claus-M. Naske, *Edward Lewis "Bob" Bartlett of Alaska: A Life in Politics* (Fairbanks: University of Alaska Press, 1979), 42–43; Telegram, Clarence P. Gainor to Bartlett, Mar. 12, 1941, RG 101 Juneau, box 489; "Statement Concerning Labor Conditions," ibid.

22. R. E. Thomas, commander, U.S. Navy, to Secretary Edward L. "Bob" Bartlett, May 16, 1941; and Bartlett to Thomas, May 22, 1941, RG 101 Juneau, box 489.

23. U.S. Commissioner Jack Martin to Anthony J. Dimond, Sept. 4, 1941; and Martin to George A. Parks, Sept. 10, 1941, RG 101 Juneau, box 562; Deputy U.S. Marshal L. Verne Robinson to General Edgar B. Colladay, Oct. 16, 1941; and Colladay to commanding general, Alaska Defense Command, Oct. 27, 1941, RG 101 Juneau, box 489.

24. General Simon B. Buckner to Gruening, Nov. 5, 1941, RG 101 Juneau, box 489.

25. Martin to Dimond, Sept. 4, 1941, RG 101 Juneau, box 562.

26. Hudson, *People,* 314.

27. This estimate is based on 1940 census data and on adult Aleuts who were likely heads of a household in "Report on Unalaska Community," RG 75 Alaska, file 7469-1944-123, pt. 1A, box 31; and "Unalaska Natives," Passenger List, RG 75 Alaska, file 27167-1943-220, box 39.

28. Excerpt from letter, Mr. Fickinger to Mr. Beatty, July 30 [1941], RG 75 Alaska, file 35086-1941-310, box 80.

29. Joseph J. White, Jr., and Dr. John P. Harrington, "Preliminary Report on Certain Conditions Affecting Natives of Unalaska and Its Environs," Sept. 20, 1941, ibid.

30. Ibid.

31. Hudson, *People,* 215–21.

32. John A. Yatchmeneff "to our President, Franklin Delano Roosevelt, and to our Delegate to Congress, Anthony J. Dimond," May 16, 1941; and Yatchmeneff to Mrs. Eleanor Roosevelt, May 19, 1941, RG 75 Alaska, file 35086-1941-310, box 80.

33. Hudson, *People,* 220.

34. White and Harrington, "Preliminary Report."

35. This and the above Yatchmeneff quotations are from his letter to Roosevelt and Dimond.

36. Assistant Commissioner William Zimmerman, Jr., to Mr. C. H. Hirst, Sept. 4, 1941; Joseph J. White, Jr., and Dr. John P. Harrington, "Report on Certain Conditions Affecting the Natives of Unalaska," Nov. 25, 1941, RG 75 Alaska, file 305086-1941-310, box 80.

37. White and Harrington, "Report," ibid.

38. Driscoll, *War Discovers Alaska,* 323–26; Ruth Gruber to Harold L. Ickes, Mar. 3 and April 6, 1942, Library of Congress Manuscript Division, Washing-

ton, D.C., Papers of Harold L. Ickes, Secretary of Interior file 1933–46, folder AK2, 1942–46, box 93; Ruth Gruber, "Report on Social and Economic Conditions at Kodiak and Dutch Harbor to the Secretary of Interior," 1942, Papers of Ernest Gruening, UAF Archives, General Correspondence 1920–1970, file Defense (Alaska), box 2.

39. Paul W. Gordon to David J. Speck, Nov. 24, 1941, National Archives, Washington, D.C., RG 126 Division of Territories and Island Possessions (hereinafter cited as RG 126 Territories), file 9-1-52, box 330.

40. Ibid.

41. Memorandum, E. K. Burlew for the Secretary, approved by H. L. I., signed Dec. 2, 1941, RG 126 Territories, file 9-1-52, box 330.

42. Ibid.

43. Ibid.

3. RESPONSES TO WAR

1. Morgan Sherwood, "Seal Poaching in the North Pacific: Japanese Raids on the Pribilofs, 1906," *Alaska History* (Fall 1984): 45; John J. Underwood, *Alaska: An Empire in the Making*, 2d ed. (New York: Dodd, Mead and Company, 1925), 268; Theodore P. Bank III et al., *The University of Michigan Expedition to the Aleutian Islands, 1948–49* (Ann Arbor: University of Michigan, 1950), 30.

2. Memo, Office of Strategic Services, Record Group 226, OSS, National Archives, Washington, D.C., file 19526; Report, Officer-in-Charge to District Intelligence Officer, 13th Naval District, June 29, 1942, Naval Historical Center, Washington Naval Yard, Washington, D.C., EG3/A16-3 serial 0339.

3. William Gillman, *Our Hidden Front* (New York: Reynal & Hitchcock, 1944), 4, 41.

4. Gruber to Ickes, Dec. 2, 1941, Library of Congress Manuscript Division, Washington, D.C., Papers of Harold L. Ickes, Secretary of Interior file 1933-46, folder AK1, 1934–41, box 93.

5. Quoted in Lt. Gen. George I. Forsythe, vol. 1 (Carlisle Barracks, Pennsylvania: U.S. Army Military History Institute, Senior Officer Oral History Program, 1974), 88.

6. Jean Potter, *Alaska under Arms* (New York: Macmillan, 1942), 47; Wesley Frank Craven and James Lea Cate, eds., *The Army Air Forces in World War II*, vol. 1, *Plans and Early Operations, January 1939 to August 1942* (Chicago: University of Chicago Press, 1948), 276.

7. Potter, *Alaska under Arms*, 48, 53.

8. Gruening to Ickes, Jan. 10, 1942, Ernest Gruening Papers, UAF Archives, Diaries, Notebooks (1930–1970), box 4; Gruening, *Many Battles*, 308–09 and 318–22.

9. Diary entries, Monday, Dec. 8; Thursday, Dec. 18; Friday, Dec. 19; and Monday, Dec. 29, 1941, Gruening Papers, UAF Archives, Diaries, Notebooks (1930–1970), box 4.

10. Gruening to Ickes, Jan. 10, 1942, ibid; Entry, Sunday, Feb. 1, 1942, Ickes Diary, Library of Congress Manuscript Division, microfilm, roll 5, frame 6281.

11. Memo, Gruening to the Under Secretary, Dec. 19, 1942, Gruening Papers, UAF Archives, Alaska General Correspondence, 1920–1970, file Defense (Alaska), box 2.

12. Ibid.

13. Ibid.

14. Dimond to Secretary Henry L. Stimson and Secretary Frank Knox, Jan. 27, 1942; and Patterson to Dimond, Feb. 24, 1941, Dimond Papers, UAF Archives, Political Correspondence Files, box 29.

15. James C. Rettie to Harold D. Smith, May 7 [emphasis original]; and Smith to Rettie, May 13, 1942, Correspondence of Frank Knox, Record Group 80, National Archives, Washington, D.C., file 4-1-5, box 2; Stimson to Smith, May 25, 1942, Papers of the Commission on Wartime Relocation and Internment of Civilians, Record Group 220 (hereafter cited as CWRIC), National Archives, Washington, D.C., file Publications and Reports, box 49.

16. *Code of Federal Regulations,* Title 3, *The President, 1938–1943: Compilation* (Washington, D.C.: U.S. Government Printing Office, 1968), 1167–69.

17. Morgan Sherwood, *Big Game in Alaska: A History of Wildlife and People* (New Haven, Conn.: Yale University Press, 1981), 1–17, 126–36; memo, Paul F. Foster to Director Plans Division, May 15, 1942, Records of the 17th Naval District (Alaska), RG 181 Seattle, General Files 1942–43, file A16-3, box 8.

18. Memo, ibid.

19. Jacobus ten Broek, Edward N. Barnhart, and Floyd W. Matson, *Prejudice, War and the Constitution: Japanese American Evacuation and Resettlement* (Berkeley: University of California Press, 1954), 134.

20. Ibid., 134–35; Conn, Engelman, and Fairchild, *Guarding the United States,* 143; U.S. Air Force Office of History, Elmendorf Air Force Base, Anchorage, Alaska, file "Censorship in Alaska During World War II."

21. Parker to the governor, Aug. 5, 1941, RG 101 Juneau, series 130, box 571.

22. Secretary of the Navy to Chief of Naval Operations, Oct. 31, 1941, Records of the 13th Naval District, RG 181 Seattle, Commandant's Office Regular Navy Files 1941, file EG3/A16, box 56.

23. Quoted in Gillman, *Hidden Front,* 55–56.

24. Telegrams, Garnet W. Martin to Gruening, Dec. 10; Gruening to Martin, Dec. 23, 1941; and letter, Bartlett to O. E. Wilcox, Jan. 27, 1942, RG 101 Juneau, file 77, box 571.

25. Bartlett to Gruening, Feb. 11; and memo, Gruening for the secretary, Feb. 19, 1942, ibid.

26. Telegram, Commandant 13th Naval District to Gruening, Jan. 13, 1942, RG 101 Juneau, file 77, box 562.

27. Telegrams, Gruening to Buckner and Commanding General Fort Mears, Jan. 14; Commandant 13th Naval District to Gruening, Jan. 17; Gruening to Guy Swope, Jan. 17; and Vice Admiral Charles S. Freeman to Bartlett, Jan. 27, 1942, ibid.

28. Captain Zeusler to Bartlett, Feb. 6; Freeman to Bartlett, Feb. 17; Bartlett to Freeman, Feb. 26; and Bartlett to George Sundborg, Feb. 27, 1942, RG 101 Juneau, file 77, box 571.

29. Letter, Oscar M. Powell to Hugh J. Wade, Mar. 13; and telegrams, Bartlett to Gruening, Mar. 13; and Gruening to Bartlett, Mar. 16, 1942, ibid.

30. Telegrams, Homer I. Stockdale to Hirst, Dec. 9; Fred R. Geeslin to Stockdale, Dec. 11; Stockdale to Hirst, Dec. 12; and Virgil R. Farrell to Stockdale, Dec. 12, 1942, ibid.

31. Secretary of the Interior to Secretary of the Navy, Dec. 11, 1941, Records of the Fish and Wildlife Service, RG 22 Seattle, General, 1941–1943, file Navy, box 12505.

32. Superintendent Edward C. Johnston to the Director, Mar. 18, 1942, RG 22 Seattle, Pribilof Island Program, file Navy General 1941–43, box 40.

33. Chief Ward T. Bower to F. G. Morton, Feb. 11; Morton to Commandant, Mar. 5; Freeman to Chief of the Bureau of Supplies and Accounts, Mar. 11; and Freeman to the Office in Charge, Mar. 25, 1942, RG 181 Seattle, 13th Naval District Commandant's Office, Regular Navy Files, file EG3/A16-3/L20-1, box 145.

34. Buckner to General John L. DeWitt, Feb. 4, 1942, RG 338 Suitland, Official Correspondence of Maj. Gen. Simon B. Buckner, 1941–44.

35. Ibid.

36. Colladay to Buckner, May 12, 1942, ibid.

4. WAR ON THE ALEUTS

1. United States Strategic Bombing Survey (Pacific), *The Campaigns of the Pacific War* (New York: Greenwood Press, 1946), 78–79.

2. Elmer B. Potter and Chester W. Nimitz, eds., *Sea Power: A Naval History* (Englewood Cliffs, N.J.: Prentice-Hall, 1960), 731; Samuel Eliot Morison, *History of United States Naval Operations in World War II*, vol. 7, *Aleutians, Gilberts and Marshals, June 1942–April 1944* (Boston: Little, Brown, 1961), 3.

3. Isobel Wylie Hutchinson, *Stepping Stones from Alaska to Asia* (London: Blackie & Son, 1937), 168–69.

4. Quoted in information, October 1945, by Donald Q. Palmer, Office of

Indian Affairs, Record Group 75-N, Still Picture Branch, National Archives, Washington, D.C., Prints: Photographs of Indians, 1909–1957, series N, file Aleut-D, box 2.

5. *Anchorage Daily Times,* Aug. 14, 1942; *Daily Alaska Empire* (Juneau) Aug. 22, 1942; Mike Lokanin, "Here Is My Lifetime's Story," in Ethel Ross Oliver, ed., *Journal of an Aleutian Year* (Seattle: University of Washington Press, 1988), 224–25.

6. Lokanin, ibid., 226–27.

7. Ibid., 227.

8. Mike Lokanin, "Aleut Tells of Jap Invasion," Nov. 28, 1945, RG 75-N Still Picture Branch, file Aleut-C, box 2; Innokenty Golodoff as told to Karl W. Kenyon, "The Last Days of Attu Village," *Alaska Sportsman,* Dec. 1966, 8; Alex Prossoff, "Alex Prossoff's Story," in Oliver, *Journal,* 242; Olean Prokopeuff, *The Aleutian Invasion: World War II in the Aleutian Islands* (Unalaska, Alaska: Unalaska City School District, 1981), 50. For a Japanese version see: Henry Stewart, "Preliminary Report Concerning the 1942 Japanese Invasion and Occupation of Attu and the Subsequent Removal of Attuans to Japan 1942–1945," 16–17, files of the Aleutian/Pribilof Islands Association, Inc., Anchorage, Alaska. The report on Jones's exhumation is in the U.S. Air Force Office of History, Elmendorf Air Force Base, Anchorage, Alaska.

9. Parascovia Wright, CWRIC microfilm, frame 585; Palmer information, RG 75-N, file Aleut-D, box 2; Lokanin, "Lifetime's Story," 230–34; Golodoff, "Last Days," 8.

10. Lokanin, "Aleut Tells"; John Golodoff, quoted in Rose Curtice Butts, "Prisoners from Alaska," *Alaska Sportsman,* May 1948, 15; Golodoff, "Last Days," 8.

11. Lokanin, "Lifetime's Story," 233–34; Prossoff, "Prossoff's Story," 242–43.

12. "Summary of Information on Japanese Names Applied to the Aleutian Islands and the Komandorskis," National Archives, Suitland, Maryland, RG 165, Department of War (hereinafter cited as RG 165 Suitland), rg 2, Regional File, 1933–44, Alaska, 6910-9185, box 51; translations of place names were provided by Dr. Frederich G. Kavanagh, Valparaiso University. Kavanagh has seen World War II Japanese maps that included the western Aleutians in Japanese territory. Intelligence Report, "The Enemy on Kiska," 53, U.S. Air Force Office of History, Elmendorf Air Force Base, Anchorage, Alaska.

13. Colby, *Guide to Alaska,* 343; entry, Sunday, June 14, 1942, Ickes Diary, Library of Congress Manuscript Division, microfilm, roll 5, frame 6281.

14. Fredrika Martin Papers, box 3, UAF Archives; Jakuo Mikami, "Aleutian Naval Operation March 1942–February 1943," Japanese Monograph no. 88, pp. 3, 18, U.S. Air Force Office of History, Elmendorf Air Force Base, Anchorage, Alaska.

15. "Operation Plan no. 2-42, pp. 1–2, RG 313 Suitland, NOPACFOR (Red Numbers), box 5279; "War Diary of Commander Patrol Wing Four, 27 May 1942, to 30 June 1942," 154–55, COMNDRWESSEAFRON (Blue Numbers), box 4593.

16. "War Diary," ibid.; Brian Garfield, *The Thousand-Mile War: World War II in Alaska and the Aleutians* (New York: Doubleday, 1969; reprint, Bantam Books, 1988), 95–97; "Naval Action at Kiska Harbor," Bill Carter to Frank G. Gorrie, July 2, 1942, RG 126 Territories, Alaska 9-1-96, file Foreign Relations. World War. General; memo, Officer-in-Charge to the District Intelligence Officer, 13th Naval District, June 29, 1942, Naval Historical Center, Washington Naval Yard, Washington, D.C.

17. "War Diary," ibid.; "Official History of the Alaska Department," U.S. Army of the Chief of Military History, Washington, D.C., n.d., n.p.

18. Alice Snigaroff Petrivelli, CWRIC microfilm, frames 570–71, 573; Poda Snigaroff, "We Left Our Village Burning," in Thomas P. Bank III et al., *The University of Michigan Expedition to the Aleutian Islands, 1948–49* (Ann Arbor: University of Michigan, 1950), 32; Alice Snigaroff Petrivelli to Dean Kohlhoff, April 7, 1992.

19. Memorandum for War Plans Division by Marshal/Chief of Staff, March 18, 1942, RG 165 Suitland, Operations Divisions U.S. Army Chief of Staff, WDCSA381, file War Plans, box 87; Morton, *Strategy and Command*, 420; "History of the Western Defense Command," Vol. 2., U.S. Army Office of the Chief of Military History, Washington, D.C., n.d., 171; Commander in Chief, United States Fleet, and Chief of Naval Operations to Commander, Alaska Sector, June 11, 1942, RG 165 Suitland, Operations Division, Decimal file 1942–45, 320.2, ADC, sec. II, box 688; Admiral Theobald to Admiral Nimitz, June 16, 1942, RG 313 Suitland, NORPACFOR (Red Numbers), box 5279.

20. Bombing Survey, *Campaigns*, 79.

21. Bower to Johnston, June 2, 1942, RG 22 Seattle, file Sealing General, 1941–1944, box 12504.

22. Notice, June 5, 1942, UAF Archives, Fredericka Martin Papers, box 3.

23. Ibid.

24. Ibid.

25. Sergie Shaishnikoff, CWRIC microfilm, frames 793–94; Flore Lekanof, frame 757.

26. George McGlashen, frames 682–87, ibid.

27. Leonty Savoroff, frames 632–33, ibid.

28. Martin to Estella Draper [Gruening's secretary], May 2, 1942; and Martin to Bartlett, May 25, 1942, RG 101 Juneau, series 130, box 567.

29. William M. Floyd to Gruening, June 18, 1942, ibid.

30. Memorandum to District Liaison Officer, 13th Naval District, from Captain B. C. Allen, June 9, 1942, RG 181 Seattle, Records of Naval Districts

and Shore Establishments (hereinafter cited as RG 181 Seattle), "General Correspondence of 13th Naval District and Components," entry 114, box 1; "Report by Claude Smith at Dutch Harbor," file Correspondence Ernest Gruening, U.S. Air Force Office of History, Elmendorf Air Force Base, Anchorage, Alaska.

31. "Report by worker Julius H. Clague, at Unalaska, June 17, 1942," RG 101 Juneau, series 130, box 495.

32. Philemon Tutiakoff, CWRIC microfilm, frames 625–27.

5. CONTEMPLATING ALEUT EVACUATION

1. Telegrams, Naval Air Station to Superintendent, Bureau of Indian Affairs [Hirst]; and Geeslin to Commanding Officer, Dec. 8, 1941, RG 101 Juneau, box 571.

2. Telegram, Hirst to Corthell, Dec. 26, 1941, ibid.

3. Telegram, Stockdale to Office of Indian Service, Dec. 16, 1941, ibid.; National Archives Microfilm Publication, "Public Hearings," CWRIC microfilm, frame 628. The estimate of Unalaska Aleut independent departures is based on the difference between those polled, 173, and those evacuated, 143, taking into account that some were not evacuated at all.

4. Stockdale to Hirst, Jan. 31, 1942, RG 75 Alaska, folder 13460-142-134, box 32.

5. Ibid.

6. Ibid.; Stockdale to Dr. Evelyn Butler, Feb. 5, 1942, ibid.

7. Stockdale to Butler; and Hirst to Commissioner of Indian Affairs, Mar. 13, 1942, ibid.

8. Mr. and Mrs. Charles R. Magee to General Superintendent, Jan. 6, 1942, ibid.

9. *Anchorage Daily Times,* Aug. 14, 1942; Gillman, *Hidden Front,* 89; Golodoff, "Last Days," 8.

10. "Excerpts from preliminary and confidential draft 'PLAN OF PROCEDURE FOR EVACUATION AND RECEPTION CARE OF EVACUEES,' Evacuation Bulletin No. 2 of the Federal Security Agency," 1–2, RG 101 Juneau, series 130, box 571.

11. Memorandum, Paul W. Gordon to Governor Gruening, Jan. 23, 1942, RG 126 Territories, Alaska 9-1-96, file Foreign Relations. World War. General.

12. "Discussion at a Meeting called March 18, 1942, by Acting Governor E. L. Bartlett on the subject of evacuation planning for Alaska"; and Bartlett's explanation of this meeting's make-up and origin, Mar. 18, 1942, RG 101 Juneau, series 130, file 77, box 571.

13. Ibid.

14. "STATEMENT OF PROBLEMS" and "Basis for Discussion at Conference of Federal and Territory Agency Representatives March 18," 1942, ibid.

15. "Discussion at a Meeting," RG 101 Juneau, series 130, file 77, box 571.

16. Ibid.

17. Ibid.

18. Ibid.

19. Ibid.

20. Bartlett to Buckner, Mar. 19; and Buckner to Bartlett, Mar. 23, 1942, ibid.

21. Hugh J. Wade to Alvin Roseman, Mar. 20; and Wade to Donald W. Hagerty and Hirst, Apr. 21, 1942, RG 75 Alaska, folder 13460-1942-134, box 32.

22. Wade to Roseman, ibid.

23. Ibid.

24. Telegram, Com Thirteen to William Zimmerman, April 6, 1942, ibid.

25. Memorandum, John Collier to Secretary Ickes, April 10, 1942, ibid.

26. Ibid.

27. Telegrams, Hagerty to Commissioner Zimmerman, Apr. 5; and Hagerty to Hirst, Apr. 9, 1942, RG 75 Alaska, folder 13460-1942-134, box 32.

28. Telegram, Hirst to Hagerty, Apr. 11; and letter, Hirst to Hagerty, Apr. 14, 1942, ibid.

29. Hagerty to Zimmerman, Apr. 11 and 13, 1942, ibid.

30. Hagerty to Zimmerman, Apr. 13, ibid.

31. Parker to Hirst, Apr. 15; and Henry W. Clark to Hirst, Apr. 21, 1942, ibid.

32. Telegram, Hagerty to Zimmerman, Apr. 18; and letter, Hagerty to Zimmerman, Apr. 20, 1942, ibid.

33. Hagerty to Zimmerman, Apr. 20; and Hagerty to Hirst, Apr. 21, 1942, ibid.

34. Assistant Commissioner Zimmerman to Hagerty, Apr. 22, ibid.

35. Ibid; Telegram, Zimmerman to Hagerty, Apr. 23, 1942, ibid.

36. Telegrams, Commander Alaska Sector to Bureau of Indian Affairs, May 7; and Geeslin to Commander Alaska Sector, May 8; and letter, Geeslin to Zimmerman, May 8, 1942, ibid.

37. Parker to Zimmerman; and Hagerty to Hirst, May 14, 1942, ibid.

38. Hagerty to Hirst, ibid.

39. Hirst to Zimmerman, n.d. [but after May 14, 1942], ibid.

40. Telegrams, Zimmerman to Hagerty, May 19; Hagerty to Zimmerman, May 20; and Zimmerman to Hirst, May 21, 1942, ibid.

41. Telegram, Hirst to Zimmerman, May 22; and letter, Zimmerman to Hirst, May 17, 1942, ibid.

42. Gruening to Ickes, June 4, 1942, Gruening Papers, UAF Archives, Political Affairs Reading File, box 1.

43. Hagerty to Zimmerman, June 6, 1942, RG 75 Alaska, folder 13460-1942-134, box 32.

6. ALEUT EVACUATIONS

1. Michael and Mary Jo Thill, producers, *Aleut Evacuation: The Untold War Story* (Anchorage: Aleutian/Pribilof Islands Association, Inc., 1992, documentary videotape).

2. Melvin C. Walthall, *"We Can't All Be Heroes:" A History of the Separate Infantry Regiments in World War II* (n.p., n.d.), appendix by Capt. Otho Rawlings (circa Sept. 15, 1942), 3; William Dirks, CWRIC microfilm, frame 579. There are several accounts of these evacuations with variant data. The attempt herein is to present what happened based on documents, some containing contradictory claims. Concordance is impossible.

3. Logbook, USS *Gillis* (AVD 12), entry Fri., June 12, 1942, RG 80, General Records of the Department of Navy, Army; National Archives, Washington, D.C. (hereinafter cited as RG 80 National Archives).

4. June 13, ibid.; "War Diary of Commander Patrol Wing Four, 27 May 1942 to 30 June 1942," 155, RG 80 National Archives.

5. Logbook, June 13, ibid.; Snigaroff, "We Left Our Village," 32–33; Logbook, USS *Hulbert* (AVD 6), entry Sat., June 13, 1942, RG 80 National Archives.

6. Logbook, ibid.; memo, Officer-in-Charge to the District Intelligence Officer, 13th Naval District, June 29, 1942, Naval Historical Center, Washington Naval Yard, Washington, D.C.; Snigaroff, "We Left Our Village," 33.

7. Lyman R. Ellsworth, *Guys on Ice* (New York: David McKay, 1952), 4.

8. Ibid., 8.

9. Ibid., 9; Logbook, USS *Oriole* (AT 136), entries Sun., June 14, and Tues., June 16, 1942, RG 80 National Archives.

10. Ellsworth, *Guys*, 10–11.

11. Logbook, USS *Oriole*, entry Tues., June 16, 1942; "Summary of the Evacuation of St. George," files of the Aleutian/Pribilof Islands Association, Anchorage, Alaska.

12. St. George "Summary," ibid.; "Summaries of the Evacuation of St. George and St. Paul," files of the Aleutian/Pribilof Islands Association, Anchorage, Alaska.

13. Logbook, USS *Oriole*, entry Tues., June 16; "St. George Island Logbook," Department of Interior, Bureau of Commerical Fisheries, Alaska State Historical Library, Juneau, Alaska, microfilm reel 17, entry Tues., June 16; "Summaries," ibid.

14. "St. George Logbook," ibid.; Papers of the War Shipping Administra-

tion, RG 248 National Archives, entry 9, Records of Allocations and Assignments, Alaska, box 2.

15. Telegrams, Commander Alaskan Sector to Lieutenant Robert Schoettler; and Schoettler to Commander Alaskan Sector, June 14, 1942, RG 75 Alaska, box 32; Navy Command to Navy Department, June 14, RG 101 Juneau, series 130, box 571; Hagerty to Zimmerman; Commander Alaskan Sector to Schoettler; and Hagerty to Hirst, June 15, 1942, RG 75 Alaska, box 32.

16. Telegrams, Gault AG ADC to Bureau of Indian Affairs; June 16, RG 75 Alaska, box 32; Zimmerman to Hirst; and Zimmerman to Hagerty, June 16, RG 101 Juneau, series 130, box 571.

17. Telegram, Hagerty to Zimmerman, June 17, RG 75 Alaska, box 32.

18. Telegrams, Hirst to Hagerty; and Hagerty to Hirst, June 17, RG 75 Alaska, ibid.; Johnston to Olson, June 17, RG 101 Juneau, series 130, box 571; Hagerty to Hirst, June 18, RG 75 Alaska, ibid.

19. Telegrams, B. F. Heintzleman to Forest Service, June 17, RG 126 Territories, file Foreign Relations. World War. Evacuation; Hagerty to Hirst; and Hirst to Zimmerman, June 18, RG 75 Alaska, ibid.

20. Telegram, Gruening to Roosevelt, June 20, 1942, RG 101 Juneau, series 130, box 571.

21. Telegrams, Gruening to Buckner, June 18; Buckner to Gruening, June 23; and Gault to Gruening, June 25, 1942, ibid.

22. Gruening to Ickes, June 20, 1942, Gruening Papers, UAF Archives, "Political Affairs," Reading File, box 1.

23. Ibid.

24. Ibid.; Telegrams, Gruening to Swope; and Buckner to District Commander, June 22, 1942, RG 101 Juneau, series 130, box 571; telegram, Stevenson OIC to Territories Interior, June 22, 1942, RG 126 Territories, file Foreign Relations. World War. Evacuation.

25. Telegram, Swope to Gruening, June 23, 1942, RG 126 Territories, ibid.

26. Telegram, Hirst to Zimmerman, June 22, 1942, RG 101 Juneau, series 130, box 571; letter, Hirst to Zimmerman, June 23, 1942, RG 75 Alaska, box 32.

27. Telegrams, Hagerty to Hirst; Hagerty to Zimmerman; and Hirst to Hagerty, June 22, 1942, RG 75 Alaska, ibid.

28. Telegrams, Pauline A. T. Whitfield to Hirst, June 16; Baish to Commanding Officer, June 19; and Hirst to Whitfield, June 19, 1942, RG 101 Juneau, series 130, box 571.

29. Telegrams, Margaret Quinn to Hirst, June 16; Hirst to Quinn, June 18, 1942, ibid.

30. Telegram, Gruening to Freeman, June 26, 1942, ibid.

31. Telegram, COMALSEC to Schoettler, n.d., ibid.; letter, Hirst to Zimmerman, June 30, 1942, RG 75 Alaska, box 32.

32. Telegrams, Hagerty to Hirst, July 2; Hirst to Hagerty, July 2; and Hirst to Zeusler, July 3, 1942, RG 101 Juneau, series 130, box 571.

33. Telegrams, Barrett to Hirst, July 4, 5, and 6, 1942, ibid.

34. Telegram, Hirst to Barrett and Zeusler, July 6, 1942, ibid.

35. Telegram, Gruening to Commanding Officer, July 6, 1942, ibid.

36. Telegrams, Hirst to Leonard Allen, July 7; Allen to Captain of the Port, July 8; Barrett to Hirst, July 8; Hagerty to Hirst, July 8; and Hirst to Hagerty, July 10, 1942, ibid.

37. Telegrams, Hirst to Zimmerman and Captain of Port, July 11; and Allen to Hirst, July 12, 1942, ibid.

38. Telegrams, COMALSEC Kodiak to DCGO Ketchikan; and Gruening to Commanding Officer, July 11, 1942, ibid.

39. Hirst to Commissioner of Indian Affairs Collier, July 31, 1942, RG 75 Alaska, box 32.

40. Papers of the War Shipping Administration, RG 248 National Archives, Entry 9, Records of Allocations and Assignments, Alaska, box 2.

41. Testimony of William Ermeloff, Dorofey Chercasen, Leonty Savoroff, Laverna Pletnikoff Dushkin, and Olga Mansoff, CWRIC microfilm, frames 633, 640, 648, 653, and 687, respectively.

42. Testimony of George McGlashen and Laverna Dushkin, ibid., frames 648 and 682.

43. Colladay to Buckner, June 15, 1942, RG 338 Suitland, Buckner Correspondence, 1941–44.

44. Hobart W. Copeland to Commanding General, Jan. 17, 1944, RG 75 Alaska, box 31.

45. Telegram, Quinn to Collier, June 23, 1942, RG 75 Alaska, box 32.

46. Hagerty to Zimmerman, June 26, ibid.; Telegram, Fletcher to Ickes, July 7, RG 126 Territories, file Foreign Relations. World War. Evacuation; letter, Zimmerman to Hagerty, July 15, 1942, RG 75 Alaska, box 32.

47. Letters, Zimmerman to Hagerty, RG 75 Alaska, ibid.; Ickes to Forrestal and Fletcher, July 9; and Forrestal to Ickes, July 12, in John C. Kirtland and David F. Coffin, Jr., *The Relocation and Internment of the Aleuts During World War II*, vol. 2 (Anchorage: Aleutian/Pribilof Islands Association, 1981), 65–67.

48. Military Police to Commanding General, Jan. 12, 1944, CWRIC, Aleutian-Pribilof Islands, file General–Ward Lake, box 51; RG 248 National Archives, Papers of the War Shipping Administration, Entry 9, Records of Allocations and Assignments, Alaska, "WSA Passenger Vessels in Alaska Pool," box 2; Copeland to Commanding General, Jan. 17, 1944, RG 75 Alaska, box 31.

49. Military Police to Commanding General, ibid; telegrams, Hagerty to Zimmerman, July 21 and 22, CWRIC, ibid. "History of the Western Defense

Command," vol. 1, U.S. Army Office of the Chief of Military History, Washington, D.C., n.d., 15 n. 1. The figure for Unalaska city passengers is derived from official passenger lists in RG 75 Alaska as already cited, minus one person who arrived earlier on the *Columbia*.

50. Letter, Copeland to Commanding General, June 17, 1944, RG 75 Alaska, box 31.

51. W. Barton Greenwood to Hirst, Oct. 2, 1942, RG 126 Territories, file Foreign Relations. World War. Evacuation; J. J. Lichtenwalner to Commandant, Nov. 4; and Charles S. Kerrick to Department of Interior, Nov. 10, 1942, RG 75 Alaska, file 27167-1943-220, box 39; J. W. Reeves, Jr., to Commandant, 13th Naval District, Mar. 23, 1943, RG 181 Seattle, "Commandant's Office, Regular Navy Files 1942–1943," file A16-3/Aleutian, box 4.

52. Greenwood to Hirst, Oct. 2, 1942; Hirst to Commissioner, Dec. 4, 1942; and Greenwood to Hirst, Mar. 10, 1943, RG 75 Alaska, box 39; James V. Forrestal to Ickes, April 7; Knox to Ickes, April 15; and Michael W. Straus to Forrestal, May 6, 1944, RG 75 Alaska, box 31; Summary, "Return of the Aleuts," RG 165 Suitland, Alaska Defense Command, box 1171.

53. Parker to H. J. Thompson, June 17, 1942, RG 101 Juneau, box 571.

54. From "Transcripts and Reference Papers" for *Alaska at War* (Anchorage: Alaska Historical Commission, 1987, film), 1–2, University of Alaska Anchorage Archives; Parascovia Lokanin Wright, CWRIC microfilm, frame 586; from Prossoff, "Alex Prossof's Story," 243.

55. From Lokanin, "Lifetime's Story," 235; Stewart, "Preliminary Report," 14.

56. Prossoff, "Alex Prossof's Story," 243; Lokanin, 235; Stewart Report, 23–24.

57. Prossoff and Lokanin, ibid.

7. IN STRANGE NEW LANDS

1. *Personal Justice Denied*, 330–31; Oliver, *Journal*, 243.

2. William Ermeloff, CWRIC microfilm, frame 658.

3. T. Hattori to Dr. Stein, Oct. 19, 1976, files of Dr. Michael Krauss, University of Alaska Fairbanks.

4. Mary L. Beech, "Refugees from the Pribilofs," *Alaska Life*, Aug. 1944, 18; Driscoll, *War Discovers Alaska*, 35.

5. Memo, Mr. Geeslin, Mr. Peters, Mr. Dale to Hirst, June 23, 1942, and "Recommendations," RG 75 Alaska, folder 13460-142-134, box 32.

6. Ibid., 2–3

7. Ibid., 3.

8. Ibid., 4–6.

9. Ibid., 7–8.

10. Ibid., 8–11.

11. Ibid., 1 and 6.

12. Driscoll, *War Discovers Alaska,* 33–37.

13. Ibid., 38–39, 46, and 49–50.

14. Ibid., 38, 50–51, and 55.

15. Ibid., 46–47, and 51.

16. Marjorie Ward, CWRIC microfilm, frame 821; Beech, "Refugees," 18; Anatoly Lekanof in *Wartime in the Aleutians* (Unalaska, Alaska: Unalaska City School District, 1977) 62; William J. Merculief, CWRIC microfilm, frame 745; Flore Lekanof, frame 749; Mike Lekanof, frame 565.

17. "St. Paul Island Logbook," Department of Interior, Bureau of Commercial Fisheries, Alaska State Historical Library, Juneau, Alaska, microfilm reel 17, entry June 27–Aug. 2, 1942; Natalie Misikian, CWRIC microfilm, frame 804; Martha Krukof, frame 812; Ann S. McGlashen, frame 709; Father Michael Lestenkof, frame 731; Mike Lekanof, frame 565; Sergie Shaishnikoff, frame 793.

18. Lekanof, ibid.; McGlashen, ibid.; Martha Krukof, CWRIC microfilm, frame 810; Natalie Misikian, frame 805.

19. F. W. Hynes, "Report of Fish and Wildlife Service Participation in the Evacuation of the Aleutian and Pribilof Islands Natives," June 25, 1942, RG 22 Seattle, file Evacuation-Pribilofs 1942–1943, box 12503; Hirst to Gruening, June 29, 1942, RG 75 Alaska, folder 13460-142-131, box 32.

20. Daniel C. R. Benson to Johnston, July 6, 1942, RG 22 Seattle, box 34.

21. Lee C. McMillin to Johnston, July 11, 1942, ibid.

22. McMillin to Johnston, July 24; and Clarence C. Olson to Johnston, July 24, 1942, RG 22 Seattle, box 12503.

23. Johnston to Bower, Aug. 24, 1942, RG 22 Seattle, box 33.

24. McMillin to Johnston, Sept. 12, 1942, RG 22 Seattle, box 12503.

25. Ibid.

26. Morton to Bower, Sept. 18; Johnston to McMillin, Sept. 22; and McMillin to Johnston, Oct. 7, 1942, ibid.

27. Memorandum, Ruth Gruber to Mr. Chapman, Oct. 15, 1942, RG 75 Alaska, box 32.

28. Handwritten notes and memorandum from A. G. H., Nov. 10, 1942 (emphasis in original), ibid.

29. Ickes to Stimson, Nov. 23, 1942, RG 22 Seattle, box 12505.

30. From research at Department of Vital Statistics, Alaska Office Building, Juneau, Alaska.

31. Driscoll, *War Discovers Alaska,* 39–40; Hirst to Gruening, June 29, 1942, RG 75 Alaska, folder 13460-142-131, box 32.

32. Driscoll, *War Discovers Alaska,* 40, 42, and 45–56.

33. Stephen E. Hilson, *Exploring Alaska and British Columbia* (Holland, Mich.: Van Winkle Publishing Company, 1976), plate 72; *Alaska Geographic* 3, no. 4 (1976): 29; *Alaska Geographic* 1, no. 3 (1973): 33–34.

34. Memorandum, Farrell to Hirst, May 13, 1942, RG 75 Alaska, folder 13460-142-131, box 32.

35. Ibid.

36. Hirst to Gruening, June 29, ibid.

37. Driscoll, *War Discovers Alaska*, 43 and 46.

38. C. Ralph and Ruby J. Magee, "Our Atka Island Experience 1940–1942," in Kirtland and Coffin, vol. 2, 16.

39. Quoted in Lael Morgan, *And the Land Provides: Alaskan Natives in a Year of Transition* (Garden City, N.Y.: Doubleday, 1974), 174.

40. Vera Snigaroff, CWRIC microfilm, frame 575; Henry Dirks, frame 581.

41. Telegrams, Walter R. Hanlon to Gruening and Gruening to Hanlon, July 3, 1942, RG 101 Juneau, box 571.

42. Hirst to Commissioner, Sept. 9; and Commissioner to Hirst, Oct. 13, 1942, RG 75 Alaska, file 27167-1943-220, box 39.

43. Hirst telegram quoted in memorandum, Greenwood for Assistant Secretary Chapman, Sept. 29, 1942, ibid.; White quoted in letter, Hirst to Gruening, June 29, 1942, RG 75 Alaska, box 32.

44. Hirst to Gruening, ibid.; from research at Department of Vital Statistics, Alaska Office Building, Juneau, Alaska.

45. "Report of Field Agent on Wrangell," July 1943, Papers of the Territorial Department of Public Welfare, RG 107, Alaska State Archives, Juneau, series 51, Central Office Files 1937–1963, box 4628; Colby, *Guide to Alaska*, 132–33.

46. Colby, ibid., 140.

47. Fred R. Geeslin, "Special Report on the Evacuation and Relocation of the Aleuts from the Native Villages in the Aleutians, under the Jurisdiction of the Alaska Native Service, Department of Interior, during World War II, 1942–1945," 2, CWRIC witness file, Seattle, folder Unalaska, Alaska, box 91.

48. Hirst to Commissioner of Indian Affairs Collier, July 31, 1942, RG 75 Alaska, box 32.

49. *Wrangell Sentinel*, July 17, 1942, 2; *Ketchikan Alaska Chronicle*, July 15, 1942, 1.

50. *Wrangell Sentinel*, Sept. 11, 1942, 6.

51. Phil Tutiakoff in *Wartimes in the Aleutians*, 54; George McGlashen, CWRIC microfilm, frame 683; Leonty Savoroff, frame 634.

52. Laverna Dushkin, CWRIC microfilm, frame 649.

53. Hirst to Commissioner, Oct. 3, 1942, RG 75 Alaska, box 39; Geeslin, "Special Report," 2–3.

54. Phil Tutiakoff in *Wartimes in the Aleutians,* 54; Hirst to Commissioner, RG 75 Alaska, box 39; Phil Tutiakoff in *Aleutian Invasion,* 107.

55. Gertrude Svarny in *Aleutian Invasion,* 107–8; Genevieve Mayberry, "Call of the Williwaws," *Alaska Life,* Mar. 1944, 49; Phil Tutiakoff in *Aleutian Invasion,* 107.

56. Katherine Grimnes, cwric microfilm, frame 704; Mayberry, "Call of Williwaws," 47.

57. Hirst to Barrett, Aug. 3, 1942, RG 75 Alaska, box 39.

58. Telegram, Zaharoff to Hirst, Aug. 23, 1942, ibid.

59. Telegrams, Geeslin to Hirst and Hirst to Geeslin, Aug. 24, 1942, ibid.

60. Telegrams, Geeslin to Hirst, Sept. 2; and Barrett to Hirst, Sept. 3, 1942, ibid.

61. Telegrams, ibid.; telegram, Harry Weber to General Superintendent Hirst, Sept. 3, 1942, ibid. From the grave marker of Mary Zaharoff, Bayview Cemetery, Ketchikan, Alaska.

62. Hirst to Commissioner, Oct. 3; telegram, Geeslin to Hirst, Aug. 24, 1942, RG 75 Alaska, box 39; Kirtland and Coffin, vol. 3, 67.

63. Geeslin, "Special Report," 4–5.

64. Colby, *Guide to Alaska,* 128–30.

65. Report, *Ward Lake Recreation Unit,* Nov. 3, 1936, file 1650, Historical Data, Tongass National Forest Southern Division, U.S. Department of Agriculture, Forest Service, Ketchikan, Alaska.

66. George McGlashen, cwric microfilm, frame 648; Geeslin, "Special Report," 5; Hirst to Commissioner, Oct. 3, 1942, RG 75 Alaska, box 39.

67. Geeslin, "Special Report," 5.

68. George McGlashen, cwric microfilm, frame 648; Laverna Dushkin, frame 650; Dorofey Chercasen, frames 640 and 642.

69. Leonty Savoroff, cwric microfilm, frame 635; Laverna Dushkin, frame 650; White to Commissioner, July 1, 1942, RG 75 Alaska, folder 00-1942-770, box 102; Mayor McCain to C. M. Archibold, June 9, 1942, RG 101 Juneau, box 572.

70. Geeslin, "Special Report," 6–7; telegrams, Senior Coast Guard Ketchikan, Alaska, to Secretary of Alaska Bartlett, Feb. 7; and Bartlett to Zeusler, Feb. 13, 1942, RG 101 Juneau, box 492.

71. *Alaska Fishing News,* Oct. 23, 1942, 1; Bartlett to Zeusler, Oct. 19, 1942; Bartlett Papers, UAF Archives, Personal Correspondence file, box 3.

72. McCain to Gruening, Oct. 29, 1942, RG 101 Juneau, box 562.

73. Dorofey Chercasen, cwric microfilm, frame 643; From "Police Blotter–Kethcikan," Apr. 1–Dec. 18, 1942, Ketchikan Museum Archives, Ketchikan, Alaska.

74. *Alaska Fishing News,* Sept. 16, 1942, 1; Kirtland and Coffin, vol. 3, 69–70.

75. Prokopeuff, in *Aleutian Invasion,* 51.

76. Stewart, "Preliminary Report," 27; Lokanin, "Lifetime's Story," 236; Prokopeuff, ibid., 52; Prossoff, "Alex Prossoff's Story," 244.

77. Prossoff, ibid., 243–45; Lokanin, ibid., 235; John Golodoff in Butts, "Prisoners from Alaska," 36.

78. Lokanin, ibid., 236; Prossoff, ibid., 244; tables in Oliver, *Journal,* Appendix 3.

79. Prossoff, ibid., 243–44.

8. MATTERS OF DEATH AND LIFE

1. Martha Krukoff, CWRIC microfilm, frame 809.

2. Reprinted article, *Daily Alaska Empire,* Juneau, Sept. 18, 1942, RG 22 Seattle, folder D, 1941–1944, box 33.

3. Ickes Diary, July 12, 1942, Library of Congress Manuscript Division, roll 5, frame 6784.

4. McMillin to Johnston, July 1, 1942, RG 22 Seattle, file Evacuation-Pribilofs 1942–43, box 12503.

5. Ibid.

6. Johnston to Barnes, July 7; and McMillin to Johnston, July 11, 1942, ibid.

7. Johnston to Bower, July 15, 1942, ibid.

8. McMillin to Johnston, July 18, 1942, RG 22 Seattle, box 12505.

9. Bower to Johnston, July 31, 1942, ibid.

10. Johnston to Bower, Nov. 26, 1942, ibid.; Jackson to Ira N. Gabrielson, Dec. 7, 1943, RG 22 Seattle, box 33.

11. Memorandum, Bower to Jackson, Feb. 8, 1942, RG 75 Alaska, file 27167-1943-220, box 39; letter, Geeslin to Johnston, March 20, 1943, RG 22 Seattle, box 12505.

12. Anatoly Lekanof, CWRIC microfilm, frames 560–63; Stefan A. Lekanof, frame 760; Natalie Misikian, frame 804; Mary Bourdukofsky, CWRIC witness file, box 91.

13. Stefan Lekanof, CWRIC microfilm, frame 807.

14. Petition; and letter, Johnston to Bower, Oct. 10, 1942, RG 22 Seattle, box 33.

15. Petition, ibid.

16. Ibid.

17. Johnston to Bower, Oct. 10, 1942, ibid.

18. Ibid.

19. Ibid.

20. Ibid.

21. Bower to Johnston, Oct. 29, 1942, ibid.

22. Fredericka Martin Papers, UAF Archives, box 3; report, Medical Department, pp. 32–33, UAF Archives, Pribilof Island Collection, folder ACC 76–74. These calculations are based on data from Department of Vital Statistics, Juneau, Alaska.

23. Vital Statistics, ibid.

24. McMillin to Barnes, July 13, 1942, RG 22 Seattle, box 42.

25. McMillin to Johnston, Jan. 1; and Johnston to Bower, Jan. 27, 1943, ibid.; Benson to Johnston, Jan. 26; and Green to McMillin, Feb. 3, 1943, RG 22 Seattle, box 33.

26. Benson to Johnston, ibid.; U.S. Department of the Interior, Fish and Wildlife Service, *Alaska Fishery and Fur-Seal Industries: 1943* (Washington, D.C.: U.S. Government Printing Office, 1944), 40–41 and 43.

27. Carl M. Hoverson to Morton, July 28, 1943, RG 22 Seattle, box 33.

28. Funter Bay visit of John Hall, Sept. 3–4, 1943, RG 22 Seattle, box 12504; memorandum, John Hall to Carl M. Hoverson, Sept. 3, 1943, in Kirtland and Coffin, vol. 3, 23–25.

29. Funter Bay visit of John Hall, Sept. 3–4, 1943, RG 22 Seattle, box 12504.

30. Henry Roden to Gruening, Sept. 20, 1943, RG 101 Juneau, box 471.

31. Gruening to Roden and Gruening to Gabrielson, Sept. 22, ibid.

32. Report of Trip to Funter Bay by N. Berneta Block, Oct. 2–6, 1943, RG 22 Seattle, box 12504.

33. Ibid.

34. Block to Johnston, Oct. 14; and Bower to Block, Oct. 23, 1943, ibid.

35. Bower to Block, ibid.

36. Hynes to Bower, Oct. 28, 1943, RG 22 Seattle, box 12503.

37. Bower to Johnston, Nov. 3, 1942, ibid.

38. Telegram, Jackson to Gabrielson, Dec. 7, 1943, RG 22 Seattle, box 33; letter, Stimson to Secretary of the Interior Ickes, Dec. 14, 1943, RG 126 Territories, file 9-1-96, Foreign Relations. World War. Evacuation; letter, Olson to Johnston, Nov. 11, 1943, RG 22 Seattle, box 38; letter, H. O. K. Bauer to Dr. J. P. Eberhardt, Nov. 30, 1943, RG 22 Seattle, box 33.

39. Data from Department of Vital Statistics, Juneau, Alaska.

40. Anatoly Lekanof, CWRIC microfilm, frame 563; Anne S. McGlashen, CWRIC witness file, box 92.

41. Geeslin to Barrett, Dec. 1, 1942, RG 22 Seattle, box 33; McMillin to Johnston, July 11, 1942, RG 22 Seattle, box 12503; Gruening to Gabrielson, May 1, 1944, Gruening Papers, UAF Archives, Governor's Alaska File "Political," box 6.

42. Department of the Interior, *Annual Report of the Commissioner of Indian Affairs to the Secretary of the Interior—Ended June 1942*, (Washington, D.C.: Government Printing Office, 1942), 235.

43. Driscoll, *War Discovers Alaska,* 44 and 45.

44. Data from Department of Vital Statistics; Official Passenger Lists, RG 75 Alaska, box 39.

45. Bill Dirks, CWRIC witness file, box 92; Henry Dirks, CWRIC microfilm, frames 581–82; Vera Nevzaroff and John L. Nevzaroff, CWRIC witness file, box 92.

46. Vera Nevzaroff, ibid.; Alice Petrivelli, CWRIC witness file, box 92.

47. Petrivelli, ibid.; Henry Dirks, CWRIC microfilm, frames 581–82.

48. Magee to Geeslin, Jan. 14, 1943, RG 75 Alaska, box 39.

49. Ruby and Ralph Magee to Dr. and Mrs. Berenberg, Sept. 20, 1943, Fredericka Martin Papers, UAF Archives, box 3.

50. Magee to Geeslin, Jan. 14, 1943, RG 75 Alaska, box 39; Magees to Berenbergs, ibid.

51. Magees to Berenbergs, ibid.

52. Hirst to Commissioner, Oct. 3, 1942, RG 75 Alaska, box 39; Magee to Geeslin, Jan. 14, 1943, RG 75 Alaska, box 39.

53. Geeslin to Hirst, Jan. 8; and Hirst to Commissioner, May 21, 1943, ibid.

54. Magee to Hirst, Jan. 14, 1943, ibid.; John and Vera Nevzaroff, Bill Dirks, CWRIC witness file, box 92; Henry Dirks, CWRIC microfilm, frame 581.

55. Vera Nevzaroff, Alice Petrivelli, CWRIC witness file, box 92.

56. Magee to Hirst, Jan. 14, 1943, RG 75 Alaska, box 39; Alice Petrivelli, ibid.

57. Mayberry, "Call of the Williwaws," 48; Reprinted article, *Daily Alaska Empire,* Sept. 18, 1942.

58. Rosalie (Yatchmeneff) Siverling, Alfred Stepetin, CWRIC witness file, box 92.

59. Gertrude Svarny, Alfred Stepetin, Walter Dyakanoff, CWRIC microfilm, frame 691.

60. Svarny, Clara Chute (Borenin), CWRIC witness file, box 92.

61. Official Passenger Lists, RG 75 Alaska, box 39. These mortality figures are based on the confirmed death of Mary Zaharoff plus four others in Kirtland and Coffin, vol. 3, 108. Vital Statistics indicate only one death at Burnett Inlet.

62. Mayberry, "Call of the Williwaws," 46–47.

63. Mayberry, ibid., 49; *Personal Justice Denied,* 350. Alfred Stepetin in CWRIC witness file, box 92, mentions two of these wives; Martha Newell was the other one.

64. Mayberry, ibid., 48; *Ang Wakum,* Aleut League Newsletter, 1 (February 1976); Gertrude Svarny in *Aleutian Invasion,* 108.

65. Svarny, ibid.

66. Long to General Superintendent, Jan. 5; Geeslin to Hirst, Jan. 8; and Hirst to Commissioner of Indian Affairs, May 21, 1943, RG 75 Alaska, box 39.

67. Martha to Kenneth, Mar. 18 and 26, 1943, CWRIC subject file A–G, box 50.

68. Kenneth Newell to Dimond, Apr. 4, 1943, ibid.

69. Geeslin to Dimond, Apr. 24, 1943, ibid.; Geeslin to Hirst, Jan. 8, 1943, RG 75 Alaska, box 39.

70. Geeslin to Dimond, ibid.

71. Edythe Long to General Superintendent, May 6, 1943, CWRIC subject file A–G, box 50.

72. Ibid.; Geeslin to Hirst, June 8, 1943, RG 75 Alaska, box 39; Kirtland and Coffin, vol. 3, 108.

73. The Unalaska Community Members to Gruening, Oct. 25; and Bartlett to Dear Friends, Nov. 3, 1943, RG 101 Juneau, box 571.

74. *Alaska Fishing News,* Aug. 31, 1942, 6.

75. Hodgman to Archbold, Oct. 17 and Dec. 15, 1942, U.S. Department of Agriculture, Forest Service, Ketchikan, Ward Lake Area file 1650.

76. Geeslin to Hirst, Jan. 8; Whitfield to General Superintendent Hirst, Jan. 17; Geeslin to Commissioner Collier, Feb. 18; and Hirst to Commissioner Collier, Oct. 3, 1943, RG 75 Alaska, box 39.

77. Whitfield to General Superintendent Hirst, ibid.

78. Luke Shelikoff, Bill Tcheripanoff, CWRIC witness file, box 93.

79. Dorofey Chercasen, CWRIC microfilm, frames 642 and 645.

80. Leonty Savoroff, CWRIC microfilm, frame 635.

81. Kirtland and Coffin, vol. 3, 69–70; burials in Bayview Cemetery, Office of the City Clerk, Ketchikan, Alaska.

82. *Alaska Fishing News,* May 10, 1943, 1; McCain to Gruening, May 19, 1943, RG 101 Juneau, box 461.

83. *Alaska Fishing News,* May 21, 1943, 1; Minutes of the Ketchikan City Council Meeting, May 25[?], 1943.

84. *Alaska Fishing News,* ibid.; J. A. Talbot to Gruening, May 27, 1943, RG 101 Juneau, box 461; McCain to Gruening, May 12, box 415; McCain to Bartlett, May 19, box 572; and Langdon White to Wayne Ramsey, May 22, box 572; Bartlett, Memorandum For Files, May 28, box 461.

85. Hirst to Talbot, June 5; Raymond L. Wolfe to Hirst, June 11, RG 101 Juneau, box 461. Hirst to Commissioner, June 18, 1943, RG 75 Alaska, box 33.

86. A. W. Hodgman to Hirst, Jan. 17, 1944, Forest Service, Ketchikan, file 1650; George A. Dale to Gruening, May 13, 1944, RG 101 Juneau, box 571.

87. *Ketchikan Alaska Chronicle,* Aug. 26, 1942, 2; Sophie Pletnikoff, CWRIC microfilm, frame 710; Whitfield to General Superintendent, Jan. 17, 1943, RG 75 Alaska, box 39; Leonty Savoroff, CWRIC witness file, box 92; Geeslin, "Special Report," 6.

88. Hirst to Commissioner, Oct. 3, 1942, RG 75 Alaska, box 39; Luke Shelikoff, CWRIC witness file, box 93; Whitfield to General Superintendent, ibid.; Geeslin, "Special Report," 6; William Ermeloff, CWRIC microfilm, frame 654.

89. *Ketchikan Alaska Chronicle,* Jan. 8, Jan. 15, and Feb. 6, 1945, 4.

90. "Police Blotters," Ketchikan Library Museum Archives, 1943–44; editorial, *Alaska Fishing News,* May 24, 1943, 4.

91. *Alaska Fishing News,* May 21, 1943, 5.

92. The term is used by Thomas R. H. Havens in *Valley of Darkness: The Japanese People and World War Two* (New York: W. W. Norton, 1978).

93. Mike Lokanin, "Aleut Tells"; Stewart, "Preliminary Report," 30–31; Golodoff, "Last Days," 8; Prokopeuff, in *Aleutian Invasion,* 52–53.

94. John Golodoff and Angelina Hodikoff, in Butts, "Prisoners from Alaska," 15 and 37.

95. Stewart Report, 45 n. 12; Prokopeuff in *Aleutian Invasion,* 53; Lokanin, "Lifetime's Story," 236–37; Prossoff, "Alex Prossoff's Story," 244.

96. Innokenty Golodoff, CWRIC microfilm, frame 589; T. Hattori to Dr. Stein, Oct. 19, 1976, from the files of Michael Krauss, University of Alaska Fairbanks; Prokopeuff, ibid.; Lokanin, ibid., 237.

97. From tables in Oliver, *Journal,* Appendix 3.

98. Ibid.; "American Civilian Internees Formerly Detained by the Japanese Govt." RG 75 Alaska, box 31; Prossoff, "Alex Prossoff's Story," 245.

99. Lokanin, "Lifetime's Story," 237; Prossoff, ibid.; Prokopeuff in *Aleutian Invasion,* 53.

100. Prokopeuff, ibid., 53–54; Lokanin, ibid.

101. From a story written by Monroe M. Sweetland, files of Lydia Black, University of Alaska Fairbanks.

102. *Watakushi-Tach: No Shogen* (As We Saw It), *Mainichi* Newspaper, Sapporo, 1974, in Stewart, "Preliminary Report," 68.

103. Innokenty Golodoff, CWRIC microfilm, frame 589; Lokanin, "Aleut Tells"; Lokanin, "Lifetime's Story," 237.

104. Prokopeuff in *Aleutian Invasion,* 52; Lokanin, "Lifetime's Story," 238; Prossoff, "Alex Prossoff's Story," 245.

105. Prossoff, ibid., 243–44.

106. Butts, "Prisoners from Alaska," 37; Prossoff, ibid., 246.

9. PRIBILOF AND ALEUTIAN HOMECOMINGS

1. "The Chuginadak Woman," 18–50.

2. Geeslin, "Special Report," 2; John L. Nevzaroff, CWRIC witness file, box 92; Leonty Savoroff, CWRIC microfilm frames 636-38..

3. Ickes to Stimson, Nov. 23, 1942, RG 22 Seattle, box 12505.

4. Memorandum for the Chief of Staff, Dec. 2, 1942, in Kirtland and Coffin, vol. 4, 7; Letter, Stimson to Ickes, Dec. 4, 1942, ibid.

5. Stimson to Ickes, Jan. 2, 1943, ibid.

6. Historical Reports, 1941–47, RG 338 Suitland, Alaska Defense Command, Alaskan Department, box Fort Randall.

7. Bower to Johnston, Nov. 11, 1942, in Kirtland and Coffin, vol. 4, 1; Johnston to Bower, Dec. 7, 1942; and Bower to Johnston, Dec. 11, 1942, RG 22 Seattle, box 12505; Director to Commandant, Dec. 28, 1942, RG 181 Seattle, Commandant's Office Regular Navy Files 1942, 1943, box 14.

8. Gabrielson to Gruening, Jan. 6; and Oscar Chapman to Buckner, Jan. 15, 1943, RG 101 Juneau, box 557; memoranda, Bower to Jackson, Jan. 13; and Johnston to Bower, Jan. 16, 1943, RG 22 Seattle, boxes 40 and 12505; Buckner to Commanding Officer, St. Paul, Feb. 21, 1943, RG 101 Juneau, box 557; letter, Johnston to Agent and Caretaker, St. Paul and St. George, Mar. 2, 1943, RG 22 Seattle, box 33.

9. Gruening to Buckner, Feb. 5, 1943, RG 101 Juneau, box 557.

10. McMillin to Johnston, Mar. 6, 1943, RG 22 Seattle, box 33.

11. Johnston to McMillin, Mar. 17, 1943, ibid.

12. Johnston to Bower, Mar. 19; and Bower to Johnston, Mar. 30, 1943, RG 22 Seattle, box 12505.

13. James W. Huston to Fisheries Division, Mar. 20, 1943, RG 22 Seattle, box 40.

14. Geeslin to Johnston, April 3, 1943, ibid.; Johnston to Bower, April 27, 1943, Record Group 22, Records of the Fish and Wildlife Service, National Archives, Washington, D.C., Johnston and Morton Correspondence, 1943, (hereinafter cited as RG 22 National Archives), box 220.

15. "An Open Letter to the Public" from Mary Jane Gaither sent to Anthony Dimond, Apr. 7; and letter, Frank Hynes to Bower, May 5, 1943, RG 22 Seattle, box 12505.

16. Acting Director to Dimond, Apr. 20, 1943, ibid.; Hynes to Bower, ibid.

17. Johnston to Bower, Apr. 27; and Bower to Johnston, Jan. 29, 1943, RG 22 National Archives, box 220.

18. Statement, Apr. 26, 1943; and letter, Johnston to Bower, Apr. 27, 1943, ibid.

19. Telegram, Bower to Morton, April 29, 1943, in Kirtland and Coffin, vol. 5, 44; letter, Johnston to Bower, May 5; and telegram, Johnston to Bower, Oct. 13, 1943, ibid.

20. "St. Paul Island Logbook," microfilm reel 8, entry May 6, 1943.

21. Howard J. Brice, "Men from St. Paul," *Alaska Life*, Sept. 1944, 31.

22. Hynes to Bower, May 5, 1943, RG 22 Seattle, box 12505; J. H.

O'Reilley to Commanding General, Sept. 7, 1943, RG 165 Suitland, U.S. Army Operations Division 1942–1945, Decimal File 680.421, box 1674; *Alaska Fishery and Fur-Seal Industries: 1943,* 40–43.

23. Carl to Fred, June 28, 1943, RG 22 Seattle, box 33; Gabrielson telegram quoted in letter, Bower to Morton, Sept. 6, 1943, box 12505.

24. Telegrams, Jackson to Morton, Sept. 8, 1943, in Kirtland and Coffin, vol. 4, 14; Gruening to Whittaker and Whittaker to Gruening, Sept. 11, 1943, RG 101 Juneau, box 557.

25. Morton to Bower, Sept. 14, 1943, RG 22 Seattle, box 12505.

26. Telegram, Morton to Bower, Sept. 21, 1943, RG 22 National Archives, box 220; "St. Paul Island Logbook," microfilm reel 8, entry Sept. 13, 1943; telegram, McMillin to Morton, Sept. 19, 1943, in Kirtland and Coffin, vol. 4, 15.

27. Telegram, Morton to Bower, Sept. 20, 1943, RG 22 Seattle, box 12505.

28. Ibid.; telegram, Morton to Bower, Sept. 21, 1943, RG 22 National Archives, box 220; letter, Gabrielson to Gruening, Oct. 13, 1943, RG 101 Juneau, box 571.

29. "St. Paul Island Logbook," microfilm reel 8, entry Oct 12, 1943; "St. George Island Logbook," reel 17, entry Nov. 22, 1943; telegram, Johnston to Bower, Oct. 13, 1943, RG 22 National Archives, box 220.

30. Telegram, Hynes to Johnston, Oct. 26; and letter, Johnston to Bower, Dec. 25, 1943, RG 101 Juneau, box 33; letter, Bower to Johnston, Nov. 3, 1943, RG 22 Seattle, box 12503.

31. Johnston to Commanding General, Nov. 9, 1943, RG 22 Seattle, box 33; Johnston to Bower, Dec. 13; and Bower to Morton, Dec. 24, 1943, RG 22 Seattle, box 40.

32. Johnston to Bower, Dec. 25, 1943, RG 22 Seattle, box 33.

33. Memorandum, Gruber to the Secretary, Jan. 12, 1944, RG 126 Territories, file 9-1-31, Pribilof Islands.

34. Beech, "Refugees," 21.

35. Ibid.

36. "St. Paul Island Logbook," microfilm reel 8, entry Apr. 28; Oscar L. Chapman to Henry L. Stimson, Mar. 25, 1944, RG 22 Seattle, box 12505.

37. Bess Winn, "Priest from the Pribilofs," *Alaska Life,* May 1943, 17; Mike Lestenkof, CWRIC microfilm, frame 733; "St. Paul Island Logbook," ibid.

38. "St. Paul Island Logbook," microfilm reel 8, entries Apr. 30 and May 4; "St. George Island Logbook," microfilm reel 17, entries May 14 and 19.

39. "St. Paul" and "St. George," ibid.

40. Bower to Jackson, May 31, 1944, RG 22 National Archives, box 220.

41. *Alaska Fishing News,* Ketchikan, Sept. 29, 1943, 8.

42. Mary Bourdukofsky, CWRIC witness file, box 91; Heratina Krukoff, box 93; Martha Krukoff, CWRIC microfilm, frame 811; Natalie Misikian, frame 807.

43. Anne S. McGlashen, Anatoly Lekanof, Jr., and Michael Lekanof, Sr., CWRIC witness file, box 92; William Shane, CWRIC microfilm, frame 776.

44. Father Michael Lestenkof, CWRIC microfilm, frame 742.

45. Father Paul Merculief, CWRIC microfilm, frame 720; Anatoly Lekanof in *Wartimes in the Aleutians,* 64.

46. Greenwood to Tyrrell, Apr. 29, 1943, RG 75 Alaska, box 39.

47. Letters, Hirst to Commissioner Collier, Oct. 2, 1943, ibid.

48. Memoranda, Zimmerman to Mr. McCaskill, Oct. 15; Benjamin W. Thoron to Mr. Oscar L. Chapman, Oct. 19; and Chapman to Commissioner Collier, Oct. 20, 1943, ibid.

49. Memorandum, Zimmerman to Mr. McCaskill, Oct. 23, 1943, ibid.

50. Telegram, McCaskill to Zimmerman, Nov. 2; and letters, Ickes to Stimson, Nov. 26, and Stimson to Ickes, Dec. 13, 1943, RG 126 Territories, file 9-1-96, Foreign Relations. World War Evacuation.

51. Copies of telegrams in letter, Geeslin to Zimmerman, Feb. 20, 1944, RG 75 Alaska, box 31.

52. Letter, ibid.

53. Memorandum, Collier to the Secretary, Dec. 1, 1943; and letter, Gruening to Collier, Feb. 15, 1944, RG 101 Juneau, box 557; Ickes Diary, Sunday, Jan. 9, 1944, Library of Congress, microfilm roll 6.

54. Geeslin to Buckner, Feb. 26, 1944, RG 75 Alaska, box 31.

55. Forrestal to Ickes, Apr. 7, 1944, ibid.

56. Telegram, Don Foster to Zimmerman, Apr. 10, 1944, ibid.

57. Knox to Ickes, Apr. 15, 1944, ibid.

58. Telegram, Zimmerman to Foster, Apr. 26, 1944, ibid.

59. Memorandum, J. Donald Kroeker, George A. Dale, and Ralph W. Mize to Commanding General; and letter, Foster to Zimmerman, Apr. 27, 1944, ibid.

60. Telegram, Gruening to Thoron, Apr. 28, 1944, RG 126 Territories, file 9-1-96; memorandum, Geeslin to Foster, Apr. 29; letters, Foster to Zimmerman, May 2; Secretary of Interior to Forrestal and Stimson, May 6; Stimson to Ickes, May 11; and "First Endorsement," Foster to Alaska Department and Com 17, May 20, 1944, RG 75 Alaska, box 31; letter, Roosevelt to the Secretary of the Treasury, Aug. 7, 1944, RG 75 Alaska, box 39.

61. Geeslin to Fickinger and Zimmerman, June 8 (emphasis in original); Foster to Fickinger, June 30; memorandum, Collier to Ickes, July 4; and D'Arcy McNickle to George Louden, July 20, 1944, RG 75 Alaska, box 31.

62. Telegram, Foster to Zimmerman, Sept. 2; and memorandum, Fickinger to Zimmerman, signed note by Zimmerman on bottom, Sept. 6, 1944, ibid.

63. Geeslin to A. M. Babich, G. E. Duffy, and F. W. Laskowski, Sept. 29, ibid.

64. Martha to Kenneth, Mar. 18, 1943, RG 220 CWRIC, subject file A–G, box 50; *Ketchikan Alaska Chronicle,* Apr. 24, 1944, 2; and Aug. 2, 1944, 2.

65. *Ketchikan Alaska Chronicle,* Jan. 16, 1945, 2.

66. Geeslin to Commanding General, Feb. 1; and Geeslin to Zimmerman, Feb. 8, 1944, RG 75 Alaska, box 31.

67. *Ketchikan Alaska Chronicle,* Feb. 28, 1945, 4.

68. Ibid., Mar. 14, 1; Mar. 16, 4; and Mar. 21, 2.

69. Ibid., Apr. 14, 1.

70. *Ketchikan Alaska Chronicle,* Apr. 17, 1945, 6; "Breakdown of Aleut Passengers—Evacuees in Southeastern Alaska to Be Returned to Their Former Homes in the Aleutians During April 1945," RG 75 Alaska, box 31; Foster to Zimmerman, Apr. 23, 1945, RG 75 Alaska, box 31.

71. "Breakdown of Aleut Passengers"; Luke Shelikoff, CWRIC witness file, box 93; Benedict to Foster, RG 75 Alaska, box 31.

72. Matrona Stepetin, CWRIC microfilm, frame 681; George McGlashen, frames 682–83; Bill Tcheripanoff, CWRIC witness file, box 93.

73. "Statement of Crozier . . . and Beebe . . . Concerning Their Observations of Akutan Village while on Duty at N.F.S. Akutan, Alaska," June 11, 1943; and Kroeker, Dale, and Mize, "Report On Akutan Village," Apr. 27, 1944, RG 75 Alaska, box 31.

74. Memorandum, Covalt to Foster, Apr. 12; and letter, Foster to Zimmerman, Apr. 23, 1945, ibid.

75. Geeslin, "Special Report," 8.

76. Matrona Stepetin, CWRIC microfilm, frame 682; Luke Shelikoff, Bill Tcheripanoff, CWRIC witness file, box 93.

77. Walter Dyakanoff, CWRIC microfilm, frame 692; "Breakdown of Aleut Passengers," RG 75 Alaska, box 31; Phil Tutiakoff in *Wartimes in the Aleutians,* 55–56.

78. Pauline Lekanof in *Wartimes in the Aleutians,* 57; Rosalie Yatchmeneff Siverling, CWRIC witness file, box 93; Walter Dyakanoff, CWRIC microfilm, frame 691.

79. The Unalaska Community Members to General Buckner, Oct. 25; and Bartlett to Buckner, Nov. 1, 1943, RG 75 Alaska, box 31; Geeslin to Dimond, April 24, 1943, CWRIC subject file A–G, box 50.

80. Unsigned copy of "Statement Concerning Housebreaking and Thievery in Unalaska Village" to Commanding General, Jan. 12, 1944, RG 75 Alaska, box 31.

81. Reports, O. H. Longino to Commanding General, Jan. 14, 1944; and Kroeker, Dale, and Mize, "Report on Unalaska Community," Apr. 27, 1944, ibid.

82. Memorandum, Covalt to Foster, Apr. 12; and letter, Foster to Zimmerman, Apr. 23, 1945, ibid.

83. Geeslin, "Special Report," 7–8. This picture was an image of Alaska made of cotton to give it a three-dimensional appearance.

84. John L. Nevzaroff, CWRIC witness file, box 92, Leonty Savoroff, CWRIC microfilm, frames 636–38; "Breakdown of Aleut Passengers"; Kroeker, Dale, and Mize, "Report on Nikolski Village," Apr. 27, 1944, RG 75 Alaska, box 31.

85. Paul Merculief, CWRIC microfilm, frame 667; Leonty Savoroff, frame 635; William Ermeloff, frame 655.

86. William N. Snouffer to Commanding General, Oct. 5, 1942, RG 75 Alaska, box 31.

87. Kroeker, Dale, and Mize, "Nikolski Village," RG 75 Alaska, box 31.

88. Harley W. Covalt to Foster, Apr. 12, 1942, ibid.

89. Geeslin, "Special Report," 8.

90. John L. Nevzoroff, Vera Snigaroff Nevzoroff, Alice Snigaroff Petrivelli, CWRIC witness file, box 92.

91. "Historical Report U.S. Troops Atka Alaska," RG 338 Suitland, Alaska Defense Command. Alaskan Department. Historical Reports 1941–47, box A; Bill Dirks, CWRIC witness file, box 92; Kroeker, Dale, and Mize, "Report on Survey of Atka," Apr. 27, 1944, RG 75 Alaska, box 31.

92. "Historical Report," ibid.; Covalt to Foster, Apr. 12, 1945; and Foster to Zimmerman, Apr. 23, 1945, RG 75 Alaska, box 31; John L. Nevzoroff, CWRIC witness file, box 92.

93. Geeslin, "Special Report," 9.

94. Bill Dirks, CWRIC witness file, box 92; Geeslin, "Special Report", 8.

95. Lokanin, "Lifetime's Story," 239.

96. Stewart Report, 33–34; Prossoff, "Alex Prossoff's Story," 247.

97. Golodoff, "Last Days," 9.

98. Ibid.; Lokanin, "Lifetime's Story," 240; Stewart Report, 33–36.

99. Prokopeuff in Aleutian Invasion, 54; Lokanin, "Aleut Tells"; Monroe Sweetland to Oscar Chapman, Oct. 16, 1945, RG 75 Alaska, box 31.

100. Lokanin, "Lifetime's Story," 240.

101. Lokanin, ibid.; Prossoff, "Alex Prossoff's Story," 248.

102. Golodoff, "Last Days," 9; Prossoff, ibid.; Seattle Times, Nov. 12, 1945, 3.

103. List and Remarks, "Surviving Attu Natives—as of September 20, 1945," RG 75 Alaska, box 31; Report, Michael Lekanof, Sr., "Aleuts of the Aleutian Chain," n.d. [circa 1981]. Aleutian/Pribilof Islands Association, WWII: Documentation File.

104. Foster to William A. Brophy, Jan. 29, 1946, in Kirtland and Coffin, vol. 4, 239; telegram, Foster to D'Arcy McNickle, Oct. 4, 1945, RG 75 Alaska, box 31.

105. Telegram, Nelson to Brophy, Nov. 13, 1945, RG 75 Alaska, box 31; letter, Foster to Brophy, ibid.; letter, Foster to Zimmerman, Dec. 10, 1945, Aleutian/Pribilof Islands Association, Interior Department File.

106. Golodoff, "Last Days," 9; Innokenty Golodoff, CWRIC microfilm, frame 591; Prossoff, "Alex Prossoff's Story," 248.

107. Foster to Brophy, Jan. 29, 1946, in Kirtland and Coffin, vol. 4, 239.

108. Lokanin, "Lifetime's Story," 240; Prokopeuff in *Aleutian Invasion*, 55.

109. Prokopeuff, ibid.

10: VICTORY AND REDRESS

1. Marion V. Benedict to Foster, June 15, 1945, RG 75-N Still Picture Branch, Aleut, box 2.

2. Public Law 100-383, Aug. 10, 1988—102 STAT.903; Alec Wilkinson, "The Uncommitted Crime," *New Yorker*, Nov. 26, 1990, 112–15.

3. Lillie McGarvey, "Aleut: People of the Aleutian Chain," *Alaska Geographic* 6, no. 3 (1979): 163.

4. Telegrams, R. B. Patterson to Gruening, Apr. 27; and Foster to Delegate Bartlett, Apr. 28, 1945, RG 101 Juneau, box 461; letter, E. W. Norris to Foster, May 23, 1945, RG 75 Alaska, box 31.

5. Foster to General Philoon, June 8, 1945, RG 75 Alaska, box 31.

6. Elbert F. Foster to Bureau of Indian Affairs, July 3; and Don Foster to Commissioner, July 23, 1945, RG 75 Alaska, box 102.

7. Telegram, Arthur J. Harris to Gruening, Oct. 20; and letter, Acting Governor Lew W. Williams to Harris, Oct. 30, 1945, RG 101 Juneau, box 562.

8. Press release, Fish and Wildlife Service, June 19; letter, Samuel R. Berenberg to Ickes, June 24; letter, Ickes to Berenberg, July 10; and note from Director to Ickes, July 5, 1944, RG 126 Territories, Office File of Benjamin W. Thoron, series 10.

9. Dr. Will F. Spears to Johnston, July 18; and Johnston to Berneta Block, Aug. 26, 1944, RG 22 Seattle, box 34.

10. Johnston to Bower, Oct. 3, 1944, RG 22 Seattle, box 40.

11. U.S. Department of the Interior, "Pribilof Islands Survey Report," 73, Oct. 8, 1949, 73.

12. Geeslin to Covalt, May 22 and July 12, 1945, RG 75 Alaska, box 31.

13. Foster to Zimmerman, Nov. 9, 1945, RG 75 Alaska, box 33.

14. Ibid; petition, Oct. 18, 1945, RG 101 Juneau, box 562.

15. Petition, ibid.

16. Henry Swanson, *The Unknown Islands: Life and Tales of Henry Swanson*, (Unalaska, Alaska: Unalaska City School District, 1982), 192; Foster to Bartlett, July 30, 1946, RG 101 Juneau, box 460.

17. Foster to Commissioner, Aug. 26, 1946, RG 126 Territories, 9-1-52, file Reservation of Lands for Natives.

18. Foster to Gruening, Aug. 30, 1946, ibid.

19. James A. Harris to Mildred Hermann, Nov. 28, 1947, RG 126 Territories, 9-1-31, file Islands–Aleutian Islands.

20. Gruening to James P. Davis, Jan. 19, 1947; and Davis to Gruening, Mar. 17, 1948, ibid.; War Claims Commission, *Report of the War Claims Commission* (Washington, D.C.: Government Printing Office, 1950), 43.

21. Combined figures from budget sheets, RG 75 Alaska, boxes 39 and 41; Foster to Commissioner, Apr. 26, 1946, RG 75 Alaska, box 41.

22. Harold E. Bowman to Commandant, Dec. 17, 1942, RG 181 Seattle, folder EG3/H-4-F, box 145; Admiral Frank J. Fletcher to Bowman, Jan. 19, 1943, RG 181 Seattle, folder EG3/H-4-F, box 15; Parsons to Governor's Office, n.d.; Bartlett to Buckner, Dec. 16, 1942; and Colonel E. C. Gault to Bartlett, Mar. 5, 1943, RG 101 Juneau, box 495.

23. Eubank to Gruening, Aug. 7, 1942; Eubank to Buckner, Sept. 5, 1942; H.R. 3668, July 3, 1945, 79th Cong., 1st Sess.; and Eubank to Gruening, Mar. 29, 1946, RG 101 Juneau, box 571.

24. Wilfred C. Stump to Bartlett, Mar. 28; Gruening to Stump, Apr. 14; and Lew Williams to Col. Rhodes, Oct. 15, 1947, ibid.

25. Sam Peckovich to Johnston, Apr. 18; Hynes to Director, May 23; and Johnston to Bower, July 10, 1944, RG 22 Seattle, box 35; Commissioner to Foster, Mar. 21, 1945, RG 75 Alaska, box 31.

26. Bower to Chief, Division of Fisheries, May 31, 1944, RG 22 National Archives, entry 269, Johnston and Morton Correspondence, box 220; memorandum, Roy L. Deal to Chief of Operations Division, General Staff, n.d. [June 1944], RG 165 Suitland, U.S. Army Operations Division, decimal file 370.05 ADC, box 1171.

27. Fortas to Director of the Budget, Sept. 19; and Roosevelt to Secretary of the Treasury, Sept. 28, 1944, RG 75 Alaska, box 31.

28. Michael Lestenkof, CWRIC microfilm, frames 742–43; Bower to Johnston, Feb. 6, 1945, RG 75 Alaska, ibid.

29. Geeslin to Commissioner, Jan. 5, 1946, ibid.; Verne Robinson, CWRIC microfilm, frames 676–77.

30. Geeslin to Foster, Mar. 18, 1946, RG 75 Alaska, box 41.

31. Telegram, Provinse to Zimmerman, June 18, 1946, RG 75 Alaska, box 31.

32. Monroe Sweetland to Oscar Chapman, Sept. 27 and Oct. 16, 1945, ibid.

33. Memorandum, Niehardt to Brophy, Oct. 31, 1945; and letters, Newman to Brophy, Mar. 14, 1946; Newman to Foster, Mar. 20, 1946; and Brust to Zimmerman, May 11, 1949, ibid.

34. Memoranda, Guy C. Williams to D'Arcy McNickle, June 7; and McNickle

to Division Directors, June 15, 1949; and letters, Foster to Commissioner, Aug. 9, 1950; and Ripke to War Claims Commission, Jan. 9, 1951, ibid.; *Report of the War Claims Commission,* 7, 60, and 67.

35. War Claims Commissioner, *Supplementary Report of the War Claims Commission with Respect to War Claims Arising out of World War II* (Washington, D.C.: Government Printing Office, 1953), 33; data from Foreign Claims Settlement Commission index cards, Washington, D.C.; *Report of War Claims Commission,* 57.

36. Sweetland to Chapman, Oct. 16, 1945, RG 75 Alaska, box 31.

37. Michael K. Orbach and Beverly Holmes, "The Pribilof Island Aleuts: Tentative Players in a Hybrid Economy," in Steve J. Langdon, ed., *Contemporary Alaska Native Economics* (Lanham, Md.: University Press of America, 1986), 77–78; Dorothy Knee Jones, *Century of Servitude,* 119–34.

38. Orbach and Holmes, ibid., 95.

39. *Native Organizations in Alaska: A Records Survey and Historical Profile* (Anchorage: Alaska Native Foundation, 1979), 39–43.

40. Letters, Lael Morgan, Jan. 7; Gary R. Frink, Aug. 18; and Forrest J. Gerard, Dec. 19, 1977, to Patrick Pletnikoff; memorandum, John C. Kirtland to Pletnikoff, July 1, 1978; and letter, Kirtland to Gregg Brelsford, Nov. 20, 1980, APIA Headquarters, Anchorage, Alaska, WWII: Correspondence, 1977–80 and 1978–81.

41. Pletnikoff to Vice-Consul Yamamato, June 2, 1978, and reply from Consul Sadao Saito; Pletnikoff to Verne Robinson, June 15, 1979; and Kirtland to Brelsford, Nov. 20, 1980, ibid.

42. Mike Gravel to Pletnikoff, Sept. 20, 1977, Mar. 1, 1978, and July 31, 1978; Pletnikoff to Gravel, Dec. 14, 1977; and Richard [of Gravel's staff] to Pletnikoff, Aug. 26, 1977, UAF Archives, Mike Gravel Papers, boxes 406 and 410.

43. William Minoru Hohri, *Repairing America: An Account of the Movement for Japanese-American Redress* (Pullman, Wash.: Washington State University Press, 1988), 2; Kirtland to Brelsford, Nov. 20, 1980, APIA Headquarters, Correspondence.

44. Kirtland to Michael Zacharof, Aug. 7 (emphasis in original); Brelsford to Stevens, June 26; and telegram, Stevens, Murkowski, and Young to Jay Hammond, June 30, 1981, ibid.

45. John C. Kirtland and David F. Coffin, Jr., *The Relocation and Internment of the Aleuts During World War II,* 9 vols. (Anchorage, Aleutian/Pribilof Islands Association, 1981); Commission on Wartime Relocation and Internment of Civilians, report, *Personal Justice Denied* (Washington, D.C.: Government Printing Office, 1982), 18–23, 317–359, and part 2: *Recommendations; Aang Angagin, Aang Angaginas* (APIA Newsletter), Feb. 1981.

46. *Aang Angagin, Aang Angaginas,* Feb. 1981, Nov.–Dec. 1981, and

Apr.–May 1982; Phil Tutiakoff, audiotaped interview by Ron Inouye, May 3, 1984, UAF Archives.

47. Videotapes, Oral History Collection, UAF Archives; "Public Hearings," CWRIC microfilm, roll 6, frames 450–822; Kirtland, CWRIC microfilm frames 478–79.

48. *Aang Angagin, Aang Angaginas,* June–Aug. 1983; Kirtland to Brelsford, Oct. 27, 1983, APIA correspondence; H.R. 4322, Nov. 4, 1983, 98th Cong., 1st Sess.

49. Memorandum, Kirtland to Board of Directors, Apr. 11; and letter, John R. Bolton to Peter W. Rodino, Apr. 25, 1986, APIA correspondence.

50. U.S. Senate, 100th Cong., 2nd Sess. Governmental Affairs Committee, "Hearings Before the Subcommittee on Federal Services, Post Office, and Civil Services," June 17, 1987, 31–42, 242–75, and 347–73; *Congressional Quarterly Weekly Report,* vol. 46, no. 32, Aug. 6, 1988, 2209; vol. 46, no. 38, Sept. 17, 1988, 2612.

51. Public Law 100-383, *An Act to Implement Recommendations of the Commission on Wartime Relocation and Internment of Civilians, Statutes at Large* 102 (1988), 911–16. Attuans had previously been denied a petition for incorporating a village on Attu under provisions of the Alaska Native Claims Act.

52. Senate, "Hearings Before the Subcommittee," 39, 41.

Index

Adak Island, 3, 164, 168, 175
Admiralty Island, 77, 79, 90
Afognak, 11
Agattu Island, 175
Ainu, 107
Akutan, 3, 8, 18, 58, 81, 99, 103–4,
    156–59 *passim. See also* Ward Lake
Alaska (ship), 83, 106
Alaska Defense Command, 27, 32, 76,
    146, 150, 151, 156, 167
Alaska Indian Service, 7, 11–12, 150,
    153, 172–73, 178
Alaska Native Brotherhood, 141
Alaska Native Claims Settlement Act, 182
Alaska Peninsula, 54, 66
Alaska Salmon Packers, 61, 72
Alaska Steamship Company, 79, 83, 151
Alaska Territorial Guards, 28, 139
Alaska Territorial Health Department, 75
Alaska Territory, 9, 17, 23, 29, 30, 35,
    36, 37, 53, 57, 172
Alaska War Council, 31–32, 74, 76, 79
Aleut Corporation, 182, 185, 186
Aleutian Campaign: military buildup for,
    16–17; importance of, 40–41; ending
    of, 149–50; damage caused by, 176
Aleutian Islands: environment on, 4, 15;
    obscurity of, 9; as possible war zone,
    15–16, 28
Aleutian Livestock Company, 6, 7, 161,
    162, 177
Aleutian Planning Commission, 182
Aleutian and Pribilof Islands Restitution,
    170, 186
Aleutian/Pribilof Islands Association
    (APIA), 182, 184, 186
Aleuts: love of home, 3–4; accomplish-
    ments, 4; adaptability, 5; villages, 5–9;
    negative attitude toward, 12–14, 28–
    29, 55, 59, 69–70, 84, 91, 92, 102, 123,
    129; blood quantum test for, 24, 83,
    124, 184; war dangers, 52–53; deaths

en route to camps, 87; efforts in South-
    east camps, 108–9; losses, 136–37; dam-
    age claims, 178–79; lawsuit, 181
Alien Property, Office of, 181
Allen, Leonard, 79, 80, 105, 129
Amaknak Island, 38
Amchitka Island, 23, 175
American Legion, 98
Amlia Island, 6
Anchorage, 17, 27, 32, 59
Angagin, Angaginas, 3
Angoon, 97, 98, 120, 121, 170
Army, U.S. *See* Military, U.S.
Army Claims Division, 178
Army Weather Bureau, 178
Arnold, Henry "Hap," 15
Artumonoff, Peter, 132
Assumption, Church of the (Seattle), 166
Atka: description of, 6; strategic position
    of, 44–46; children mentioned, 46;
    evacuated, 70–71; Aleuts return to,
    163–64. *See also* Killisnoo
Atlantic Richfield, 185
Atsugi Air Base, 165
Atsuta Island (Attu), 43
Attu: description of, 5–6; proximity to
    Japan, 18; Japanese occupation of, 41–
    43; motivation for evacuation of, 85–
    86; not resettled, 87, 136; Aleut war
    claims, 180–81. *See also* Otaru

Baranoff, Makary, 147, 178
Baranoff Island, 74
Barrett, George T., 78, 79, 102, 103
Barrow, 11
Bartlett, Edward L. "Bob," 19–20, 57–
    59, 119, 126–27
Bayview Cemetery, 103, 128
Beck, George, 129
Beebe, Mr. and Mrs. Chaney O., 162
Benedict, Mr. and Mrs. Henry W., 131,
    158, 173

228

post-war conditions on, 172–73. *See also* St. George; St. Paul
Prince of Wales Island, 79, 80
Prince William Sound, 66
Prokopeuff, Olean, 107, 132, 165, 168
Prokopioff, Alfred, 42
Prokopioff, Alfred, Jr., 181
Prossoff, Alex, 40, 43, 86, 107, 133, 134, 166, 167
Public Health Service, U.S., 75
Public Law 96-317. *See* Commission on Wartime Relocation and Internment of Civilians
Public Law 100-383. *See* Aleutian and Pribilof Islands Restitution
Public Welfare, Alaska Department of, 36

Qisagunax, 4
Quinn, Margaret, 77, 82, 83

Ransom, Jay Ellis, 12
Rat Island, 175
Reagan, Ronald, 186
Reconstruction Finance Corporation, 175, 176
Red Cross, 133, 166
Reindeer Service, 11
Rettie, James C., 31
Revillagigedo Island, 104
Robinson, Verne L., 20, 22, 25, 159, 160, 182
Roden, Henry, 116
Roosevelt, Eleanor, 22
Roosevelt, Franklin D., 22, 125, 154, 155, 160, 176, 178, 180
Russian Orthodox Christianity, 5, 44
Russians, 101, 166
Russo-Japanese War, 15

St. George: description of, 8; in wartime, 47–49; evacuated, 72; Aleuts return to, 147–48; post-war conditions on, 172–73. *See also* Funter Bay
St. Lawrence Island, 75, 79
St. Matthew Island, 47
St. Mihiel (transport), 163
St. Paul: description of, 8; in wartime, 47–49; evacuated, 71–72; Aleuts return to, 147–48; post-war conditions on, 172–73. *See also* Funter Bay
Salvation Army, 98

Samalga Island, 135, 175
Sand Point, Alaska, 58
San Francisco, 32, 142, 166
Sapporo, 165
Savoroff, Leonty, 49, 105, 128, 161
Savoroff, Sergie, 161
Saxman Village, 157
Sealing operations: on the Pribilofs, 8; in World War II, 115; Atkans refuse to join, 122–23; use of military in, 141; effects on Funter Bay, 143–45
Seattle, 35, 62, 65, 74, 92, 93, 142, 145, 166, 167
Sedanka Island, 7, 78, 81
Segum Island, 175
Semichi Island, 175
Seventeenth Naval District, 153, 167
Seward, Alaska, 58, 59
Shaishnikoff, Sergie, 49
Shane, William, 149
Shapniskoff, Anfesia, 124
Shelikoff, Luke, 128, 130, 157, 158
Shikanai, Takeshiro, 133, 165
Shinto shrines, 44
Shoemaker Bay, 100
Siberia, 47
Siems-Drake-Puget Sound Company, 19–20, 29, 38, 83
Sitka, 17, 29, 122
Skagway, 58
Skowl Arm, 80
Snigaroff, Andrew, 70, 122
Snigaroff, Cedar, 46
Snigaroff, Poda, 46, 70, 71
Snigaroff, Vera, 98, 121
Social Security Board, 75
Spanish-American War, 15
Squaw Harbor, 58, 65
Stepetin, Alfred, 184
Stepetin, Matrona, 157, 158
Stevens, Ted, 183
Stimson, Henry L., 30, 137–38, 151
Stockdale, Homer I., 37, 54–55
Sundborg, George W., 57
Svarny, Gertrude Hope, 102
Swanson, Henry, 174
Sweetland, Monroe, 180

Tacoma Indian Hospital, 105, 166
Talbot, J. A., 129
Tanaga Island, 175